IT WORKED FOR ME

MY LIFE SEIZING OPPORTUNITY AND BUILDING SUCCESS

It Worked For Me
My Life Seizing Opportunity and Building Success
By Jeff Burgess

Copyright © 2025 by

Published by
Munn Avenue Press
300 Main Street, Ste 21
Madison, NJ 07940
MunnAvenuePress.com

Paperback ISBN: 978-1-960299-66-6
Hardcover ISBN: 978-1-960299-67-3

Printed in the United States of America

*Dedicated to my late father, Oscar William (Bill) Burgess.
I have always admired him; however, it took writing this to realize
that he was the greatest, most inspiring man I will ever know.*

*And of course, Joanne, for giving me the most wonderful life
imaginable, and for keeping me alive more than a few times along
the way.*

*Special thanks to Michael Lewis, Jamie Malanowski,
and Elizabeth Austin for their guidance along my two-year
journey in completing this business biography.*

IT WORKED FOR ME

MY LIFE SEIZING OPPORTUNITY AND BUILDING SUCCESS

JEFF BURGESS

DISCLAIMER

Having a photographic memory was both a blessing and a curse. In recapturing decades of my personal and professional life, I had no written notes; only my memory to rely on. Therefore, any discrepancies are unintentional; rather, just how I remember them.

PREFACE

In 1979, I was living with my best friend Gary in a two-bedroom apartment in my hometown of Skokie, a suburb just north of Chicago. I was 22 years old, a few months removed from my sophomore year at Illinois State University – and I say "removed" literally, since the Dean of Students had strongly pointed out that school was not the best choice for me.

Gary and I both had "floater jobs" which covered our monthly rent, weed, beer, and food, in that order. (Our landlord would likely have put rent and weed in reverse order.) Basically, I seemed to be pursuing the destiny first noted in my eighth-grade yearbook from Oakview Junior High, where I was dubbed "town clown." My mom was horrified.

Me? I took it as a badge of honor, one that I kept wearing through high school and my short stint in college.

It was a typical September Sunday. Gary and I were lying around, recovering from hangovers, and planning our next downtown Chicago adventure. Around four o'clock, the phone rang. It was my dad.

"Hey, Jeff, are you busy?"

"Well, a little. Hanging out."

"I really need to speak with you. Can you come over?"

I was at that age when I did not have anything against my parents. I would see them for birthdays and holidays, and whenever I wanted to conduct a secret withdrawal from the packed meat freezer they kept in their basement, but I did not see the need to spend any extra time with them. "Is it important?"

His answer was firm. "It is important enough that I'm asking you to come over – now."

That was good enough for me. I quickly jumped into the shower to wash off the after-aroma of the previous night's parties. As the hot water rushed down, my mind began spinning with scenarios. What did he want to talk about? Abruptly, it dawned on me that maybe he was going to tell me he was dying. My mind always moved at a mile a minute, but suddenly it came to a screeching halt.

Why else would he need to talk to me? My dad was an ordinary man – 52 years old, husband, father of five, owner and CEO of an envelope company, recovered alcoholic, and my hero. He was my rock, and he more than made up for my distracted mother. How would I survive without him? We always shared this unspoken bond of my inheriting his OCD gene. While he never appreciated my roles as town clown and high school fuck-up, he admired my underlying work ethic. When I did put my mind to something, I took it to completion, whether it was shoveling neighbors' sidewalks in those Chicago winters or mowing their lawns in the summer. Even as an eight-year-old.

If I had suddenly kicked the bucket at age twenty-two, that would have been the story of my life – a human oxymoron who had a great work ethic yet couldn't hold down a job.

Dad hugged me when I came through the door and told my mom to let us be. We went upstairs to my parents' bedroom, which was decorated with a complete Brady Bunch-era motif: matching avocado and orange bedspread and curtains, beige shag carpeting, and large imitation Picasso paintings on the walls. We sat together on the bench seat at the bottom of the bed, connected at the hip. He started to put his arm around my shoulder, and I began to cry. *"Dad, please do not die on me!"* I said, sobbing.

Startled, he jumped to his feet, then put his hands on my shoulders. "Listen to me! That is not what this is about. I am not dying! But now that you mention it, you are killing me." I started to say something, but he went on. "Seriously, I need you to listen to me."

He started speaking to me in an authoritative tone, unlike anything I had heard from him before. It was two decades before his time, but when I remember my Dad's voice now, it was James Earl Jones speaking to me. It was clear I had either upset or disappointed him. I quickly learned that it was both. "You are wasting your life," he said. "You have always had an outstanding work ethic, along with an incredible quick wit. If you were ever able to use that wit to think on your feet instead of just being a smartass, you could bring great value to some company one day." He looked me directly in the eye. "I did not send you to college to be a fuck-up. You have a gift, and I cannot allow you to waste it. You need to get your collective shit together."

I was stunned, and very upset. Not so much about what he said, but because I knew it was dead-on.

My mind jumped back to a moment two summers before when I was working in his company warehouse. The combination of my 17-year-old male hormones and the female members of the warehouse staff had been too much for me to overcome, and I devoted far more time to chasing skirts than fulfilling my work responsibilities. He fired me. I know that memory was painful for both of us. I had let him down, and now here I was, letting him down again.

I drove back to the apartment. The aroma of cannabis greeted my arrival. Gary passed me the loaded pipe as I entered. "You look like you need one," he said. But I already had what I needed. My dad was my hero, and I had been forced to confront the reality that I was failing him and failing myself. "No thanks," I replied, echoing the words my dad had just said to me. "I just need to start getting my shit together."

The very next day, I started searching for the Help Wanted section in the *Chicago Tribune*. Some company called Tek-Aids, two towns over, was looking for a warehouse worker. I had never heard of them, but I knew I wanted that job. I am not sure why, but the ad called out to me. Maybe I just wanted a job quickly so

3

I could get back into my dad's good favor. For the interview, I put my best foot forward, wearing the blue blazer my mother bought me for high school graduation and borrowing a paisley tie I had bought Dad for Father's Day.

Tek-Aids was a family business, about five years old. A computer peripherals distributor, they sold printers, monitors, and bins full of internal parts. Jud Beamsley, the founder and CEO, gave me a tour of the 15,000-square-foot facility. I could tell he had great pride in his operation, and I was impressed that he knew every employee on a first-name basis.

The warehouse was sloppy and seemed a little disorganized. I knew I could fix that. I was surprised to see that they also had a tech area in the warehouse, run by a guy wearing a lab coat and glasses with thick lenses. He looked like a mad scientist. They were building student tech systems for community colleges, based upon Ohio Scientific's Challenger 1P single-processor computer systems. ``A warehouse *and* tech?" I said to Jud. He did not reply.

I did find it interesting that he was already introducing me to the workers. After the tour, he also introduced me to his wife Lorayne. Together, they ran through the job responsibilities. I was trying not to jump the gun, but it sure seemed like I was already hired. And I hoped I was because I felt like I was looking into a crystal ball and seeing my future.

Perhaps I was willing it to happen by confidently adding, "I look forward to hearing from you sometime tomorrow."

Lorayne gave me a strange look, perhaps due to my presumptuousness. ``The blazer and tie will not be necessary when you come back," she said. At that point, I knew the job was mine. I was already reorganizing the sloppy warehouse in my head.

I started two days later. Within two years, I was promoted to vice president of sales. Twenty years and three days after my dad's sermon, I founded my own IT server-building company. We morphed into the video surveillance recording market in 2009, and by the time of my retirement on my 66th birthday on July 21, 2023, I had built a company that is now the world's largest supplier of purpose-built surveillance video recording appliances. We have installed more than 250,000 devices recording video surveillance from more than four million cameras in 91 countries around the globe, at the most secure sites and the coolest companies in the world.

Here is the story of how that happened.

PART ONE

CAREER

CHAPTER 1

GENTLEMEN, START YOUR ENGINES

———

May 1979

I was excited to start the new job, and confident that I would succeed. Given my strong record of messing up, that confidence may seem undeserved. But I had worked in the warehouse at my dad's paper manufacturing company, Burgess Envelope Company, for three of my high school summers. Based on that experience, I was pretty sure I knew how a warehouse operation should operate.

I also was pretty sure how I ought to operate. Even though I had been the "boss's kid" during those summers, I knew better than to act like I was a know-it-all. At Tek-Aids, I just wanted to fit in, work hard, and be one of the team.

Right from the first day at Tek-Aids, I felt I was being given a wide berth. There was no written job description. Nobody was dictating a list of priorities. So, I walked around the office and warehouse and introduced myself to everyone, then went through the warehouse again taking notes.

What I saw was a lot of parts – parts whose names were unfamiliar to me, parts whose functions I did not understand, parts whose relationships with one another were a mystery to me. But what I noticed more than anything was the concrete floor. It was dusty and dirty and speckled with trash and cigarette butts. Just from that, I could tell nobody was paying attention to what went on in that room. Nobody took responsibility, and nobody cared.

Some people may have found such conditions discouraging. I found them inspirational. When I went back to the apartment after work, Gary asked me how my day had gone. "I could run that place one day!" I replied.

"Funny," he said and laughed. But I was not kidding.

The next morning, under my authority and without enlisting anyone's help, I used the manual pallet jack to move all the skids that had products on them over to one side of the 6,000-square-foot warehouse. I swept and then wet-mopped that side of the warehouse. When I pallet-jacked the skids back in place, I took care to put the ones with the fewest computers or printers on them closest to the shipping dock. These were the computers from Altos and Dynabyte, and the dot-matrix printers, primarily from Okidata Corporation. I put them up front on the hunch – correct, as it turned out – that if a skid did not have much product on it, that was because those were the best-selling units. It would save time to keep those items closer to the dock. I then swept and wet-mopped the other half of the warehouse. Within three hours, I had my domain tidy and under my control.

Now that the floors were spic and span, it was time to organize things. I have always needed to have things in their right places, a need surely fueled by my OCD gene. Although I was never a clean freak, I was always a neat freak. (It still drives my wife Joanne nuts.)

I took all the items off the metal shelves and restocked them one by one, with products from each brand in the same area, close to any skids holding products from the same manufacturer. I read all the product labels – font wheel, fabric ribbon, and mylar ribbon. I had no idea what they were, but I began to understand that they went together.

Within the first few weeks, I felt on top of the back-end operations, but I still needed to work on learning the various product lines. Our top three vendors, Okidata, Altos, and

Wyse, each came to see us three or four times a month, which made me think Tek-Aids must be very important to them. Jud would sometimes bring the reps back to meet me. They seemed to be reassured to see their products so readily available in our warehouse, and it made me proud that they appeared impressed by my work. They always asked me about which products were shipping the most. I was gaining quite the education without realizing it.

It was exciting. And I was excited to be excited. This company was consuming me (although my team members may have thought I was slightly crazy.) I spent hours peppering my colleague Jerry Clark with questions. He was the lead tech who oversaw customizing systems for customers. Jerry was always so analytical, even to the point of testing something three times before moving forward. I was the exact opposite, just running on my instincts.

Over time, Jerry started asking *me* questions about what made some products more important than others to our customers. I found this fascinating, and I challenged myself to become Jerry's source of information, instead of the other way around. Soon, people in sales began asking me questions as well. That confused me, considering they had so much more access to information than I did.

Jud soon had me overseeing the entire back end. That included maintaining the inventory needed for the tech area, as well as managing the company's two drivers. One driver, Steve, had been driving our Ford van to Ohio Scientific in Chillicothe, Ohio, to pick up our orders and then drive back to Chicago. It was known, via word-of-mouth and his breath, that Steve had a drinking issue.

Steve was around my age and had been with the company for just over a year. Although he had a full-time salary, he seemed to be more of a part-timer, as he only came to work when there was a planned pickup. Before his first trip after I became manager, I warned him that drinking on his route was dangerous and could put the company at risk. Nevertheless, when Steve returned and backed the van up to the dock two days later, he opened the driver's door and dropped a brown paper bag, shattering an empty quart bottle of Schlitz beer on the concrete dock.

I had no choice but to take him to Lorayne, the company matriarch. She fired him. I felt bad, but he did it to himself.

Once Steve was gone, the light bulb went over my head. Why were we driving four hundred miles to and from a suburb of Cleveland, Ohio to pick up goods? Why were we driving anywhere? We had a second driver, Bill Long. One day, I saw that we had Bill scheduled to take a load in our larger step van to El Paso, Texas. Have you ever driven to El Paso from Chicago? It is easy – you drive 18 hours to San Antonio, turn right on I-10, then drive another 550 miles through desert and scorpions.

And what were we delivering to El Paso? A cathode-ray tube (CRT) computer monitor. A single $500 CRT.

It dawned on me that of the eight to ten trucks that came to our dock every day, I had never seen one from UPS or Federal Express that was handling freight. Overnight letters, yes, but no freight. I had enough confidence to raise the issue with Jud and Lorayne. "I bet it's expensive to transport this stuff ourselves," I said. "The driver, the truck, insurance, gas. Did you ever consider UPS or Federal Express?"

"It never occurred to me," Lorayne said. "I thought they were strictly residential. Do they handle commercial freight?"

"Why, Lorayne, I believe they do," I replied, knowing full well that they did. They permitted me to investigate switching.

I was in overdrive now. Not even two months in, and I was already finding ways to save the company time and money on freight. I had prevented a potential catastrophe by bringing the issue of a drinking driver to Lorayne's attention. And what made me most proud, I had turned the warehouse into the focal point of all vendor visits.

I had found my destiny!

CHAPTER 2

BE LIKE A SPONGE

June 1979

I suppose some people learn about an industry from the top down. I learned about computers and the market for them from the inside out.

I was always fascinated by technology, particularly audio technology. At 15, I was one of those guys who bought the Heathkit build-your-own spehaker kit. My brother had one of the first quad-speaker stereo systems. When Pink Floyd's "Money" came out, I parked in front of his system, just so I could hear the cash registers in the song going around the room. Talk about separation! So cool for 1972!

New things fascinated me, and I was intrigued by the way parts worked together to form a larger whole. For somebody like me, the Tek-Aids warehouse was the perfect playroom, and I had all the toys I could ever want.

To learn the product lines, I studied the packing lists we generated in the warehouse to see who was buying what, and with what other products. Eventually I began to see why they were buying certain things together. Packing lists became my textbooks. I wanted to saturate myself in this industry.

My mind was in overdrive, mirroring the speed of the evolving technology. Before long, I could read a packing list the way a conductor reads music. I could see the products fitting together like notes blending in harmony. Every morning, I would grab my coffee and stand before the shelves to look at all the options and combinations I had read about the day before.

I acquired even more knowledge about the industry just by listening. It seems like listening is a lost art these days. (Thanks, Google.) But listening allowed me to pick up a new language of computer terminology – CPU, RAM, hard disk drive, floppy disk, hardware, software, firmware, user-friendly. I would do a deep dive to find those words on packing lists and the vendor-supplied product datasheet. I wanted to go beyond definitions to learn the differentiators within each one. For instance, CPUs (central processing units) had different chipsets (Intel and Motorola, for example), and different processor speeds. After a while, I began to understand how the computer companies sought to distinguish themselves from one another.

Eventually Jud began to send vendors to the warehouse to talk to me. They would ask me which of their products were moving, and how their items compared to their competitors' versions. I knew the vendors were likely able to get that information just from reading monthly sales reports. But it became obvious that Jud trusted me to share information, and that meant a lot to me. At the end of every day, I would head back to the apartment coasting on another new level of confidence.

After I had been with the company about six weeks, Tek-Aids won the largest deal in its history. This contract was with the State of Texas to supply CRT terminals to connect all the state colleges to the statewide Amdahl mainframe computer system, housed at Texas A&M University in College Station. It was a three-year contract that was expected to involve at least 7,000 CRT terminals.

I was shocked – not just because we won, but because we had made a deal to supply a product that we did not even carry. It turns out that every other bidder had quoted a price to supply the requested DEC VT-52 CRT straight from the Digital Equipment Corporation (DEC) catalog. But as it turned out, the bid request called out for a "DEC VT-52 CRT or equal."

Jud, the Tek-Aids president, had won the contract by quoting the price for the "equal" version that met the product's specifications but was one-third less expensive. I was perplexed, confused, and uneasy. "Sounds great," I said, "but we do not carry that brand."

> **Jud responded with the most important lesson I ever learned in business, which I carry with me to this day. "First get the deal," he said. "Then worry about it. Too much time is wasted on plotting and planning for deals you do not even win. Once you win them, everything will fall into place, because once you have the deal, the vendors will beat a path to your door."**

Then he shared a secret. Two weeks before the bid went in, Jud called Micro-Term, a St. Louis-based CRT manufacturer. The call was completely out of the blue; we had never done business together. Without mentioning the Texas bid (to avoid drawing attention to it), he asked for a price quote on a single CRT unit that, coincidentally, happened to match the Texas bid specification precisely. "All I needed was their worst price to win the bid," Jud said. "Now I will get their best one."

The very next day, the Micro-Term sales team drove the four hours up Interstate 55, with champagne and a contract in hand, to celebrate the multi-million-dollar win. We bought the terminals from them, then sold them to Texas. Everyone was happy.

As we sipped the champagne, my new mantra kept repeating in my head. "First get the deal. First get the deal." It has never failed me.

CHAPTER 3
THE MASTER MAVERICK

October 1980

I absorbed so much from Judson Beamsley. He was a maverick. Earlier in his career, he repossessed cars and televisions in Omaha and East St. Louis, Illinois. Talk about having balls!

Jud founded Tek-Aids in the 1970s in the basement of his apartment building. He always believed that his focus on keeping up with industry trends separated him from his competition, and he continued to study those trends for as long as I knew him. His two sons, Jeff and Jim, joined him in the venture. Jeff had been the manager of Amazingrace, a legendary folk music venue in Evanston, on the Northwestern University campus. (He became good friends with jazz guitarist Pat Metheny.) Jim came from an operations background within the Chicago banking industry. To make the company a full family affair, Lorayne managed the expenses. She was very frugal. Okay, she was cheap.

Lorayne and I did not always mesh. But Jud and I did. He liked to talk, and I liked to listen. When I knew him, he was a man in his fifties, the boss. He did not care that I was just a shipper and a kid; apparently, he liked my work ethic and my curiosity. He always seemed so worldly to me, with such interesting ways of seeing things. For example, when he was negotiating a loan from a bank, he would always try to get approval for more than he needed, and then not use it. It was like a challenge to him. When workers wanted to leave the company, he always tried to line up jobs for them with our suppliers. He did not mind people leaving, but he hated the thought that any of them might join one of our competitors.

Jud always had an angle. He kept three different sets of business cards in his desk. One of the cards had his actual title, "President." Another card gave his title as "Vice President." He used this card when he was having an initial meeting with a new vendor. If Jud was not ready to make a deal, he would present the vice-president card to the vendor and say, "Let me check and get back to you." It bought him time to think it over, and it was not necessarily untrue, as he occasionally might have wanted to run it by the rest of his family. But I always wondered what that vendor thought once he realized Jud was the company president. Perhaps Jud was the first Undercover Boss?

The third card? It did not include his name or title. It only had the Tek-Aids Industries logo, company name, and the tagline *"We're those whores you keep hearing about."* Like I said, Jud was a maverick.

> **Jud helped me to form the two fundamental principles that have led to my success: "Know Thy Customer" and "Know Thy Competition." The prerequisite for both these principles is preparation, and Jud was always prepared. Jud taught me to be ready for anything, and to always have an alternative plan.**

Here is a perfect example. In late 1980, almost a year after I joined the company, Jud signed Tek-Aids to carry a new dot-matrix printer brand, Citizen (the watch people). We already carried Okidata, which was far and away the world leader in dot-matrix printers with their Pacemaker series. We were shipping Okidata printers to customers all over the country.

At the time, automobile dealerships were among the largest

consumers of dot-matrix printers. Odds are, even today, if you are buying a car, when the time comes for you to sit in the finance office and sign papers, you will have seen (and heard!) an Okidata Pacemaker 2350 printing out those seven-part finance forms. The Okidata printers were such rugged machines that they called them "Tank-Tough." To emphasize the point, Okidata came out with a desktop printer stand made from a heavy-duty plastic version of two tank-tread tires. Talk about driving the message home!

When Citizen launched its dot-matrix printer initiative, the company recruited several sales executives from Okidata's corporate office in Mt. Laurel, New Jersey. At that time, Citizen was also based in Mt. Laurel. For a while, this little town 19 miles east of Philadelphia was the dot-matrix capital of the world.

Although Tek-Aids was Okidata's largest distributor, Jud knew that Citizen would come knocking on our door. It was obvious (at least if you were as smart as Jud.) The newly poached sales managers knew we already had relationships with customers buying dot matrix printers, and they knew that any sales Citizen got through us would be sales taken away from Okidata. Recruiting Tek-Aids would be a double win for them.

Jud saw them coming. So, when Citizen came in, Jud explained that while we were interested in signing with them, we would be putting our relationship with Okidata at risk. Therefore, if they wanted us to carry their printers, we would require a one-year exclusive territory contract on their product line. Much to my surprise, Citizen agreed. They probably figured they had nothing to lose. We had the customers; we knew the technology. Why not?

To my delight, I witnessed this discussion in person. Jud had invited me to attend this important meeting – only to listen, he stressed, not to talk. I thought it was very cool that he had included me, although his two sons – also in the meeting – clearly did not feel the same way. I never took it personally, as I did not want to get involved in whatever family dynamic was going on. I just appreciated that Jud was an open book with me, and I was a happy learner.

After the meeting, I pumped Jud for information. What was so important about having an exclusive territory agreement? "Nothing, really," he replied. "I have known those guys from their Okidata days. They will say anything. Exclusive does not mean you are the only dealer, just that you are the first. I doubt Citizen will even honor it." I was shocked by all this maneuvering. "So why bother to demand it?" I asked.

"We will use it as leverage against Okidata."

"For what?"

"Larger territory. Better pricing."

So, we were going to make a bad deal with Citizen to get a better deal with Okidata? That seemed unlikely. But Jud knew his customers, and he knew his competition.

Tek-Aids soon received their first stocking order from Citizen – maybe $500,000 worth. (This was a large order back in the 1980s.) Two weeks later, Citizen signed up Kaltronics – Tek-Aids' biggest competitor, a company located a mere three miles from our front door. Jud and Harvey Kalman (the "Kal" in Kaltronics) were each other's Lex Luthor. So much for exclusive territory. Citizens had pulled a "Jud" on Jud!

Or so you might conclude if you did not know Jud. He had fully expected Citizen to break its exclusivity commitment. When they did, he grabbed the opportunity to destroy the Citizen marketplace before it even got started. He instructed his marketing department to create a flyer (again, it was 1980 – no Internet, email, PDF, etc.) that we sent to all 3,000 Tek-Aids customers. The flyer listed the Citizen cost per printer, along with our cost, although he had made this cost significantly below each item's actual cost.

While I had to be impressed by Jud's spite and retaliation, this did not look like a completely clean victory. When I pointed out that we were losing money by selling under cost, his answer stunned me.

"There is no cost, if you do not intend to pay the vendor," Jud replied matter-of-factly. Sure enough, he never paid for them. Instead, he sold out his Citizen inventory at 25% below their cost, dropped their product line, and sued them for breach of contract. When they settled, his victory was complete. The memory of this lesson in being prepared (and playing hardball) has stuck with me these past 40 years.

Jud's ruthlessness, which he may have developed from repossessing cars, did tarnish my admiration for him a bit. My first thought was, "My dad would never have done that!" Seeing this side of Jud did not damage our relationship or diminish my hunger to learn from him, but it certainly opened my eyes. I wanted to be a maverick, too, but only in a good way.

CHAPTER 4

THE QUEEN OF MAVERICK

———

February 1981

At Tek-Aids, I lived in two worlds. The warehouse was my domain, and I took pains to keep it organized and clean. Jud was always bringing visitors through whenever he gave office tours, and I felt such a sense of pride when he took the time to introduce me to his guests. Beyond the warehouse, Jud was exposing me to the many facets of the business. As he painted the big picture with his broad brush, I kept connecting the dots, one packing list at a time. It was as if the external and internal worlds within the company were colliding, and my brain was a sponge absorbing it all. The more I learned, the more confident I became. More and more, I felt part of the future. The future of what I was not sure, but I knew it was my future.

At some point, instead of going through the sales department, customers started calling me in the warehouse directly. Many of these questions had to do with shipping; I seemed to be the only one in the company who knew how to get a product from point A to point B and how long it would take.

Many other calls were for "sneakerware" stock checks. Customers would call to see if a product was in stock. Today, of course, all somebody must do is look at a screen. But back then, I would have to put the customer on hold, run back to the bin – that is where the "sneakerware" came in – do a stock count, then run back to the phone and report the information.

These runs to check the shelves expedited my learning curve on products. Fairly early on, I realized that a customer who asked about one product frequently then asked for another – or at least meant to. For example, NEC pinwheel printers used more than a hundred different hard fonts that fit inside the printer. They also had two types of inked print ribbon options. It was almost automatic; if someone was buying printers, they were also going to be buying fonts and ribbons. If only to save wear and tear on my Converse All-Stars, I learned that when I was asked to take an inventory check, it made sense to do a quick count of the complementary parts customers usually asked for next. I could tell that the customers appreciated my proactiveness. This translated into more sales for Tek-Aids, and more "attaboys" for me. And nothing drove me like "attaboys." All these years later, they still do, even more than the money.

But it was not just the customers who called me. I also started getting queries from our own salespeople. I even got questions from the techs. I loved being the hero coming to the rescue. I felt like Superman managing the warehouse, the Caped Crusader coming through on stock checks. I absolutely loved the buzz that gave me.

As time went on, I developed a bond with Donna Panfil, a sales manager at Tek-Aids who reported to Jeff Beamsley, the vice president of sales. She ran the inside sales desk, and she was a fireball of spirit and personality. Donna was beyond bold and brash in an incredibly positive way. She was fearless!

In the early 1980s, the women's rights movement was challenging business head-on. Donna never waited for business to catch up. She charged ahead, regardless of who else was in that meeting. With her business acumen, she commanded and earned the respect of her peers, male and female. She was an expert at problem-solving.

The way she handled one problem is forever etched in my brain.

We had a customer who bought two Altos computer systems worth roughly $23,000. He agreed to pay cash on delivery, via UPS. That is not quite what happened. It took two weeks after the delivery before the check finally reached our bank, where it bounced for insufficient funds.

Donna immediately called the customer, who blamed cash flow issues. That excuse has since become a trigger for me. I fucking hate hearing, *"My customer has yet to pay me,"* from people who bought my products and have not paid for them. I did not sell that product to his customer, he did. If the payment terms of his purchase order had stated "Will pay you when I get paid" instead of net thirty or net sixty, no one would accept it – and rightfully so.

Donna did not care what happened or why it happened. All she wanted was the remedy. The customer promised to pay within 15 days.

To no one's surprise, least of all Donna's, the customer did not honor his 15-day payment pledge. Another few weeks passed and still nothing but crickets. Putting icing on a cake that needed no further icing, the customer was also ducking Donna's call.

Finally, 60-some days later, the customer called Donna back. Unbelievably, he was not calling to talk about his missing payment. He wanted more products. His customer needed just one more of the same system to finish the project. Once that was done, his customer would pay him, and he would pay us. Guaranteed.

Donna played it very cool. Sure thing, she told him, we can fill this order. She made it clear, however, that we could only ship the order as a C.O.D. certified check shipment. In addition to the new $11,250 purchase, the outstanding $23,000 would have to be added to the certified check total. So, when the customer received the shipment he would have to hand over a certified check for $34,250. The customer was not happy, but he had no other choice than to agree to the terms.

This is where Donna's unique approach to problem-solving came into play – and then some. She had the techs pull the requested server unit out of the carton and put it off to the side, keeping it wrapped in its original internal covering. Then Donna put the now-empty carton on the floor and began filling it up with old computer trade magazines – roughly seventy pounds of magazines, equal to the weight of the system.

The carton reached the customer four days later. A few minutes later, our phone rang. The dealer was livid, claiming he was ripped off. Donna disagreed. "I was very clear with you," she said. "I told you the shipment was coming as a certified COD check. I never said order, or computer, or system. I said "shipment."

She concluded the call by telling him that after the check reached our bank by UPS, she would settle the matter. And she did exactly that – precisely 71 days later, the same amount of time it had taken him to pay us originally. He cried and complained, but he was stuck. Since he had already paid for the order, he was not in any position to cancel it. All he could do was stew and try to avoid the angry calls of his client. When the server finally arrived, there was a personalized note from Donna inside the carton. *"Let's see how you fucking like it,"* she had written, just before she closed his account.

While there might have been "cleaner" ways to resolve the issue, her scorched earth approach taught me a valuable lesson: Always have an alternative solution, should your original plan go sideways. Without her certified check move, we might never have been paid. Teaching the customer a lesson he would never forget was just, um, icing on the cake.

A quick history lesson: It was about this time that HP, along with other companies, started developing laser technology for computer printers. The clarity of these documents was amazing – sometimes too amazing. Millions of dollars' worth of bogus checks later, carriers like UPS stopped accepting C.O.D. shipments, whether the checks were "certified" or not.

CHAPTER 5

"YOU MAY GO TO HELL; I WILL GO TO TEXAS" –DAVY CROCKETT

————

May 1981

After those first two years at Tek-Aids, I could comfortably say I had made a home and a name for myself. I was part of the team. To all my colleagues, I was the dependable warehouse supervisor and shipping clerk, a guy who captained a tight ship. To many customers and sales reps, I was an easily accessible source of information. To the Beamsleys, I was the kid who would listen for hours while Jud expounded on his theories. And me? I was just happy to go to work every day, happy with my job, and motivated to excel.

It was Donna Panfil who saw what I was becoming. She saw my growing confidence. She also saw the confidence the customers had in me, and how they often bypassed the inside staff to talk to me in the warehouse. Recognizing that I was doing more to help the company than a lot of the actual sales force, Donna proposed moving me from the warehouse to the sales desk, so that I could be even more accessible to customers.

I was blown away. I idolized Donna, and her belief in me meant everything. Only one thing would have mattered more – if Jud

Beamsley had agreed with her.

Which he did not. Even after all those meetings we had shared, even after all those lessons he imparted, neither Jud nor any of the other Beamsleys thought I was up to the task. They came up with all kinds of pushback. "He is just a shipper. No college. Besides, he has a stutter. Hard to see us having a guy in sales who stutters."

It was true. I had a stutter; sometimes I still do. When I was a kid, I stuttered every time I opened my mouth. It made me an easy target for mockery; people who stutter appear weak or unsure of themselves. So, I got picked on, which naturally led to more anxiety and more stuttering. My solution was to steer clear of groups. I never had more than one friend at a time. I also tried to handle the stutter by being a wise-ass funny guy. I figured if they were laughing *with* me, they were not laughing *at* me.

But over time, I learned that I could control the stutter by controlling the pace of my speech. I had been trying to talk as fast as my brain moved (which was fast!) and I ended up tripping over my words. I learned to listen longer and to talk slower. I also began to realize that people liked me, even with the stutter, which gave me more confidence. And the more confidence I had, the less I stuttered. By the time I got to Tek-Aids, my stutter was mostly under control, mostly because my outlook was under control. I stuttered sometimes. So what? What people thought of me was their business, not mine. (Had I only had such wisdom in junior high and high school...)

Most of these criticisms came from the Beamsley boys, Jeff and Jim. I somewhat understood it; I am sure they were concerned that Jud treated me with a warmth that he never seemed to show them, at least at work. But Jud went along with it, which surprised me – and hurt me, too. He had made me feel that I had potential. This rejection seemed so cold, 180 degrees from the way he'd made me feel during all those lessons he had shared with me.

Whatever. I was happy enough at my warehouse job. Over the past few years, I had worked too hard and come too far to quit over a single rejection, no matter how painful.

Donna did not quit either. She seemed almost excited by the challenge before her. I heard it in her voice. She told me to keep my head up. "Just keep doing what you've been doing," she said, and she would take it from there.

She asked me which customers called me in the warehouse most frequently. Over the following couple of weeks, she called those customers, mentioned she was considering moving me to the sales desk, and asked them why they called me instead of their assigned territory manager. I do not know exactly what anybody told her, but less than six weeks after Jud first passed me over, I got the job on the inside sales desk. I was a salesman at last.

"Sales is 99% confidence and 1% bullshit." I have said that a thousand times. Some people think I came out of the womb saying it, but I learned it from my father.

On the afternoon he fired me from my summer job at his company, I had to sit in his office for three hours, waiting for him to drive me home. There was no place for me to go, nowhere to hang – I just had to sit there. Just sit there. For three hours. Doing nothing except watching him work.

I am sure I spent some time squirming, maybe even pouting, but after a short while, I got into it. My dad was impressive, working behind his desk, multi-tasking on various documents while talking with customers and vendors. Maybe for the first time in my life, I was seeing him in his true element – not mowing the lawn, lighting the grill, or watching my ball game, but running his company. He had a real sense of confidence when speaking with people on the phone, displaying an assurance that obviously came from knowing his company and his product in deep detail. I had seen how confidence filled my father with authority, and I wanted to be like Dad.

As I took on this new role, having Donna on my side gave me even more confidence. Once I had been afraid to even open my mouth for fear of being mocked. Now there was someone here who wanted me to talk to customers as my primary job. No customer would ever hear me stumbling and fumbling around, forcing him to play "Rolodex Roulette" in search of another vendor to call. Customers would hear me speak about products with authority, and they would want to work with us.

Equipped with all the information about the products I had studied, enlightened with the insights I had learned from Jud, and empowered by the faith Donna had placed in my abilities, I picked up the phone. The more I spoke, the more confident I became.

I did well at the inside sales desk assisting customers. I really liked the action and the buzz.

My introduction to the world of sales gave me a new appreciation for some of my old favorite movies. Most salespeople would likely name *Glengarry Glen Ross* or *Wolf of Wall Street* as their favorite sales movies of all time. But for me, it was a mix of *Used Cars* and *Miracle on 34th Street*.

Used Cars was a 1980 Steve Spielberg-produced, Robert Zemeckis-directed comedy starring Kurt Russell as Rudy Russo, a super-slick used car salesperson with an incredible gift for deflection.

> **Deflection is the art of flipping the conversation in your favor. Anyone who wants to succeed in sales should develop this skill. Nearly every customer you will ever encounter will come in with a list of reasons to buy your product, and a list of reasons not to. If you are in sales, your job is to get the customer to focus on the reasons to buy and to ignore the reasons for them to abstain.**

I began learning this art of deflection at the knee of my father, who was a master. Once, during the late spring of my sophomore year in high school, I shot a Roman candle down an empty hallway, a stupid and heedless stunt. The dean, whose office was halfway down that hallway, called my dad at work to come to the school. "Mr. Burgess," said the Dean, "this is a very serious offense, and we are strongly considering having Jeff retake sophomore year." My Dad immediately shot back with, "Dean Reiter, with all due respect, are you sure you want him around for an extra year?"

That awed me. What a comeback! What a deflection! What a way to turn the conversation into your favor! My dad was the king of deflection! He became my hero all over again. I was so awed by the immediacy of his turn-the-tables reply, I barely heard the Dean's response: "You know, Mr. Burgess, you make a lot of sense here. Instead, we will give him two weeks of detention."

I was delighted to get off so easily. In one fell swoop, I went from retaking sophomore year to two weeks of detention. But more importantly, it made me realize something. I, too, had a quick wit. Maybe I could figure out a way to use it to my advantage, or even make a living from it.

Later, when I saw *Used Cars*, I recognized that Russo was even more skilled at deflection. When a high school principal realized that the $20,000 worth of cars the school had purchased for Driver's Education classes were pieces of junk, Russo responded quickly, "They will be great for your auto body class to practice on." Unbelievably, that worked.

The classic *Miracle on 34th Street* showed me an approach even better than deflection. Anyone who has seen the movie will remember the scene where a customer learns that Macy's does not carry the toy fire engine her son wants. Instead of trying to sell her a different toy, Kris Kringle (working as Macy's Santa Claus), sends the customer to a rival store that has the toy in stock. At first, the store's executives are horrified. But when hundreds of customers express their appreciation, Macy's adopts a new sales policy: If Macy's doesn't carry the product you want, we'll help you find the store that does. "Macy's is the store with a heart," becomes the new slogan.

As a salesman, that became my approach. I took the attitude that I could find anything, and the customers ate it up. (Keep in mind that this was more than a decade before Google was founded.) Customers appreciated my helping them obtain what they were looking for, even if we did not carry it. This enhanced my reputation; I would often hear from new customers who had been referred to me by those I had helped. My network expanded. For many customers, I became their one-stop shop.

I began to realize that I was not selling products; I was selling service.

If the shipment was going to be late, I gave them a heads-up. If there was a price change coming, I gave them advance warning. If an upgrade was right around the corner, I let them know. And I always honored my commitments. The last thing I wanted was for customers to think of me as a supplier. I wanted them to think of me as their supporter, their ally, their hero.

Donna's vision was vindicated. I felt happy in my work. The company profited, and I loved the commissions that fattened my W-2 at year end. Only sixteen months later, I was presented with a new opportunity.

When we signed that big contract with the University of Texas, we had agreed to staff a location in Austin. Jud offered me the job. Within two weeks, I had shipped my belongings ahead and taken off for Austin.

After staying overnight in Oklahoma City, I headed south on I-35 in my black-and-tan Toyota Corolla, with Rush's "New World Man" blasting out of the stereo. *Yee-hah!*

CHAPTER 6
FROM BBQ TO CHEESESTEAKS

June 1981

I did consider myself that new-world man. New assignment, new territory, new people. For the first time, I was truly moving away from home and establishing real independence. Independent, but still connected, especially to my dad. He and I always had an unspoken bond. I knew how proud he was of me, and nothing could motivate me more than that!

The first person I met in Austin was Mike Parkhill, a Texas Tech graduate whom Jud had spotted at the Thrifty Car Rental counter during the numerous visits it took to finalize the contract with the State of Texas. Mike's job consisted of handling the paperwork at the rental counter and walking customers to their cars, but his spirit and energy caught Jud's eye.

Mike and I clicked. Technically, I was his manager, but there were no egos involved here. We were just two sales guys looking to do business.

The timing was incredible! Just a few months after we established the Austin office, IBM announced its first personal computer – or PC, as they were soon known to just about everyone. A new generation of PC clones appeared almost immediately thereafter. The whole distribution world had changed. Our entire business had been selling devices connected to mainframes and servers, such as printers, tape systems, and monitors. Now people can have computers right on their desks. It was a game-changer.

Austin had already earned nationwide recognition as a technology hub. The University of Texas at Austin is a renowned technology research institution, which had drawn both IBM and Texas Instruments to Austin in the late 1960s.

This second wave of technology in the early 1980s made for an exciting time. Customers were having a feeding frenzy. If San Jose was Silicon Valley, Austin was becoming Silicon Gulch (and this was still three years before Michael Dell founded his namesake computer company from his UT Austin dorm room.)

Tek-Aids picked up two of the first IBM clones to be released – the Columbia MPC (multi-personal computer) and Eagle Computers' 1600 series. Both came with hundreds of computer programs available on separate floppy disks.

Critical for all these computer manufacturers was the ability to run on Microsoft's MS-DOS operating system. That made the machines compatible with third-party business software applications, such as accounting and word processing.

Eagle Computers launched their systems with the choice of a single or dual floppy disk drive system. That was the extent of their storage for about six months, until they introduced hard disk drive versions. Customers did not want to wait that long, so they gobbled up the floppy disk versions as soon as we received them.

Columbia Data Systems was not technically a clone, as it had more features than the IBM PC. In addition to coming standard with twice the 64 KB of random-access memory (RAM) offered by IBM, it also included Digital Research's MP/M operating system, which offered compatibility with the same third-party applications. The MP/M operating system was a multi-user operating system, the same one Altos used in their data center computer.

Columbia had brought multi-user computers to the desktop, and our branch sales of Columbia Data were four times greater than the sales of Eagle Computers. The following year, Microelectronics and Computer Technology Corporation (MCC), a consortium of leading tech companies, was established in Austin. Their presence attracted even more technology businesses to the city. We began seeing startups emerge, focusing on chip-making, software development, and computer systems design.

Shortly after IBM revolutionized the computer industry, Houston-based Compaq announced their original portable PC. Weighing in at a hefty twenty-eight pounds, it was less of a "portable" and more of a "luggable." But between the PC clones and the Compaq "luggable," the personal computer market was erupting. Just within our regional territory, which covered Texas, Oklahoma, Louisiana, and Arkansas (TOLA), these business engines were being installed in retail stores, hospitals, real estate offices, insurance offices, colleges and universities, heavy manufacturing, government offices, and even at Mike's old employer, Thrifty Car Rental. We talked and sold to new and existing reseller customers every day, making the distribution business pulsating and fun.

The business expanded fast. We had started out with more warehouse space than we needed, and I really enjoyed building out from a blank canvas instead of simply reorganizing. As things were moving so rapidly with new products and even newer technologies, we tweaked the space daily, always making room for more incoming shipments.

We even carved out space for system-building. We brought in tech benches and enough voltage to power those systems on the benches. We then hired some gearheads with the technical chops to build the systems. This was my first venture into value-added selling – setting up the system for the customer prior to shipping it.

One of those warehouse hires with technical aptitude was Willy. He and I hit it off quickly. He shared my work ethic, and we liked to party together after work as well. It was his idea to mount speakers to the ceiling so we could work to the beat of a rock and roll soundtrack, and I let him run with it. Rock on!

And rock on we did. The place had such an electric atmosphere, and not just because of the music. That merely provided the backbeat (albeit a loud backbeat.) We had so many new computer retailer customers vying for these new, revolutionary products, and we had them in stock! Perhaps having our wall-sharing neighbor being the Texas Department of Aging explained why they never complained about the music?

There was a certain level of competition going on between my branch and the corporate office. Tek-Aids now had seven other branch offices, stretching from Phoenix to King of Prussia, but those were of no interest to me. I focused solely on the corporate office in Illinois and Jud's son Jeff, the VP of sales. I wanted to stick it to him for trying to squash my career growth while I was still "just a shipper." By our third month, our branch sales were only 12% behind the head office's. I made up my mind that we would not finish behind them again. And we did not!

The next month, we smoked them. We ranked as the top sales office in the company. It drove Jeff nuts. He berated his branch sales team. Even better, Jud loved it. And why wouldn't he? We were making money!

Mike and I were really in tune with the entire Austin branch team. It was not just the rock and roll music driving us. We were all very much in sync. All eight of us felt a part of something special within the friendly confines of our office and warehouse location at 10108 North Interstate Highway 35. We wanted to be great. And our tight connections extended to the local vendor sales reps, the trucking hubs, and our customers.

To truly maximize our proactivity, we needed to get better insight into our inbound deliveries. After all, we could not get it out the door until we got it in the door. When it came to order turnaround times, every day mattered.

Today, online customers routinely expect to be able to track their packages and to know when goods will likely arrive. Back in the 1980s, however, that kind of precision was unheard of. Customers were used to hearing something like "Our inbound product shipment is on the way; we will let you know when it arrives," or "Your order will probably arrive by the end of the month" – nothing more than vague estimates that left a ton of wiggle room.

Mike and I wanted to remove the guesswork from the equation. So, we became "freight-crazy," obsessively looking for those inbound shipments. Most of our inbound LTL (Less Than Truckload) shipments arrived via Yellow Freight, either from the home office in Arlington Heights, Illinois, or from Micro-Term in St. Louis. Mike and I became best buds with the local team at the local Yellow Freight hub in Austin. Every other day, we would arrive at their offices at 8 a.m. with coffee and donuts, then park ourselves at a couple of empty desks and check on the status of each of our incoming shipments.

Armed with Yellow Freight's data, we could tell our customers when the goods had hit the road and when they would reach us. We could anticipate and prepare, so we could pre-schedule the bench time necessary to set up the systems, and – most importantly – make certain we had the other components on hand to complete that system when those goods arrived. That meant we could tell customers when their goods would be ready for shipment or pick-up. Being proactive works. That's a lesson I never forgot throughout my entire career.

Jim Foster, the procurement director for the State of Texas, said our ability to timetable his CRT deliveries down to the day and time was unlike anything he had seen anywhere else. This became an incredible value-add for us.

Our ability to function successfully as a business within a business gave us a whole new level of confidence, and that confidence quickly became contagious.

I was bubbling over with happiness. The hop in my step at work was evident outside of work as well, including my life-changing time spent socializing in Austin. I was making $43,000 a year ($149,000 in 2024 dollars) back then and Sixth Street was the main drag. The bars, the live music, the Tex-Mex and BBQ, the women, and the whole party scene. It was quite a culture change from the northern suburbs of Chicago! I even learned how to BBQ properly – low and slow – however, I never learned to drink anywhere near as much beer as those Texas pitmasters did.

Although I was the branch manager and focused on sales, I spent a lot of time in the warehouse, helping to finish off systems on the bench and then pack and ship. Apparently, you can take the shipper out of the warehouse but you cannot take the warehouse out of the shipper. One day, I was back there when we had lots of shipments going out. As I jammed on my air guitar to the music blasting in the warehouse, I shouted, "Let's get this shit Out The Fucking Door today!"

Impulsively, I suggested that we stamp OTFD on every completed packing list going forward. The warehouse team loved the idea; it was totally random, but it showed our confidence, enthusiasm, and sense of urgency. On the way home, I stopped at a toy store and bought a set of alphabet blocks and a red ink pad. The next day, I created our OTFD stamp by wrapping those four letter blocks together with Scotch tape.

Customers loved the OTFD stamp on their shipping documents, and they loved the confident attitude behind it. We received several calls from people who commented: "You have an attitude unlike any other business in Texas." (Apparently, even in Texas, "low and slow" has its limits.)

My time in Austin lasted roughly three years. In August 1984, I was transferred to Philadelphia, home of Tek-Aids' poorest performing branch. (The actual site was King of Prussia, about forty-five miles from the city.) The company needed someone who could provide more sales leadership, and my accomplishments in Austin made me the logical choice. Still, I was not crazy about the idea of trading BBQ for cheesesteaks.

I did welcome the opportunity to "be the hero" and flip the script on this poorly performing location. I told Jeff Beamsley I would go to Philadelphia, but that I was not going to hang around. Once things got moving and we found a suitable manager, I would

IT WORKED FOR ME

be moving on, likely to another branch. In my mind, I figured it would take no more than three months.

It is not easy to become the new manager of a place that is on a losing streak. On the one hand, you want to be reassuring, to persuade everyone that there is a way to improve results. On the other hand, you want to make them understand they must do better, and you must believe in them yourself.

In Texas, we won over a lot of "laid-back" customers when they recognized that our urgency set us apart from other lackluster companies. I was sure that approach would work everywhere. At least in Philadelphia, no one would refer to me as that "pushy Yankee."

I began by meeting individually with each of the seven employees. I wanted them to understand that I had come to Philadelphia to help them get bigger commissions, not unemployment checks. I identified myself as someone who came up through the ranks. "And now, here I am," I told them, "still learning, just like you are.

"My way does not work for all," I acknowledged, "but if you let me, I can help you be more successful. I promise you only one thing: Whatever you put into it, you will get double in return."

My meetings with five of the six salespeople went very well. The sixth, not so much. He was incredibly negative, and he wanted a raise in salary. It was an uncomfortable conversation. I tried to explain that, for a salesperson, the salary is just a base. His focus should have been on his W-2, which included his commissions. I was there to help increase the size of that year-end document.

I knew it was a waste of breath. His body language made it obvious that he wanted nothing to do with my vision, and that he was going to just stay around until he found something else. But that was not going to work. He was a major Debbie Downer, and employees like him are cancerous to an organization. He was gone within three days – my choice, not his. (As it turned out, no one had liked him anyway.)

When I talked to the sales reps about their major customers in the region, they were surprised to learn that, although I wanted

37

to hear the good points about each relationship, I really wanted to focus on the bad.

If we wanted a fresh start, we needed to erase negative impressions from the customer's memory bank. The reps hated this; the last thing they wanted to do was relive the screw-ups. But you do not know what killed somebody if you do not do the autopsy. We talked about how things went wrong, and why. And what they could have done differently. There were some tough conversations, but the reps and I both learned a lot about the business and about one another.

The following week, I went with the reps to meet each of our seven key customers. I asked each one to tell me where we had gone off-track. "Your business is important to our business," I stressed. "We are focused on growing this territory. Please tell me how we can do better." Most of the customers were willing to give us another try. Only one of these seven customers completely shut the door. His sales rep? The person I had just fired. In the end, he proved me right.

I used to cringe whenever people referred to me as impatient. That is untrue. I just happen to run at a different speed than you. Thankfully, a sense of urgency was not a problem in Philly. Within the first two weeks, I had gained the confidence of the staff. They liked my hands-on approach, and that I never let things fester. They appreciated that I was always available to help them with a customer project. Most of all, they bought into my OTFD approach. Proactivity bests procrastination every single time.

In my first full calendar month, the branch tripled its sales. In all fairness, the bar was set low. But our combined efforts moved the branch from last place to sixth place, out of eight branches. Momentum is momentum! And the branch seemed energized. Team members were coming in early, staying late, and reaching out to me for ideas on how to tackle opportunities.

From the beginning, I had made it clear to the home office in Illinois and to the team in Philadelphia that I had no intention of hanging around for the long run. Jud had told me he had a sales management role in mind for me in Illinois. I had some serious questions about how I would fit into the scheme of things, but the idea was intriguing, Meanwhile, I was syncing very well with one of the sales reps in the office, Kurt. He was a great listener, very comfortable and assured in front of customers. Seeing him as a potential manager, I invested more time in grooming him as my successor, and he progressed nicely, as did the whole team.

Ninety days after my arrival, the Philadelphia office was the fourth highest-producing company branch and, most importantly, it had a new positive energy. Kurt was named the new acting manager, and I headed back home to Illinois to become whatever Jud had in mind for me.

CHAPTER 7

THE LIFE-ALTERING ROMAN CANDLE

May 1973

Remember that Roman candle escapade and my dad deflecting the Dean? I did not know it at the time. But when I lit that fuse, I began the countdown to the most important moments in my life.

Let us review. It was May 1973, my sophomore year at Niles East High School. The school consisted of two buildings connected by a 200-foot-long glass bridge. The office of Kenneth Reiter, Dean of Students, was halfway between the two connected buildings. In a random act of spontaneity, I had decided to bring a 10-ball Roman candle bottle rocket to school that day. I had no definite plan. I just thought somehow it would end up being funny. And every day, being funny was my goal, my cause, and my hope for acceptance. Being funny was my buffer, my status, and my reputation. It was how I tried to avoid being harassed for my stuttering.

As the morning went on, I hatched my plan. Around 12:30 p.m., when everyone was at lunch and the glass corridor was empty, I wedged the rocket into the vents of a school locker that was facing that long, empty bridge hallway. Why? Do you not think it would be funny to see a missile fly down a corridor? Do you not think it would be cool to see it shoot right past the dean's office? Especially if the dean was at that very moment hanging his head out the door? Hilarious, right?

I lit the fuse. At that point, anyone with half a brain would have run. (Of course, anyone with half a brain would have left the thing at home.) Instead, I yelled "Hey, Dean Reiter, you suck!" and just stood there. No plan from *The Man from U.N.C.L.E.* or *Mission: Impossible* ever worked more perfectly. The moment the dean popped his head out of the office, the fuse ignited the rocket and off it went, "boom, boom, boom" down the length of the hallway. Five decades later, I still shiver as I realize that I could have taken his head off, while thankful Homeland Security was yet to be created.

Dean Reiter was so angry, he might have taken my head off. Instead, he called my parents. For the first time, I grasped that this stunt might cause me to suffer some very painful, long-lasting consequences. However, it led to two of the most important, and most positive, developments in my life.

I have already mentioned the first, when my dad's quick wit saved me from being sentenced to an extra year in high school and reduced my sentence to two weeks of detention.

I started serving my punishment on the following day. My fellow detainee was some guy named Gary. He certainly did not look like a hardened criminal, just a typical Niles East male student, around six feet tall, with black hair and a light tan. His crime had been bringing a pair of karate nunchucks to school and demonstrating how to use them in the hallway. Nunchucks? I would have liked to have seen that. We became best friends almost immediately.

A few years later, we were roommates, aimlessly wandering into adulthood. Our friendship remained strong even after I moved away, and Gary (who was now working for a company that installed custom lighting for discos), was the first person I called when I learned I would be returning to Chicago. As soon as I shared the news, he said, "Have I got a girl for you!" I laughed it off as just "Gary being Gary."

It took six weeks for me to complete the move out of Philly, and Gary never let up. "You have to meet this girl; she's perfect for you," he said. Her name was Joanne, and she was a sorority sister and best friend of Gary's fiancée Monique. "She is terrific!" he stressed.

He wanted to arrange a blind date when I got back. "Gary," I answered, "I am sure she is nice and all, but I do not do blind dates." That became my daily (yes, *daily*) answer. "You have got to meet her," he insisted. "You will marry her and name your kids after me." Finally, and only to shut him up, I caved. "Fine, Gary, I will meet her, but only on a double date with you and Monique. Now get off my fucking back about it!"

I made the 10-hour drive from Philadelphia to Chicago on a Saturday the 28th. Gary being Gary, he set up our double date for Sunday evening, the 29th. He was allowing me no time to plan a getaway. I called Joanne in the early afternoon that Sunday and apologized for Gary's pressure. Hoping to avoid awkwardness, I offered to pick her up on the way to meet Gary and Monique.

For a guy who did not like blind dates, I found myself surprisingly eager to make a good impression. About two months earlier, I had bought a henna red BMW 318i with a black rubberized spoiler, gold BBS tire rims, and sunroof. On that afternoon before the date, I hand-washed, hand-waxed, and then conditioned the leather interior of the car. If anything makes a better first impression than a shiny, waxed car, I would like to hear about it.

Of course, height also helps. As I was walking up to the front door, I heard her father inside yell, "He's a big one!" When I got to the door, I realized why. Her dad, Howard, was 5' 7", so to him, at 6' 5", I was towering.

I was sitting in her family room when Joanne first came down the stairs. I had my back to her as she glided into the room. Therefore, as she is still aware to this day, it really *was* love at first sight, as the first thing I saw was her butt. But seriously, she was beautiful. Unbelievably, Gary had been right. Joanne was actually very nice, and very easy on the eyes.

We sat for about 10 minutes with her mom and dad. While I politely answered their questions about my background and my livelihood, I kept one eye lasered on Joanne, sitting across from me with her shoulder-length jet-black hair brushing her fire engine red crewneck sweater. I'd always liked how black and red looked together; since that conversation, it has been cemented as my favorite color combination. As we got up to leave to head off for our double date, I was already wishing it were just a single date. She looked so cute in her jeans and Frye boots. The attraction was immediate – and seemed mutual.

We had a little time to kill, so we decided to stop for a drink. I took that as a good sign, a chance to get those basic first-date questions out of the way. Instead, it almost turned into a disaster. "What was your major in college?" she asked.

Not a strange question, and one I should have seen coming. Instead of simply answering, I began to overthink, knowing she was a college graduate but not knowing whether she was aware that I barely finished freshman year. Images of Jackie Gleason going *"homina, homina, homina"* in *The Honeymooners* ran through my brain.

Any good lawyer will tell you to just answer the question, and do not expound. Not me! I tried to lighten the load with humor. "I was a sociology major," I answered, "and sociology majors graduate college just one rung up the ladder from English majors. All English majors do is drive taxis."

She made a somewhat startled (but still cute) face and took a sip of her Amaretto Stone Sour. "I majored in English," she said. Though she looked amused, she was not exactly laughing. My brain immediately went into full deflection mode with the *Mission: Impossible* theme playing in my head. Very quickly, I changed the subject!

"What kind of music do you like?" I asked, urgently trying to escape the hole I had dug for myself. I was hoping she would say progressive rock – even after sixty-eight concerts with Gary, the English rock band Yes is still my favorite. That was a hopeless wish; 99.3% of women would never give "Yes" as their answer, and Joanne was not part of that 0.7% minority. Her answer: The Who.

"The Who is great," I responded, "but I really love Pete

Townshend's solo stuff."

Joanne's energy picked right up. "I love *Empty Glass*," she said. "I play it over and over."

Empty Glass had just been released a few months earlier. I was back, baby!

We shared our family info. We were both one of four children. We chatted about our college experiences; I mostly listened, since she had over four times more college experience than I did. As we were talking about previous relationships, she said some of her Jewish sorority sisters had given her grief for being pinned to a guy from a non-Jewish fraternity. I grasped the irony of this; I was raised in Skokie, a predominantly Jewish community, yet I had never dated a Jewish girl in my life.

Off we went on our double date, meeting Gary and Monique at Doc Weed's, a restaurant not far from Gary's apartment. After potato skins (a 1980's delicacy) and drinks, the four of us ended up back at Gary's place sitting on his carpet playing Trivial Pursuit (again, it was the 1980s).

Joanne and I were a perfect combo – I knew all the sports and entertainment questions, and she knew all the arts and literature ones. "We're a good match!" she exclaimed as we racked up another win. I was having the same thought – but it had nothing to do with the board game.

As we got back into my car, I considered whether to wait for a good night kiss when I dropped her off. *The heck with that*, I thought. So, I went for it. I turned towards Joanne, slowly framed her face with my hands, her skin was so warm, drew her to me, and passionately kissed her. She pulled back slightly, if only to look into my eyes, then initiated the next kiss, which felt like it went on for five minutes. After I dropped her off and headed back home, in one of those occurrences that had to be more than coincidence, "Let My Love Open the Door," the big hit off her favorite Pete Townsend album came on the radio. I could literally hear that doorknob opening my door in my head and my heart.

As Joanne tells it, when she got home, her mom was still up

and asked how the date was. Joanne said, "It was nice, I guess." Her mom said, "You're going to marry him, aren't you?" Joanne said, "Yes, I think I am."

I moved a bit more slowly, but not much. Six whole weeks passed before I proposed to the love of my life at Lou Malnati's pizzeria in Lincolnwood. Six months after that first date, we married at the Armour Mansion in posh suburban Lake Forest. Now here we are, four wonderful decades later, with three wonderful, happily married kids, and a never-ending string of "I told you so's" from Gary.

So, while I am not likely to try firing a Roman candle down a hallway again, I still look back on that thoughtless prank as the smartest, most life-changing move in my life. It led to my discovery of my dad's mastery of the Art of Deflection, my five-decade friendship with my fellow detainee Gary (call that the Art of *Detention*), and my introduction to Joanne, the love of my life.

I did not merely fire off that Roman candle. In many ways, I am that Roman candle.

CHAPTER 8

HOME IS WHERE THE HEART IS

———

September 1984

After my date with Joanne that Sunday, I was floating on air. The next day, when I returned to work at Tek-Aids, I came back down to earth.

I did not crash. From many colleagues, I received a glowing welcome. Tek-Aids had moved into a new building since I had left for Texas, and it was cool to see the new headquarters. I saw some fresh faces, but everywhere I went, there were warm hugs from old friends. In no time, I felt right at home.

By far, the biggest hug of the day came from Donna. I was particularly happy to see her again and to see that she was still the sales manager. Right away, she introduced me to her friends Gerry and Bobbie Nedlin, spouses who worked, not as a sales team, but as two independent sales reps with their own accounts and territories. They must have had great "How was your day?" rides home.

Almost everyone I saw seemed to ask me the same question: "Why are you here?" I really did not have an answer. When Donna and I went to lunch with the Nedlins, I tried to pump Donna for information. She had known I was coming back to Illinois two weeks before I did, but she still did not know exactly why.

Unfortunately, the warm welcome was not unanimous. The

greeting from Jud's sons, Jeff and Jim, was definitely chilly. I assumed they saw me as a threat, although I had no plan to challenge them. I just did my job to the best of my ability. Whatever happened after that was up to Jud.

That first day, and for a good long while after, I was undirected. I spent a lot of time on the phone. I called Mike in Austin and Kurt in King of Prussia to let them know that I had landed, and to encourage them to continue to use me as a resource; now that I was at headquarters, I might have even more influence. I filled my time calling my old customers, like Jim Foster from the Texas State Board of Procurement, just to update them on my journey and let them know that I still had oversight into the region and was always available to him.

I also made sure the customers knew that anything I sold to them counted for the local vendor sales rep, to whom they tended to show loyalty. I wanted to be clear that I was not poaching on the account. Then I went even further back and called those manufacturer vendor reps who had come into the warehouse to chat with me years before. It was a chance to reintroduce myself to them and learn about the customers in their territory. Many of them told me they were not surprised to hear from me and that Jud had spoken about me often. That made me feel good and gave me even more confidence.

Even back in 1984, I knew the value of building a relationship with the local vendor sales representatives. Each of them had at least ten customers, some as many as one hundred. Befriending the vendor reps meant gaining the trust of dozens, if not hundreds, of customers. I was happy to position myself as the reps' point of contact for any customers who wanted product or pricing information. The value to them was a trusted one-stop shop for their customers. I made sure doing business with Tek-Aids was easy.

The heart of that relationship was transparency. A manufacturer's sales rep needed to trust me to talk directly to his customer, either with or without that sales rep on the phone. It was a tightrope of being both open and cautious. You are only as good as your last interaction, and if during that interaction I inadvertently mentioned that we carried a competitive product, it would have ended everything. Worse, like a brush fire, word of that misstep would have blazed throughout that vendor's company; none of his peers there would ever trust me again. But when the relationship worked, everyone benefited.

My key tool was data availability, based on point-of-sale (PoS) reports, which all manufacturers use. This is how it works: Every product has a serial number. Consumers usually encounter these numbers only when they have warranty issues, but in fact, they have many applications. A serial number is like the DNA of a product. With the number, manufacturers can tell who bought the product, how and where it was purchased, the price at which it was sold, and the freight tracking number for the delivery. It can be used for warranty purposes and to combat counterfeiting. In short, the number tells the manufacturer everything that happened to the product after it left the factory.

Importantly, the PoS provides compensation data to the field sales force. The manufacturer's field salesforce gets paid based on everything that lands in their territory or is assigned to their account list, not just what that rep sold individually. They rely on vendors, like Tek-Aids, to report all the sales they have made, listing the serial numbers as evidence. We were contractually obliged to keep them informed, and we did so, automatically, at the end of every month. We also sent that data to individual customers to use as a reconciliation tool.

I began to proactively share this data directly with the vendor sales reps, in real time. They were going to see that same data when their company sent it a month later, so why not? Armed with this information, they would know what had landed in their region the previous month, which would empower them to make business decisions, budget their finances, and maybe even take their wives out for a special dinner.

I was able to use the point-of-sale report to show the local sales rep I wanted to be his reliable back-end engine, in the hope that the ease of doing business with me would entice him to route all his customers my way. Knowing that he would be copied on all communications with his customer reassured him that we were being entirely above board about everything. This freed him up to work on opening new opportunities, which in turn would also come my way. My open door, transparent communications, and commitment to proactivity became the cornerstones of my career success.

The relationship worked both ways, with some surprising benefits. I learned a lot from the vendor reps about what was happening in my own company. Although the vendor reps assumed that I was in the Tek-Aids inner circle, that was not entirely the case.

Often, they would refer to something that Jud or Jeff or Jim had shared that came as news to me. From what I was able to pick up from these conversations and from Donna directly, I picked up that Jud's sons were not happy with the way Jud was running the company. They disagreed with his growth plans, his marketing initiatives, and his vision of how to best move the company forward.

Both Beamsley sons were analytical by nature. Jim had joined the company shortly after Jud founded it, bringing a systems analyst background from the Chicago banking and financial industry. Whenever I walked past his office, his door was cracked open just enough to see in. He was always there, hunched over and pounding away on his keyboard. Most of my interactions with Jim involved getting the month-end point-of-sale reports that were so vital to my success.

I had more interactions with Jeff. He had well-developed social skills, perhaps tracing back to his days managing that music venue. He was an okay guy. Early on, we got along favorably; he even came to my apartment to watch a televised boxing match with me and Gary and some of our friends. He and I were just wired differently. He was analytical, and I liked to trust my gut. He was a software guy, very into writing programs and code, while I was more into hardware.

Jeff was looking to take Tek-Aids in another direction. He had been customizing software code to work with our Ohio Scientific student tech workstations. This had been a revolutionary approach, based on the early 1980s Open Systems Interconnection (OSI) software that allowed computer systems to connect over a network. Jeff saw that this was quickly becoming the new standard for all major computer and telecommunications companies. In many ways, he was trying to move us forward by bundling the computer hardware with software. For some reason, Jud did not share Jeff's vision. Over time, the tension between father and sons thickened.

Meanwhile, one of my best vendor partners, a Unisys manufacturer sales rep, brought me into a unique opportunity. Unisys had cut a deal with Goldstar in South Korea to take their personal computers and relaunch them in the United States under the Unisys brand. Their mainframe salesforce, then the big dogs of the company, looked down on selling these contraptions. They felt that pushing PCs was beneath them and would damage their reputations with their chief information officer (CIO) mainframe customers, who included some of the largest name-brand companies in the United States.

But PC sales certainly were not beneath me. When Jud asked me to develop a plan to bring this line into the company, I relished the opportunity. True, it seemed more of a great one-off than a career upgrade, but who was I to argue – especially when I knew those Unisys reps would dump all these sale requests on me? All I needed was a huge catcher's mitt!

The deal fueled an incredible boom in new revenue for the company. Soon we were selling Unisys PCs to 90% of the Fortune 500, and we provided that important monthly reporting of every sale back to Unisys for trickle-down compensation to the assigned sales reps.

But as sales kept growing, so did the tension in the office. There were more and more private meetings involving the Beamsleys; we couldn't really tell what was going on, but when we passed the closed doors, we could hear the bickering. Sides had been established, Jeff and Jim on one, Jud and Lorayne on the other.

Donna remained my chief advocate and my chief source of information, but she was feeling frustrated. Jeff and Jim had always barely "put up with her," and now Jud and Donna were not getting along at all. She had grown more and more frustrated that her voice was ignored by both Jud and Jeff. One day she confided, to my complete shock, that she had received several job offers and might be moving on.

Meanwhile, Jud was still open with me, and still happy to share his thoughts and theories. I know he valued our relationship, and that in some way he felt almost parentally proud of my career growth within his company. But overall, Jud seemed weary.

By this point, it had been almost three months since I landed back at headquarters. I had made a lot of sales, brought in dozens of new customers through my Unisys relationships, and I had learned a lot of new sales techniques from Donna, Gerry, and Bobbie. But for the first time in my young life, I realized I might have to move forward in my career without Jud's mentorship, Donna's inspiration, or Tek-Aids' protection.

My only comfort was that I had Joanne to offer me all those things – the mentorship, the inspiration, the protection, the everything. Joanne was always my safe zone. And so, following her advice, I asked Jud for a one-on-one meeting.

We met in his office the following morning. I thanked him for bringing me back to Illinois; if nothing else, it had brought me to Joanne, and for that, I would be forever in his debt. I told him that while I liked being part of the front office, my role here offered me no upward path; the "building a business within the business" opportunity that running the Austin and Philly branches had provided me was much more to my liking. And, certainly, more valuable to the company.

I was trying to give him the opening, hoping he would free me to fix one of the low-performing branches in Phoenix or Atlanta. I was more than ready to go, and confident that I could bring Joanne along with me.

On the contrary, while I was speaking, his facial expression turned serious. I think he thought I was about to tell him that I was leaving the company. He cut me off and said, "I was hoping you would ask. You will find out more within a few days, but between now and then, just know that I have important plans for you."

The scheduled one-hour meeting lasted a whopping 10 minutes. I really could not have been happier. Even though I had no idea what he had in store for me, I had no reason to think it was not going to be something favorable.

The next week, Jud totally overhauled the company, firing both Jeff and Jim. The sons had been trying to force Jud and Lorayne out of the company. Dad and Mom were blocking the sons' attempt to move the company more into software. In the end, the parents won. Jud stayed on as CEO, overseeing company operations along with Lorayne.

I was promoted to the position of vice president, with full autonomy to manage sales activity in the corporate office and all the branch locations as well. Of course, I worked WITH Donna; it remained business as usual for us.

I was mostly ecstatic, but I did have a few misgivings. Jim and Jeff were not bad guys. I felt somewhat uncomfortable that my success had come at their expense. Jeff went on to build and sell several software companies, while Jim returned to the financial and banking sector. A couple of months later, there was another change: Donna left the company, becoming a regional sales manager at a nationwide computer reseller. We continued to stay in contact and were able to have a lunch or two every quarter.

I felt very confident with Jud's backing, but I sensed that Lorayne was not quite sold on me and never had been. I knew I needed to fix that somehow. But how? Jud had always seen more of his spirit and attitude in me than he saw in Jim and Jeff, while Lorayne was devoted to her sons. But none of that had anything to do with sales, which were booming. By the second month of the change, we achieved a record month at $3 million, roughly a half-million over the previous high. We went on to have month-over-month success.

Sometimes, however, success blinds you to what is not working.

In addition to managing the accounting, Lorayne was the keeper of all supplies, all locked in a shelved closet. She would hand out those 19-cent Bic pens one at a time. If your pen no longer worked, you needed to bring it to her, and she would test it to see if there was still ink in it. Only then would she grant you a new pen. (Luckily, she never tested them for white powder, as the warehouse employees went through them faster than anyone. It was 1985, after all.)

To be fair, frugality ran in the family (maybe because they had lived through the Great Depression.) Once Joanne and I were invited to Jud and Lorayne's house for dinner. It was very pleasant, with lively conversations. However, they served generic milk with dinner, rather than the name brands like Dean's and Borden's. Joanne and I both just drank water.

After dinner, Joanne and I helped to clear the table, while Jud poured his remaining half-glass of that generic milk back into the generic milk carton. This confirmed two things: First and foremost, I was happy that Joanne and I both chose water for dinner. Secondly, Jud and Lorayne were cheap. Who would pour used milk back into the carton, generic or not? It did make for an interesting conversation between Joanne and me on the 40-minute drive home, that is for sure!

Jud had another frugal habit. He would keep a long piece of floss in the pocket of his tweed sport jacket. After a meal, while still at the table, he would reach into that pocket, floss, then put the string back in the pocket for next time. It had to have been a tough Depression for his family.

Jud and Lorayne attended our wedding in May of 1985. Our venue, the historic Armour House, had been built as a summer home for J. Ogden Armour, the meatpacking magnate, and it featured a beautiful marble staircase and spectacular formal gardens. It was a perfect setting for marrying the perfect girl. The best man I ever knew held that same lofty title at the wedding. That, of course, was my dad. Safe to say, with my dad as the best man, the bachelor party was, happily, pretty tame – a table for eight at a great rib joint. After the wedding, Joanne and I enjoyed a beautiful honeymoon in Las Brises, Mexico. We traveled back there a decade later to celebrate our 10th anniversary.

Over the next few years, Jud and I meshed well. He was the yin to my yang. We showed 7% company sales growth in 1985, our first year within the new regime. This was followed up in 1986 with 15% growth. We were able to attract more outside salespeople by calling on new accounts in new regions, and we continued to receive good press from the industry trade publications.

One of the newer lines we picked up was Wyse Technology's personal computers. Wyse was known for monitor innovation, and was among the pioneers in green, amber, and white text on the black screen monitors. We had been selling those for years. Wyse had come out with their IBM-clone personal computer a few years earlier, and they were rapidly gaining popularity.

Bernie Tse was the CEO. He was such an energizing person to be around – young, smart, and assured. He always traveled with his wife Grace, and they seemed like such a powerful couple to me. Bernie and Grace were in our offices four or five times a year. They would take Jud, me, and our wives out to dinner whenever they were in town, and it was a wonderful learning experience listening to Bernie and Jud talk about the marketplace. (Although truth be told, I had more fun listening to the dinner conversations between Joanne and Grace.)

I loved the fact that Bernie would ask me questions directly, even with Jud in the room. He truly valued my opinion and asked great follow-up questions, so he was clearly listening to what I had to say. Even better, Bernie listened to my opinions on the market, the pros and cons of their product line, and customer input. I never felt out of place or out of my safety zone. It was a very cool experience, as he was the first CEO I ever really talked to, other than Jud. Perhaps that was where the seeds of my "two guys just having a beer in a bar and shootin' the breeze" customer conversations came from. Relaxed conversations with your guard down.

Wyse Technology had two strong salespeople in our region: Bob Bates, our assigned account manager, and Bob Derizinski, the Wyse Midwest regional sales manager. Joanne and I had a great relationship with the two Bobs. They introduced us to a wonderful restaurant, Tavern in the Town, an old-school steakhouse in Libertyville, about 15 minutes from our home. Tavern instantly became Joanne's and my "romantic evening night" spot, and we still enjoy it some 40 years later.

Even though Jud and I were getting along well, I struggled to win over Lorayne. Perhaps there was some bitterness about Jud choosing me over her sons. I had hopes that things would improve in October 1987 when Jud and I, along with our wives, attended the annual computer show in Las Vegas, COMDEX, (COMputer Dealer Exhibition). It was the biggest computer exhibition in the United States, and second in the world only to Germany's CEbit. I was hoping Lorayne and I could click better outside the confines of the Tek-Aids corporate headquarters. Lorayne loved this event. At the nightly dinners with business partners, she would get all dressed up in a two-piece outfit, which was a velour tracksuit fancied up with a large brooch pinned to her top. Jud and I were always in suits, and Joanne was always fashionable and stunning.

While at COMDEX, I tried to treat Lorayne as just another customer to win over. At the dinners and shows, I would try to engage with her about her business career prior to Tek-Aids, how she met Jud, and other more personal things. But all I received back were clipped, one or three-word replies. I chalked it up to the mother lioness protecting her cubs; every time she saw me, she thought of Jud replacing her sons in the company. But whatever the real reason was, I tried. And failed.

When we got back from the COMDEX show, Bobbie Nedlin

came into my office, closing the door behind her. She started crying; Donna had been diagnosed with terminal pancreatic cancer. I sucked it all in and tried to maintain my composure, getting up from behind my desk to go hug her. At that point, we were both crying. Once I composed myself, I called Joanne with the news, and we both lost it together on the phone.

My sadness over Donna's condition soon soured into bitterness. She had left the company two years before. Although we stayed in contact and saw each other occasionally, our relationship was just not the same. I always attributed the upward mobility of my career to two women: Donna Panfil and Joanne Aronson (now Joanne Aronson Burgess). Selfishly, unaccountably, and irrationally, I faulted the entire Beamsley clan for robbing me of Donna's mentorship over these past few years, even though she left on her terms.

My hard feelings gave me an edge, a negative edge. Even Joanne called me on it. I had a tough time shaking it off. I was short with co-workers, and only a little less short with vendors and customers. I am grateful that my co-workers, especially those who were on staff when Donna was there, understood what I was going through.

Cancer took Donna in February. She left behind an 11-year-old son and a seven-year-old daughter. Her funeral was one of the toughest days of my life; thankfully, Joanne was with me squeezing my hand. I stood there wondering where my life would have gone without Donna's intense belief in me. Would I even still be at the company? If so, would I still be in the warehouse? And most importantly, would Joanne be sitting next to me clutching my hand?

The next months were difficult. My mind kept wandering more than ever. I dug hard into my work to try and combat it, and for a while that seemed to work. I was able to get some computer trade magazines to do interviews with Jud, as well as with Jud and me. We worked well together on those pieces. But I could not get over my frustration with Donna's exit from the company and the internal conflicts that brought it on.

My only salvation during those painful times came when I returned home each night to a beautiful, loving wife who greeted me with a "How was your day?" I tried to put a positive spin on how things were going, with a vague reply of "All good, nothing special." Unfortunately, she knew me too well and would come back with "I do not believe you," or even "Bullshit. What aren't you telling me?" I certainly should not have been surprised that she could read me like a book, what with all the book clubs she was in.

I was losing my focus on my day-to-day responsibilities and getting too caught up in all those petty things that happen within a company. Jud and I still had a good relationship at work, but I began misdirecting my anger at Lorayne. I was less than patient with her. Whenever she began to open her mouth, she could not help but see my face tighten, while I braced myself to hear her bring up something "beneath me."

What I failed to consider was that Lorayne was the matriarch of the family-owned company, while I was a mere vice president. I also failed to consider the likely outcome of being curt to the person who had dinner nightly at her kitchen table with the family patriarch. Jud was probably hearing about my rudeness every day, not only at their dinner, but on the ride to work and the ride from work. Talk about failing to "Know Thy Customer!"

I managed to keep it all simmering beneath the surface until November 1989, when impulsively – and in hindsight, unfairly – I exploded at the ever-thrifty Lorayne for interrupting me with a minor expense question while I was working on submitting a final bid for a multimillion-dollar customer project.

Here I was, with Jud's blessing and leadership, helping to grow sales revenues by the millions, when in came Lorayne to "bother" me with what I saw as a petty question about a $35 company expense that had nothing to do with me. "Get the hell out of my office with this stupid crap!" I erupted. It was the stupid act of an immature man, and I paid the price.

I had always said that Jud treated me like a son. In the end, he proved it. He fired me, just as he had fired his sons Jeff and Jim three years earlier. I would have been naïve to think he would side with me over his wife, just as I would never side with anyone over my wife.

Without any expectation of job recovery, I immediately apologized to Lorayne and told her that I deserved to be terminated. She gave a half-hearted acceptance of my apology, but she clearly did not mean it.

At the time, Joanne was seven months pregnant with our eldest, Alexander. In what we perceived as some kind of payback, Lorayne decided to play not-so-nice with our insurance, by taking her time sending us the COBRA information and ignoring our written requests for continuing insurance coverage. Of course, by law, she had to do this, but the two weeks she took to send us the paperwork for the filing upset my very pregnant wife, who was due sometime after Christmas.

I was furious. Joanne had been an innocent bystander in all of this. Mess with me all you like, but never mess with my wife, especially my pregnant wife.

Luckily, I knew I had options.

CHAPTER 9

HELL HATH NO FURY

February 1988

Robec Distributors out of Horsham, PA, was a company that had a lot in common with Tek-Aids. Both were national microcomputer distributors that served value-added resellers with microcomputers, video displays, disc drives, printers, accessories, networks, and assorted software. Both were family businesses. Both were owned by people of Scottish heritage. Most importantly, from my perspective, both Robec and Tek-Aids offered Altos, Wyse, and Unisys products. The two companies were fierce competitors.

Robec was expanding across the United States, establishing new outposts in Phoenix, Houston, and Asheville, North Carolina. Conspicuously, they had no branch in Chicago. I found it intriguing that they had bypassed what was then the country's second largest marketplace, but I assumed there must have been a reason. Now I was beginning to think it was maybe destiny – or at least my family's need for health insurance – that led me to Robec's door.

I called Bob Beckett, Sr., the company founder. "Jud and I have had a falling out," I told him. "I see how Robec is expanding, and I cannot help but notice that you have a gap in Chicago." I got straight to the point. "I know the products, and I know the territory. Can you think of a better candidate to open Chicago for you?" Two days later, Bob flew me into the Horsham headquarters, and we struck a deal.

We had a branch office up and running in the northern suburbs in no time. I was always happiest when I was putting a branch on an ascending trajectory, and the Robec Chicago branch was a prime example. I was full of new-branch adrenaline.

A few weeks after opening, I was visited by Wes McKinney, Robec's de facto operations manager, who reported to Bob Beckett, Jr. Wes was on his way to visit the Houston branch and wanted to do a walkthrough of the facility. Because we were going to have millions of dollars' worth of products in inventory, he wanted to check our building security and walk us through their company computer system and reporting processes.

Once Joanne learned he was coming and staying overnight, she suggested I invite him over for dinner. I did just that, and made us a filet and shrimp dinner, with some veggies and a nice bottle of red wine. Wes showed up wearing a sweatshirt, so I was glad he felt so casual and comfortable. He was a very engaging guy, until he started asking me what I considered personal questions.

Wes mentioned that he really liked our townhouse. I told him we were outgrowing it and had been looking at a four-bedroom home in the same area. He then asked, "Do you already own the townhouse free and clear?" He saw and liked the cars in our garage and wanted to know if we had paid those off as well.

Respectfully, I asked him, "What's with all these questions on what we own?' Wes apologized. "I'm not trying to be intrusive," he said. "I'm just glad to hear you do not own these things. In my opinion, there is no greater motivator for a salesperson than debt!" Another business life lesson I never forgot, and that I still use to this day.

Although we did not know it at the time, our lives were about to undergo another massive change – a hard and painful one. In 1986, Joanne's wonderful mother, and my incredible mother-in-law, Lucille, had had a medical procedure done at Edgewater Hospital in Chicago. Back in 1982, she needed a blood transfusion during the operation. Although we had been hearing news reports about AIDS for a while, hospitals had not yet begun screening blood for contamination by the HIV. Through the transfusion, Lucille contracted HIV. The disease festered within her undetected for a few years before manifesting itself. Right after Alexander's birth, she was diagnosed with AIDS. It was a horrible disease, but she lived long enough to see and hold our sons Alexander and Max. She passed away in February of 1993. Our daughter Lizabeth, born in 1994, was named after this wonderfully warm person. Lucille was the mother I had always wished I had.

That time in our life was especially traumatic for Joanne, who cared for her mother during her last years. In hindsight, I was a selfish husband, leaving all this to her while I was laser-focused on work. In fairness, Lucille could not have been in better hands, but I will never forgive myself for failing Joanne miserably during this worst tragedy in her life. Granted, I always had dinner waiting for the two of us – fresh, never reheated in the microwave – whenever she came home for the day; sometimes, not until 8 p.m. But that was the easy stuff. Joanne did all the hard stuff ... alone.

In 1987, however, we couldn't see those dark clouds on the horizon. I was excited to set up the new office for Robec. When colleagues from Tek-Aids reached out to me looking for opportunities, I hired a warehouse person, a technician, and a salesperson. Since Robec offered many of the same products we sold at Tek-Aids, we easily signed several of our former customers. In no time, we were owning the territory.

> **Any business – whether a sales company, gas station or hot dog stand – faces the same basic problem: competition. There are thousands of businesses doing the same thing, selling the same thing. Selling on price is fleeting, as someone can always undercut you. The best way to stand out is to offer outstanding customer service. That was our value-add.**

From my earliest days at Tek-Aids, I developed a sense of urgency when it came to looking out for the customer's interests. At Robec, I took that urgency to another stratosphere. We emphasized conveying a positive outlook to the customer. We set high levels of expectations for response times and lead times – and then we beat them. We spoke proactivity as our primary language. In a short while, we became the metric. We did not just raise the bar; we became the bar.

At Robec, I began focusing my attention on the account managers for their most important Midwest vendor partners – Altos, Okidata, Wyse, and Citizen. These four vendors represented over 65% of the revenue at both Tek-Aids and Robec. I had built relationships with each of them based on two principles: proactivity and transparency. They knew I was someone who got things done promptly and correctly the first time, and that I had a reputation for trust, credibility, and effectiveness. Now I wanted to take these business relationships to the next level.

These account managers had huge client lists. They had so many customers that they needed multiple sales reps on the same account. Okidata, for example, had three reps covering the state of Illinois: one for Chicago, one for northern Illinois, and one for everything south of Interstate 80. My goal was to turn those account managers' customers into my customers. I intended to do that through customer service. We would always make sure that everyone was happy with all aspects of the purchase. If anyone ever needed anything, we responded with urgency. Procrastination was never in our vocabulary; we were always in the "now" business.

In short, we made it painless for the reps to deal with us and profitable for them to refer customers to us. I was offering to streamline the business and expedite delivery while ensuring that those reps got the appropriate credit for their sales. Before long, the reps were bringing us along on "buddy calls," on-site meetings where they introduced us to customers. By the end of that meeting, the vendor rep would encourage the customer to buy everything from me. This was key, as customers felt very loyal to their vendor reps, and hearing their endorsement was so much more powerful than hearing a pitch from me.

My success at Robec was an early demonstration of the "Know Thy Customer" rule. Listening to our vendor's account managers and learning their concerns was the key.

No disrespect intended, but while vendor reps want their customers to be happy (and want to get paid for the transaction), they do not want to process orders themselves. It's the part of their job that is most tedious and aggravating. So, we took care of it. We made sure they never had to circle back and check on the order. Most times, they never had to do anything. By knowing our customer's pain point, we could remove it. I could claim it was genius, but it was only common sense. And it seemed so obvious, especially when we saw that it worked.

While Robec grew, Tek-Aids foundered. The company had taken its eye off the ball. They spent time complaining to Okidata, Wyse, and Unisys about market saturation and the increasingly crowded territory, losing focus on service. It did not take long for customers to notice, particularly since the buzz on Robec was so strong.

Before long, Tek-Aids was spiraling. Within two years of my termination, Midwest Bank called in their note, and Jud filed for Chapter 7 bankruptcy. Jud and Lorayne moved to Fort Wayne, Indiana, where they lived for the rest of their years. They passed in 2022, within three months of each other, after 78 years of marriage.

I was sincerely sorry to see Tek-Aids go under, as I learned a tremendous amount about the business and about myself during those years. I am grateful for the opportunities they gave me. But they did fuck with Joanne when she was pregnant. And that was unforgivable. (Although I guess I forgave them a little bit when our blessing, Alexander, was born on Jan. 3, 1989.)

I was flourishing. I felt so energized that I could barely get to the office fast enough every morning to start my day, especially now that I had another mouth to feed. As I had done previously in

Austin and Philly, I was achieving success by simply running the branch as a business within a business.

But gradually my focus shifted. I enjoyed meeting the new customers introduced to me by the account reps, and hearing about what they needed. I felt I was at my absolute best talking to them about how we could meet their requirements, while confidently walking them through the process. I found myself visualizing selling directly to corporations without an introduction from a vendor's sales rep. I began wondering why I needed to be under someone else's roof, instead of my own.

CHAPTER 10
EXPANDING MY HORIZONS

April 1990

Time flies when you have a kid. It was hard to believe that Alexander was 15 months old already!

When I opened the Robec Schaumburg location, my first move was to focus on the manufacturer sales reps of the big four computer companies: Altos, Wyse, Okidata, and Unisys. Of the four, I was most interested in Unisys. I had an inner sense that they would offer the greatest opportunity. The bigger the company, the greater the confusion. And I had worked with a number of those same Unisys reps while at Tek-Aids.

Unisys came into existence in 1986, the product of a merger of two great American corporations, Sperry UNIVAC, and Burroughs. For decades, Sperry was a major electronics and tech company. Burroughs, a century-old firm, developed the first adding machines and, in the 1950s, moved into computers. The name for the combined firm was selected from 31,000 entries in a company-wide internal competition contest. The winner, a systems manager in the newly merged company's Atlanta office, said it stood for "Unified Systems." For naming the multi-billion company, he was awarded a whopping $5,000.

When Burroughs bought Sperry for $4.8 billion, both were major manufacturers of mainframe computers. Roughly three years later, the new Unisys decided it wanted to get in on this personal computer fad that was getting everyone so excited. They began by cutting a deal with the South Korean electronics company Goldstar to make Unisys-branded personal computers. This turned out to be one of the first original equipment manufacturer (OEM) deals in the PC industry. But who was going to sell Unisys's new PCs?

I had seen this opportunity when I was back at Tek-Aids. I knew some of the company's salespeople from computer shows and had even joined some of them on customer calls. These were high-end salespeople with equally high numbers on their year-end W-2s. They sold large, powerful mainframe computers to large, powerful companies, and they received large, impressive commissions that fed their large opinions of themselves. I did not think their egos were going to allow them to hawk $3,000 PCs to their multimillion-dollar mainframe accounts. I decided to do it for them.

That was all the help I ever needed. There is nothing greater than having a free sales force driving customers to your door. Soon the rewards rolled in: Keebler, Kellogg's, and Hanes were only a few of the blue-chip brands that reps dropped in our laps.

Again, the key to making that happen was the vendor sales rep. A Unisys account manager in Michigan invited me to a meeting with Kellogg's in Battle Creek to walk through the new Unisys PC product line. This was an impressive first opportunity for me at Robec. Kellogg's was a multimillion-dollar annual customer of Unisys, but they did not even have an account set up on Robec's books. By the time the two-hour meeting ended, however, Kellogg's had Robec on board as their "PC vendor." On that special three-hour drive home, I heard the *Beverly Hillbillies* theme song playing in my head. I was a tech Jed Clampett, who went out "shooting for some food" and wound up striking oil.

Soon the word-of-mouth network within Unisys took over, and other mainframe-focused Unisys sales reps sought me out to dump their PC "garbage deals" in my lap. Suddenly we were selling hundreds of these systems monthly. We immediately became Robec's top-selling branch of Unisys PCs, grossing $3.25 million in our first 12 months. So immense were our sales that we consistently wiped out the stock in Robec's warehouse in Horsham PA. As a result, Robec's corporate office began ordering stock from Unisys directly to our warehouse, while all the other branches were stocked out of Horsham. That is respect!

Like that brush fire, the chatter spread throughout the region. All the Unisys reps wanted in on the program – and all the free revenue that went with it. It was a salesperson's dream to walk into a 10-state Midwestern territory, full of PC opportunities and lacking any competition! Unisys customers were loyal to Unisys.

Of course, there were other distributors, including Tek-Aids, who also carried the brand. But they were dealing with Unisys's newly hired PC reps, all baby-faced recent college graduates. I had the attention of all the big-hitting mainframe account reps, and they had the largest accounts. The larger the account, the more employees there were who needed a Unisys PC on their desk. The original trickle-down economics, and I benefited.

And benefited and benefited some more. It got to the point that the mainframe reps had me join them on calls with their customers as their "Unisys PC vendor." They invited me to speak about the merits of these systems, and their advantages versus other PC brands at the time – Wyse, Columbia, and especially IBM, Unisys's fierce mainframe rival. Those Unisys reps especially loved when I highlighted the systems' merit versus IBM!

Seldom did the Unisys rep even have to learn the features of the products, as they always had me for the deep dive. I loved that, as it gave me more control. If they chose to listen, they learned more about their own products by being on those calls than they would have gained through internal corporate training.

Virtually every Fortune 500 company back then had either a Unisys or IBM mainframe running their Enterprise Resource Planning (ERP) operations, so this was truly a mass-market opportunity sitting right in front of me. I spoke on-site as the

Unisys PC manufacturer rep to the chief information officers (CIOs) at scores of companies, including Keebler, Sherwin-Williams, FedEx, and Kellogg's.

As they say, practice makes perfect. All that repetition of the Unisys pitch made me pretty damn good at it. I must have been, as they kept parading me in front of their biggest customers. I really did know it inside-out. I was able to speak with so much confidence, it sounded as if I had engineered their machines myself. (*Note to Self: Sales really IS 99% confidence and 1% bullshit.*)

Working with this multi-billion-dollar corporation was fascinating, and my daily interactions kept my creative juices flowing. To say Unisys's left hand did not know what the right hand was doing was a cosmic understatement. Their left hand and right hand were seemingly reaching in from different planets. Internally, we used to refer to Unisys as UNICEF – since, like the United Nations International Children's Emergency Fund, Unisys seemed committed to working as a non-profit organization.

Here's just one example that illustrates the inexplicable inefficiencies of their internal systems – and the costs of those inefficiencies.

Unisys had roughly eight branch locations in Illinois, each with a different purpose. The Lombard office oversaw procurements and purchase orders, while the Bensenville office was a sales/warehouse combination. These two offices were just over eight miles apart.

Normally, a customer's order for PCs would come into the Lombard office, which would send the order to Bensenville, which would then send us PCs for customization and shipment to the customer. It always kind of reminded me of a routine double play, with Lombard as the pitcher, Bensenville on first, and me on second base.

We kept a supply of their ready-to-customize products on hand in our warehouse, so we could quickly drop ship their branded PCs to other customers. But one day, Unisys received a big order from Coors Brewing Company, the Colorado-based beer maker. Coors wanted 250 PC units, custom-built to their own specifications.

Normally, the order would have come in to Lombard and been relayed to Bensenville, which would have sent us the order to customize the units per Coors specifications and drop ship them out to Colorado.

Because the size of the order exceeded our stock on hand, Bensenville shipped us 250 additional units for customization. When they were complete, the Lombard office directed us to send them back to the Bensenville warehouse. Which Bensenville then shipped BACK to us for drop shipment to Coors.

Obviously, we could have drop shipped those units in the first round. Or Bensenville could have shipped them directly to Coors and bypassed us. It made no sense whatsoever.

But it was not our job to straighten out their internal inefficiencies (thank goodness.) So, when the truck with those 250 systems from Bensenville backed into our dock, we told the driver to go get himself a cup of coffee in our breakroom. Then we went to work. The goods never left the truck. Armed with shipping labels and a bill of lading, we went through every box, slapping our labels over the Unisys ones and replacing their bill of lading with one of our own.

When the driver came back from his coffee break, he was a little confused to see the goods still sitting on the truck. But when we explained what we did, he said "I love you, guys! That is awesome." We saved him hours of sitting around waiting. Talk about OTFD! These things were never *in* TFD!

Because we were so nimble and efficient, our branch was cranking out just under 900 total PC systems a month, which made Unisys's Midwest territory the company leader in PC sales. Robec also led Wyse's Midwest territory in PC sales. (Of course, we never sold a Wyse PC to a Unisys mainframe customer, as that would have instantly ended that Unisys relationship.)

Our goal every quarter was to beat the forecasts. In the last week of the first quarter of 1991, however, we were short roughly

$350,000 of our quarterly expectation. Fortunately – *amazingly* – a $400,000 order came in for 200 Wyse PCs with optional hard drives, each needing to be fully installed prior to shipment.

The order would put us over the top for the quarter. There was just one hitch. In the early 1990s, each hard drive held about 40GB of information and was manufactured by either Western Digital or Seagate Technology.

All personal computers and servers had 3.5" bays where internal drives could be installed. Every drive came with rail kits in the carton. The proper left and right rail brackets had to be installed on the drive before they could slide into the machines. Those rails never came attached from the factory. That would have been too easy.

Normally, it would take our three techs about three days to mount 200 drives, load the data onto them, and then test the unit. But for the order to count in the quarter's results, we had two days to get the 200 units out the door. So, the techs got cracking. That gave us a couple extra hours, so by the next morning, we had about seven hours left and 55 units to go. Then they saw that the next system on the bench was missing the left rail kit; it only had the right bracket. As it was a "do not partial" order, we had to ship all of them or none of them. We had no spare unit to substitute.

The lead tech messaged me in my office with the issue. I went through the warehouse, into the tech room, and over to the bench location. I could see the drive dangling slightly in the system. I asked the tech if the system recognized the dangling hard drive. He said it did.

So, I grabbed a large 3M Post-it note, gave it some origami-style folds, wedged it in on the left side of the chassis as a brace for the drive, and stepped back. It seemed stable. "Is the system still recognizing both drives?" I asked the tech.

He may have figured out early where this was going, as he smiled and replied, "Absolutely!" I told him to pack it up and put it with the rest of the order. He literally high-fived me, and that paper-folding trick earned me a new rock star status among the crew.

Ultimately, I did not ad lib that Post-it note fix to beat the forecast. I did it for the team, to show them that I respected their work and their effort, and that I was willing to back them up. They would have been completely deflated if all their effort had gone for naught because one system was missing some two-dollar rail kit.

Telling people that you respect their efforts is important. But showing that you respect those actions is far more meaningful. On one level, I used a Post-it note inside a computer, for Christ's sake! What was I thinking? On another level, I put my reputation on the line, trusting that the units were built so well, none would fail – especially that special one!

I enjoyed those first 18 months at Robec and learned a great deal. I realized I was fairly astute in turning a branch into a mini-company and running it that way. More importantly, I came to understand that as much as I liked running the branch, I liked selling so much more.

Selling was like having an electric current running through my body. The more I met with customers, the more I learned. The more I learned, the more the company could offer in return. I began to see that people valued what I had to offer, and that my comfort zone was working with the best of the best at the biggest of the biggest.

There really was no career path for me at Robec unless I wanted to go open or salvage another branch. Like Tek-Aids, Robec was a family business, but there was zero chance Bob Sr. was going to do with Bob Jr. as Jud had done with Jeff and Jim.

I was ready for something else. I wanted to be responsible for me, and not for others who might not share my same passion. I had built a wonderful network of computer customers, and I trusted myself to deliver new business opportunities and find new customers wherever I landed.

Luckily, I had Joanne's support; she was 100% on board. Joanne always had a gift of knowing me better than I knew myself. My feelings came as no surprise to her, as she knew that I really was not happy on the inside even before I did. But she also knew I needed to figure it out for myself, just as Dorothy had on those ruby slippers the whole time.

With Joanne, it was never about the money; it was always about me feeling happy, respected, and productive. She could see that for the last few months, I had felt like a caged beast, pacing impatiently until a Unisys rep let me out of my cage to meet with a customer. Only then did I feel free.

My Tek-Aids experience ended on a sour note. When I came to Robec, I was on a mission to prove myself. I did that. Now I felt that I had something else to prove. When a new opportunity came into sight, I left on my own terms. No cages required; no cages accepted.

CHAPTER 11

"CHANGE IS INEVITABLE. CHANGE IS CONSTANT." –BENJAMIN DISRAELI

September 1991

At the start of my career, computer sales were dominated by a two-tier distribution system. Tech companies like HP and Wyse would sell to regional distributors like Tek-Aids and Robec, or national ones such as Microamerica, who would resell the machines to authorized computer resellers. They, in turn, would sell to corporations or mom-and-pop electronics stores that sold to individual consumers.

Although I had been successful working in that environment, I was feeling frustrated. Joanne felt it, too. She's always had that sixth sense. In addition to the multiple touches in the chain, I did not like having to rely on some IT reseller having to make a sale for me to make mine. I did not know that reseller well enough to want to rely on their selling skills.

Of course, all this was swirling around as Joanne was eight months pregnant with our son, Max. As she has often said, "You always change jobs when I'm pregnant."

I wanted to be that IT reseller selling to that mom-and-pop store or Fortune 500 company. I had much more confidence in my own selling abilities than theirs – I saw that first-hand when Unisys brought me in to sell their desktop computers. I was confident I could control my own destiny better by selling directly to the end customer.

Joanne, always looking to protect me, walked us both through the pros and cons. We agreed: the pros won it by a landslide. She had ultimate faith in me, even though we had another son coming within a month. The only question was when. Fortunately, we did not have to wait long. The answer appeared the very next day, on a Friday afternoon.

On that ordinary Friday, I took a random call from a new reseller looking for the price on a single hard drive. I always try to offer options to a customer whenever possible; it's a way of proactively adding value. I just never want to hear, "*I wish you had told me before I bought it.*" I told him he had a choice: you can buy a single drive for $138, or a 10-pack for $1,300.00, or $130 per drive.

Apparently, he was all about value as well. To my value proposition, he replied "If you can get me that drive for $137, I'll pick it up Monday."

As if it happened yesterday, I remember cupping the phone, mumbling to myself, "Are you fucking kidding me?" The man wanted to save a dollar! One one-hundred-thirty-seventh of the purchase price! He wanted to lop off 0.000073% of the sell price!

Sure enough, I caved and knocked the dollar off his price, if only to get his sorry ass off the phone. Also knowing I was not long for the world there.

I stewed about my caving over that $137 hardware sale all weekend. It seemed like only a month ago I visited the corporate headquarters of Fortune 500 companies to meet with chief information officers who wanted to make multimillion-dollar purchases, and now I'm bargaining over a dollar? Was this now my destiny? I realized then and there that there had to be better choices for me out there.

By the time I returned to work on Monday, I knew the answer. I had made my last sale at Robec, and hopefully my last sale ever in the two-tier arena. If I had any doubt, it disappeared when the customer showed up in a taxi – *and he was the one driving it*. I handed in my two-week notice.

Mr. Save-A-Buck may have been the last straw, but I had been contemplating my next move for a while. One of those local customers to whom I had been selling a large amount of server hardware was Business Systems Solutions (BSSi).

BSSi's customer base was primarily accounting firms, ranging from local family businesses to Arthur Anderson and Price Waterhouse. While selling them dozens of higher-end Altos computers while at Robec, Joanne and I became dinner-friendly with one of their co-founders, Bruce, and his wife Jill.

One night, a few weeks before I left Robec, the four of us were having dinner, and I softly pitched the idea of us working together. I could come to work for him, which would give me a chance to learn the direct-to-the-end-customer ecosystem. In return, I could add incremental business to his company through my vendor relationships. I would only request a minimal "cover the bills" salary and some commission plan on those sales that I brought in.

As we were enjoying a casual dinner with the wives, I left it there, although he did confirm that I had given him food for thought and that he would discuss it with his partner Scott. We then went on with our dinner without any more business talk.

Bruce reached out to me that next Monday afternoon. I reiterated that I was interested in a one-year relationship. I would use his company to learn about all those things that go into end-user sales and installations, from procurement to deployment. BSSI would get the profit from the incremental hardware sales and services I would bring. A win-win. Three days later, we had a deal.

I wanted an education from BSSi, and I got one, from the ground up. I went out with their company installers and did everything they did, from pulling cable through drywall to connecting devices to the customer's network. I manned the phones for customer service and made follow-up calls to new customers, making sure everything was satisfactory. In my spare time, I contacted my hardware vendor rep contacts at Altos, Wyse, and Okidata, introducing them to my new position.

My first call went to the local Wyse rep, Bob Bates. He and I had done several deals together, at both Tek-Aids and Robec. He was so excited about my new role that he walked me into a new customer on his account list, Ringier America. This became the jackpot of buddy calls, which over time would become my norm.

Ringier America published magazines, the largest of which was National Geographic. So large was National Geographic's circulation in that pre-digital era that the postmaster of Corinth, Mississippi, where the magazine was printed, was then the third highest-paid postmaster in the United States, due to all that volume.

The company had a new CTO named Brad, who was very receptive to our visit. They were looking to upgrade all the production plants with next-generation PCs. It was a mutual sweet spot for us both. Over the next 10 months, Ringier bought 450 Wyse-branded personal computer desktop systems for $1.8 million, all through BSSi.

This was my first proactive hardware sale, where I was able to add additional customer value beyond the hardware, and it couldn't have been easier. We went smoothly from concept to whiteboard to execution.

In addition to hardware, I also arranged for software application training for Ringier's nationwide employees on Microsoft Word and Excel. I enjoyed arranging this service, and it enhanced an already great relationship between Brad and me.

The deal with Ringier cemented in my mind the importance of selling a complete solution to a customer; once you've made yourself a one-stop shop, the customer has no reason to look elsewhere. Looking elsewhere for pieces and parts is how they find someone willing to undercut you on price.

Working the Ringier deal also confirmed something I already knew. I liked being in front of the customer, and I loved being in the hero business. When my self-imposed one-year learning project with BSSi ended, I took all the knowledge I had acquired and headed for my next adventure. As it turned out, I left at a perfect moment.

CHAPTER 12
A BUSINESS WITHIN A BUSINESS

———

October 1992

When my year at BSSI was just about up, I was approached by a man named Reo Oravec, who worked for a company called Elek-Tek. Everybody in Chicago back then had heard of Elek-Tek. In the early 1990s, it was *the* retail computer store brand in Chicago. The company had retail locations all around the area. In fact, the Elek-Tek flagship retail store, in Lincolnwood, was next to Lou Malnati's, where I had the greatest sale of my life, with Joanne Aronson accepting my marriage proposal.

Elek-Tek basically owned the back page of the Sunday *Chicago Tribune*, running impossible-to-miss full-page ads for HP LaserJet printers.

Reo Oravec had news he wanted to share with me. Elek-Tek wanted to branch out beyond retail storefront sales and establish a corporate division. He had asked vendors to recommend someone who could help, and my name kept coming up. I wound up being his first hire for the new division.

As a salesperson, it's great when you can rely on some form of brand recognition to open doors. Elek-Tek had it all – wide brand name recognition, a reputation for quality, and a retail division that carried everything from cables to computers. Elek-Tek was a Swiss Army knife, with multiple blades for multiple markets.

Regardless of what the customer was looking for, we had it!

Best of all, I was walking into another feeding frenzy. In 1992, laptop technology matured, and delivered the Second Coming of the PC revolution, as IBM launched the original ThinkPad laptops and Toshiba countered with its Satellite series.

Elek-Tek stuffed its warehouse with both laptop brands, and soon I was selling truckloads of each, both to end-user companies and computer resellers. Most notable among these resellers was MPK Consulting. The "MPK" stood for Michael P. Krasny, who would soon open a company called CDW – Computer Distribution Warehouse – which launched just in time to ride the internet boom to multi-billion-dollar status.

As the corporate division of Elek-Tek grew, I got to work with some impressive talents. One of those was Paul Skordilis, who was savvy, smooth and a little cocky. I saw him as both my peer and my rival. I was a little cocky, too. You need to be, to a certain point, to be good. The goal to be Number One was always a healthy one for me, and I benefited from the presence of someone who could keep my internal competitive juices flowing.

Paul and I developed a bond over time. Despite our always-healthy competition, we decided to double up on some accounts to use a "strength in numbers" approach. We split the commission, and our customers were delighted to have not one, but two senior business development managers working on the accounts.

My favorite end customer story from this period may have been the first of the "Know Thy Customer" lessons for me, a commandment that ranks right next to "Know Thy Competition" in my sales bible.

At the time, KPMG Peat Martwick was a mighty global accounting firm – one of the "Big Six" (now, as KPMG, one of the "Big Four.") With headquarters in Chicago, the firm's IT director was Mark Martorano, a former detective in the Pittsburgh Police Department. Mark was notorious for not returning phone calls. (Keep in mind, this was in the days before email.) But we had heard from our local account manager at IBM that Mark loved a Chicago restaurant, Houston's, that specialized in the three-martini, prime rib lunches that kept freewheeling, free-spending tech execs happy and well-fed for most of the decade.

So, one morning, when we left yet another voicemail for Mark, we did not ask him to call us back. Instead, I left the message, *"Mark, we will meet you at Houston's at 12:30 p.m. for lunch. Much to share! Call back if you cannot make it."*

By 11:45 a.m., we had yet to hear from Mark. Nevertheless, off we went from suburban Skokie to Ohio Street in downtown Chicago – a 15-mile trip that took close to 45 minutes, thanks to Chicago traffic. Sure enough, when we arrived, Mark was already at the table, with a drink already in hand.

We had a great first meeting, walking Mark through all the corporate products and services we could deliver, along with the "clout" of having two account managers at his beck and call. KMPG Peat Marwick became a $2 million customer that first year, and one of IBM's largest PC notebook customers. And, thanks to Mark, "Know Thy Customer" is forever cemented in my brain!

I developed some other downtown Chicago accounts, most notably Swiss Bank and Homart Development.

Swiss Bank occupied the entire 8th floor of the Chicago Board of Trade building, plus a data center on the 29th floor. Swiss Bank's brokers also traded options on the floor of the exchange. (Visualize the frenzied trading floor scenes of the movie *Trading Places.*) To give their brokers an edge in this hectic and highly competitive environment, Swiss Bank was always on the prowl for compact handheld and micro-PC units. Elek-Tek had them.

Homart Development was at the time the largest owner of shopping malls in the United States. I had a great relationship with them. For seven years, before Sears sold the company to General Growth Properties, I sold Homart millions of dollars' worth of HP servers, despite the best efforts of every computer reseller trying to capture Homart's business.

The key to my Homart relationship was "location, location, location," as they say in the real estate business, combined with my great love of Italian food. Homart's offices in downtown Chicago were just down the block from Italian Village – a legendary, three-story establishment that claims to be Chicago's oldest Italian restaurant. Early in our business relationship, Homart's procurement manager, Shelly, told me that Italian Village was her favorite lunchtime spot. That was all I needed to hear. From then on, we met there for lunch every other week, and we talked about everything in the world, except work. After a while, she began bringing other managers and team members to lunch with us. They saw that Shelly liked me, and that she trusted my advice. So, as time went on, Homart's spending with us grew significantly.

Another of my customers at the time was the Loyal Order of Moose, the national fraternal and service organization founded in 1888. They were yet another Unisys mainframe customer that found itself needing Unisys PCs in each of its 2,000 locations.

Who would guess that the Loyal Order of Moose would procure more Unisys PCs than Keebler and Kellogg's combined? Their local IT headquarters was in their own village, Mooseheart, close to St. Charles, Illinois, and about an hour from my office. In addition to being their IT hub, Mooseheart also served as a residential facility for children and teens in need. I went to Mooseheart to work with their IT staff at least a couple of times per month.

This is what makes selling so exciting! Every customer is unique. KPMG, Homart, and Loyal Order of Moose all used the very same product, but in very different ways.

The key was just to let them talk, and to listen with my ears, not my mouth. You can never assume one size fits all. But what I *did* realize was that hanging around Unisys was a "gift that kept on giving!"

The term "market disruptor" was not around back then, but that would describe what I had ended up doing, at least internally. Elek-Tek had been a 100% retail shop. As they had taken the initiative to open a corporate division, I saw the opportunity to positively disrupt the largest retail sales organization in the United States. They opened the door; my job was to see just how wide that door could open.

For example, IBM had two different platforms for their ThinkPads, one for consumers and one for business. The corporate ThinkPads were more robust, with a higher-level Intel processor, the powerful OS/2 operating system, higher-quality dynamic memory computer chips, and the TrackPoint pointing button device in the center of the keyboard – the predecessor to the mouse.

Elek-Tek was only stocking the retail versions, but American businesses were devouring the corporate model.

I do not believe in telling customers we cannot sell them what they want, and we began selling a fair number of corporate ThinkPads. But that meant we had to purchase them on an order-to-order basis. The process of placing those piecemeal orders was aggravating and time-consuming, and we lost some orders when the customer found them in stock elsewhere in the meantime. It was a frustrating mess.

If I was going to be successful, I needed the full buy-in of Elek-Tek's leaders – especially Vice President of Merchandising and Purchasing Steve Goldman. Steve was in his mid-thirties, with long black hair and a bit of a rock 'n' roll vibe. He was always approachable, and he seemed like a decent guy.

When I explained the problem, and that I was trying to bring more business to ElekTek, he was not completely sold. He was concerned that, by adding the corporate machine to the product line, we'd be cannibalizing our sales of consumer machines. If we were going to rob Peter to pay Paul, Steve had to be sure that Paul would end up at the right end of the deal.

Within a month, Steve began to adjust. He even started letting us place stocking orders for corporate models, so we could turn those orders around quickly. Basically, he trusted us (or he was giving us enough rope to hang ourselves.) But I took that first show of trust as a personal challenge to never fail him.

Thanks to Steve, a new door was open. My brain started whirling with new ways to leverage my relationships with hardware manufacturers to break open some old markets. But which vendor to choose? Wyse had a strong presence in PC sales, but they also had a PC-savvy sales force. They did not need me. Unisys was lagging in the PC market, but that meant they needed my help more. They also had established relationships with virtually every Fortune 500 customer in North America. If they opened the door again, I knew I could take it from there.

By the spring of 1993, Elek-Tek had already established itself as a highly successful retail store for Unisys products. Now I wanted Elek-Tek to open a new "store within a store," dedicated to selling Unisys PCs to existing Unisys mainframe customers, with all leads and introductions generated by the Unisys direct sales force. The dream relationship.

There was just one catch: Unisys classified Elek-Tek as a reseller. To sell directly to corporate customers, Elek-Tek would need to be classified in the Unisys system as "industrial distributor." This designation would ensure that Unisys account managers would make commissions on future PC sales that Elek-Tek made to their existing mainframe customers. Basically, it would add thousands and thousands of dollars to those account managers' W-2s at the end of the year. Thanks to my reputation within Unisys, it only took about a week for my friends and allies there to sell Elek-Tek's new designation up the chain. Phase one was complete.

Now came the tricky part – convincing Elek-Tek's management to back my vision for that new "store within a store." Elek-Tek was owned by Mort Goldman and his son, Hal Goldman. Mort thought he knew a lot about selling, based on his experience as the fabric buyer at Spiegel's department store, back in the 1950s.

Mort no longer had much to do with the day-to-day operations of the company, but he was anything but a silent partner. Mort made Hal's life miserable by second-guessing every decision Hal made. Mort also was not fond of the man who hired me, Reo Oravec, which made me potentially guilty by association.

I knew I needed to be ready to overcome Mort's objections. I met with Mort, Hal, Steve, and Vice President of Operations Cam

Estes. Hal's secretary, Donna, was there to take notes. I took that as a positive; Hal wanted to focus on what I was presenting and have Donna document it. I did not bring any handouts or slides. I wanted them to focus on what I was saying, instead of tuning me out while they read.

I explained my plan in detail: The go-to-market strategies with timelines, the total available market (TAM) that corporate PC sales represented, as well as the saleable available market (SAM), which was basically the slice of that total market that Elek-Tek could capture.

Conservatively, my initial 12-month forecast called for $1.5 million in the SAM, plus another $1 million in accompanying peripheral items—monitors, printers, surge suppressors, even desktop PC stands—all shipped from Elek-Tek. This represented a 6-7% increase in sales over the prior year and would add at least 75 new customers to our roster. Because almost all these customers would be Fortune 500 companies, the credit risk was virtually nil.

I stressed one further point: I would be doing all this while continuing to work my territory, selling the full range of Elek-Tek products to local Chicago companies. Unisys had no expectation of exclusivity, beyond an agreement that we would sell only Unisys PC products to those customers they brought to us. (This agreement was not as strict as it sounds. If one of their customers wanted to buy a product other than a PC – a printer, or a surge suppressor – I would just reach out to the Unisys rep before accepting the order. It was almost never an issue, but my "Mother, may I" approach strengthened their trust in me.)

Looking at the faces of those Elek-Tek execs, I could tell I had their attention, but Mort seemed skeptical. So, I ended my presentation with my ballsiest close ever. "I hope you are in," I said, "because the Unisys reps are going to start sending us their purchase orders next week, as soon as Elek-Tek is set up as a designated vendor in their procurement system."

I could see the dollar signs in their eyes. The smart play was to accept this new path and make Elek-Tek the entrepreneur of the computer reseller world. Now they had to choose between accepting those lucrative purchase orders and moving into the future or looking like idiots in front of one of their biggest customers.

They bought in. At least Hal, Cam, and Steve bought in. But even after I explained the plan four times, Mort still had concerns. Mort and Hal adjourned behind closed doors to discuss my presentation, and we could all hear Mort berating Hal, calling him weak and accusing him of allowing "some newcomer" to destroy the successful company he had founded. Elek-Tek had experienced year-over-year growth for over a decade, Mort pointedly told Hal. Why was he caving in to a radical idea that carried so much risk?

To me, this was not radical, or even especially risky. It was an opportunity as obvious as Washington's face on Mt. Rushmore. I was not about to passively sit by and allow Mort's outdated ideas to stand in the way of the company's growth . . . and my own success. So I made yet another ballsy move. I reached out to Mort directly and requested 30 minutes of his time.

We met in his office at the end of the day. I understood that I needed to turn my sales commandment, "Know your customer," on its head. To persuade him, I had to give my most important new customer, Mort, a chance to get to know me.

We had some important things in common. We were both salesmen raised in the Jewish tradition. So, I started telling him about my own family history – about my grandfather, who sold pencils and office supplies on Devon Avenue, the heart of a Jewish immigrant neighborhood in Chicago. About my Uncle Max, who opened the first Toyota distributorship in New Orleans (and who notably married Mickey Cohen's former mistress.) I also talked about my dad, and the summers I spent working for the manufacturing company he owned. I wanted Mort to understand that he and I shared a heritage, an entrepreneurial spirit, and an incredible work ethic.

I promised Mort that I was not trying to disrupt the company he'd worked so hard to establish. Rather, I was trying to build on his success to bring his company into new markets, and I felt in my bones that we could succeed. I told him that I had made my numbers everywhere I worked and that I would keep him in the loop on every deal that came in.

I ended with a heartfelt pitch. "Mort, I need you on my side for this to fully work. So, give me 60 days to put up or shut up."

He told me he appreciated what I had to say, and he called me a "mensch" (a Yiddish word that basically means a "stand-up guy.") Then he told me I had his blessing, and I went to work.

I kept my end of the deal, and then some. The Elek-Tek company "store within a store" sold over $4 million of the Unisys corporate PCs in the first six months, and we ended the year with sales 38.5% higher than my (very) conservative 12-month forecast. That did not include the countless peripherals we sold. The company also added a few hundred new accounts.

Steve Goldman, my rock 'n' roll vice president, became the president of my fan club. Hal told Steve I was a hero, which I regard as the ultimate "attaboy!" While Mort never really understood what the hell we were doing, he was very pleased. (With good reason.)

Building that "store within a store" was the kind of maverick move my old mentor, Jud Beamsley, would have approved of (and probably tried to steal.) I smiled every time I thought about the way I had created a single-tier distribution company, from initial vision through execution to ultimate success. My adrenalin and confidence were both sky-high. However, fate was getting ready to teach me another difficult but valuable lesson.

CHAPTER 13
FROM TRAGEDY TO TRAJECTORY

———

July 1994

Mort may have liked the money we were bringing in, but that was not enough to keep him happy. Mort disapproved of just about every decision made by his son, Hal. Although Hal was a charismatic leader and widely respected throughout the company, Mort could not deal with the fact that Hal was gay.

Despite the conflict between Mort and Hal, business kept booming. In 1993, Hal took the company public – in part to reduce his father's control. Unfortunately, the company ran into some headwinds. Its second-quarter earnings in 1994 came in lower than expected, and the stock plummeted.

On a long-distance conference call with the Elek-Tek board and investors in New York following the earnings report, Mort reportedly erupted at his son. "You're not man enough in your personal life," he spewed, "and you're not man enough to run a company."

Hal put his phone on hold and left the office. On his way out, he told Donna, his executive assistant, "I will not be back." He went home and hanged himself.

After Hal passed away, the company began to die. Mort retired as chairman less than two weeks after Hal's death and moved to Nevada with his wife. Cam assumed Hal's role, but he was devastated by the loss, and he couldn't prevent the company from going into a tailspin.

By 1996, Elek-Tek's NASDAQ stock had fallen from its IPO price of $10.75 to $2.75, and the company was forced to begin layoffs. In 1997, Creative Computers bought the Elek-Tek name for $43 million, but they soon closed the three Chicago offices and moved to Internet-selling only.

I couldn't stick around for the sad finale. The disarray and despair at Elek-Tek were well known, and I was soon fielding multiple offers. Luckily, I had Joanne as my voice of reason, and we both knew it was best never to jump at the first offer. Joanne was newly pregnant with our daughter, Lizabeth, and as Joanne always correctly pointed out, I seemed to only change jobs whenever she was pregnant.

The most interesting opportunity came from Hartford Computer, a huge IBM business partner based in Inverness, an affluent suburb about 20 miles from our home. The Graffia family owned Hartford. Tony Sr., the CEO, had made his fortune a decade earlier in leasing. His son, Tony Jr, was the number two in the company and the vice president of sales, while his daughter, Andrea, ran the reseller division.

I met with "the Tonys" in the father's large, wood-paneled office. Tony Sr. led off by presenting his background and giving an overview of their market strategy, stressing their clout within IBM. Then Tony Jr. talked about their ambitious plans for the future. "We want a lot of growth in the next two years – accelerated growth." To achieve their vision, they had identified the top salespeople in the area; their plan was to hire all five. I was the first one on their list.

Then they got down to the nitty-gritty. Their compensation plan included a $420,000 base salary, plus commission. "Our intent is that you double your salary in year one," Tony Jr. said. Truth be told, he had me at $420,000. It was four times my Robec base, and even more than I had made in total – salary plus commission – the previous year.

This was a salesperson's dream. They had the cash, they had the vendor clout, and they had the compensation plan. "I see no reason we cannot come to terms" I replied, "but nothing happens without my wife's buy-in. Let me get back to you within the week."

Tony Sr. was a salesman, and he was determined to close the deal. "Why not call her now? Use the phone on my desk." The Tonys left the room, and I called her.

Joanne asked the same questions she always asks when it comes to job decisions: "Will this make you happy?" and "Will they respect you?" I answered yes to both questions, adding, "If I do what I am supposed to do."

A few minutes later, the Tonys reentered and asked if I had time for lunch. "Aren't you curious what my wife said?" I asked. Tony Sr. laughed: "She was not going to say no, was she?" I told him she definitely did not say no. On the contrary, I told her we were going out to lunch, and she and I could discuss it over dinner. And they will have my answer first thing tomorrow. And that I would be worth the wait.

Joanne and I discussed the offer further that night. Pros and Cons, as we always do. The salary figure alone made it a no-brainer, and the opportunity to make even more was exciting to me. Joanne was excited to see me so motivated and excited, plus, and the fact Hartford's health insurance plan offered full family coverage on day one had sealed the deal.

The next morning, I formally accepted the offer. After spending years representing IBM competitors, I was now joining one of the top two IBM shops in the Midwest, with the responsibility of making it grow. This was big-league stuff.

The first year at Hartford went very well for me. I blew past my quota number and doubled my W-2. In fact, I was the only one of the five "heavy hitters" that made their numbers. For some reason, that really ate at me. On some level, I would have been happier finishing in fifth place, with all of us blowing through our quota numbers.

It was not just that the other four guys did not hit their quota numbers. It was that they did not even try. Granted, a $420,000 base in 1995 was substantial, to say the least. (Adjusted for inflation, this equates to roughly $775,000 in 2024.) But why would you not make your best effort? Instead, they seemed primarily focused on enjoying the free golf.

Maybe it bothered me because I felt the company left money on the table. Who knows what we collectively could have accomplished? Why settle for Hartford being one of the Midwest's largest IBM resellers, when we might have been one of the biggest in the nation? If you are not willing to make your best effort, why are you even in the game?

None of them shared my love of the challenge of outsmarting any competitor, never with price, but with service or savvy. I saw none of that moxie in these so-called "peers" of mine. In hindsight, I just wish I had been more challenged, as Paul and I did back at Elek-Tek. I just missed that internal competition.

> **Throughout my career, I have always been all-in or all-out. I never gave it 78% effort, or even 95%. It was always 100% or nothing. So, here I was the top earner in what, disappointingly, seemed like a one-horse race.**

Frankly, I was a bit embarrassed to be lumped in with them when others talked about Hartford's big hitters being not so big. (More like big shitters, perhaps.)

What made it most confusing was that I cared more about our overall sales performance than the company owners themselves. Tony Sr. and Tony Jr. just idled the days away, shooting the shit with these guys for hours at a time. I guess the Tonys had developed a "country club mentality" from their years as members at Medinah Country Club, an expensive and extremely exclusive club that had hosted PGA championships.

But what could I do about it? After stewing about it for a while, I finally listened to Joanne's advice to stop focusing on things (and people) I couldn't control. She reminded me that I was always at my best when I was focused on growing my base of accounts. So, I decided to do what had always worked for me in the past: cozying up to the regional vendors' end-customer account reps and making them part of my sales arsenal.

This time, I had an exceptionally helpful ally. In the small world department, Joanne had attended the University of Illinois with Ray Rummle, who was now the IBM reseller rep. He had account responsibility both for Hartford and for Comark, our bitter rival. So, Ray had his hands full.

Virtually every bid opportunity for IBM ThinkPad computers ended up with three finalists – Hartford, Comark, and somebody else. If Hartford won, Ray caught an earful from Chuck and Phil at Comark; if Comark won, he got a furious call from the Graffias. Both sides always suspected him of cutting the other guys a special price. God help him if the third party ever prevailed. (They never did.)

I always meant to ask Ray for his post-award strategy. Did he celebrate with the winner first, then drive the 20 miles to the loser to get his ass kicked, or did he get the ass-kicking out of the way first and then go celebrate? I guess it did not matter. Regardless of who won, Ray won. Nice gig!

At that time, the largest procurer of PCs and notebooks in the United States was State Farm Insurance, based in Bloomington, Illinois. State Farm was known as a "lotto account," because when a vendor got in with State Farm, it was like winning the lottery. State Farm had 1,826 agents, which meant the purchasing department had a 1,826 multiplier. If State Farm's human resources director deemed that agents needed new ergonomic chairs, some lucky furniture salesperson was about to receive a purchase order for 1,826 chairs.

Working with Joanne's old classmate, Ray, and our IBM account manager, Craig Evans, I made State Farm my prime target. With their introduction to open the door, I started heading downstate every other week to spend a morning at State Farm's Bloomington headquarters.

Those morning meetings at State Farm were golden. I was always given free access to the IT and Procurement departments. I could walk through the office, thank the buyers in person for their business, and have 10-minute sit-downs discussing upcoming projects with each one of them. They could tell me what was working in the relationship, and more importantly, what was not. That gave me the information I needed to eliminate the customers' pain points, at least where Hartford was concerned.

Working with State Farm was a new experience for me. I had never worked with a client that took technology so seriously. State Farm was always hot for the newest and fastest technology, to give their agents a speed advantage over their rivals at Allstate.

Until this point, I was often able to take advantage of the knowledge imbalance between the client and me. The client knew about his business; I knew how the product could help him conduct his business faster, more efficiently, and more profitably. But State Farm did not need my help in finding the right product for their needs. They knew what they wanted, when they wanted it, and how they wanted to use it. It was an exact science to them.

They were very deep into bandwidth, and the effect it had on data performance. At that time, if too many of their agents got on their IBM ThinkPad laptops and tried to access the State Farm servers in Bloomington at the same time, the system could crash. To prevent that, State Farm put servers in their regional hubs, splitting the data streams and becoming one of the first users of distributed technology. It was impressive.

And they backed their convictions. Whenever IBM and Hewlett-Packard migrated Intel's latest generational chipset into their products, State Farm upgraded all their notebooks and servers to new units. This meant swapping out all the HP servers and workstations in Bloomington and the regional hubs and buying everybody new laptops.

What did State Farm do with all that redundant equipment? Like everything else they did, it was well thought out. They shipped it all to Florida. Whenever there was a hurricane alert for that region, State Farm would set up *M*A*S*H*-like tents loaded with that "newer" previous-generation equipment, so their agents were ready to process insurance claims as soon as that hurricane plowed through.

The great part about dealing with State Farm was that they were the largest purchaser of HP servers, PCs, and IBM notebooks in the United States. The worst part about dealing with State Farm was that they knew it.

Their sheer size entitled them to some extremely elevated expectations from our company, and from me personally. Some days I felt like I was scrambling up a very steep learning curve, and some days I felt like I was earning combat pay. The methods I employed on my way up were no longer very useful. I had built my success on being a "trusted advisor" to my customers, their go-to guy. Now I was dealing with a customer who knew exactly what they wanted, as well as how, why, and when they wanted it. I really had to be at the top of my game.

State Farm's depth of knowledge translated into pricing demands. They could be brutal in pushing their advantage to get themselves the best deal.

Most tech manufacturers find ways to keep their biggest customers happy when it comes to pricing. If you're a lawyer in a small practice and you're buying five new computers for your firm, you might pay IBM or HP $1,000 apiece. If you're a hospital and you're buying 50 computers, you'll probably get a volume discount, to win your business and keep you coming back. For an enormous corporate customer with State Farm's buying power, the special pricing on each project got very complex, and nobody exploited the complexities like State Farm.

All the major computer manufacturers offered special pricing to their biggest customers who bought directly from them. However, those customers usually preferred to procure through the reseller channel, which offered faster delivery times than these large companies could provide. But these Fortune 500 companies did not want to pay a premium for these expedited deliveries; instead, they expected the best of both worlds – premium lead times at or near the same prices they would have paid for direct purchase.

To keep these huge customers happy, manufacturers set up individual special pricing letters that allowed an authorized reseller to buy directly and pass on the "favored nation" pricing to the customer.

These pricing letters were incredibly complicated, with a long list of specific discounts that came into play under various specific conditions. These were more like mathematical formulas than a price list. This complexity made it very easy to cite the wrong cost and miscalculate when putting together an offer, resulting in a potentially very costly error.

I made a few early math mistakes. The first time I realized that I had entered the wrong price, I reached out to State Farm's procurement director, Bill Jolliff, and let him know about the mistake and how it happened. He gave me a mulligan on that one – but not on the second offense, which amounted to a $387 (x 100) pricing error on a $812,000 deal. Bill was a nice guy who was just doing his job, but that is how brutal the buying margins were. (And he likely had cost savings built into his annual bonus plan.)

On one occasion when we miscalculated in their favor, State Farm took full advantage of the error and increased their order, multiplying the impact of our math mistake on our bottom line.

Pretty quickly, I learned to prepare mistake-free bid requests. My attention to detail earned the respect of Bill and his team, especially IBM buyer Sally Waller. She oversaw State Farm's biggest purchase orders, which meant that she had all the resellers clamoring for her attention. With all that financial control, she could have been arrogant and difficult (as were many people in her position at other companies.) But she was always the nicest, friendliest person you would ever want to meet.

In addition to running the department, Bill oversaw the HP product line. Sally issued the purchase orders for IBM laptops and peripheral items, such as mousepads, network adapter cards, and surge suppressors. Although those may seem like trivial items, I still have a framed State Farm purchase order hanging on my home office wall, from September 1997. It was an order for 34,163 mousepads, network adapter cards, and surge suppressors, which totaled just under $6 million. Nothing about State Farm was ever trivial.

At Hartford, our pricing structure for IBM, as well as HP and Compaq, included only a tiny margin – cost plus 1/4 to 1/2 of 1%. Our prices for other companies called for margins 30 times higher.

Why did this apparent "give-the-goods-away" deal work for the Graffias? It was simple; the tiny profit was augmented by back-end reseller rebates from the manufacturer to Hartford – eight points from Hewlett-Packard, and six points from IBM. From Hartford's perspective, this was free house money, which was separate from their salespeople's compensation plans. Even after paying my 1% commission on all net revenue from my sales, Hartford was still making from 5.25% to 7.25% on every deal.

During my three-year hitch at Hartford, State Farm bought over $100 million in products from me. When you consider my sales revenues and all those back-end manufacturer rebates, Hartford Computer must have netted more than $15 million in profits, even though they were selling many of those products for less than 1% gross profit.

Working on the State Farm account, and seeing the numbers it yielded for Hartford, taught me an incredible lesson: Always look at the big picture, and make sure you're in the picture. Otherwise, you wind up on the outside, sitting on the sidelines and pining for your next opportunity to get back in.

Personally, I was never much of a piner. I knew that selling goods at a profit of less than one point was not going to work for me in the long term, especially since all those rebates were going to the business owner, not me. I realized that, wherever possible, I needed to establish other value-adds that could make my customers see beyond price as the only measurable in their decision processes.

My value-adds were primarily "soft" products, such as low-cost extended warranties, pre-installation of additional options into the PC or workstation, and other enhancements that served as "random acts of kindness" that made customers feel taken care of while enabling me to charge a little more. These tactics succeeded because I made sure my customers saw that added value – the positive impact of these soft products on their business. Often, they were less interested in top-line financial savings than in making life better for their IT staff and supporting their organization overall.

Even with those narrow margins, I couldn't complain about my paychecks. During my three-year hitch at Hartford, State Farm bought over $100 million in HP and IBM products from me. I finished 1997 with a W-2 of just under a million dollars.

I also was building a strong network of people I liked and respected. I'm still holding on to dozens of those old State Farm business cards, artifacts of good relationships and jobs well done. Some are so old that they show only phone and fax numbers – no company Internet URL or email address, and certainly no mobile info! (I continue to keep in touch with some of those team members, thanks to LinkedIn.)

Make no mistake; I was not kidding when I said my State Farm commissions included a significant amount of combat pay. When you're talking about orders that amounted to millions and millions of dollars, people's careers were on the line (including my own.) Beyond the stresses of keeping my customers in Bloomington happy, I also had to deal with the even greater burden of dealing with Hartford's corporate office.

Two or three times a week, Ray Rummle came by to brief the Tonys about our account, and about the Midwest region. I hated it, because I always liked to keep my plans and my deals close to the vest; I did not want any of the details to leak. Let me be clear: I was not worried that Ray would run off and reveal my pending opportunities with Comark. Even though he worked with both of us, I trusted him to keep my confidence.

The real problem was that I did not want to have the two Tonys in my face, grilling me about various rumors they'd heard from their many contacts inside IBM. With other people, in other circumstances, that level of interest from the boss might have helped to keep me on my toes; here, it felt intrusive. I found myself on the defensive 80% of the time. It made no sense; even though I was delivering millions and millions of dollars on the account, they kept scrutinizing my work and calling me on the carpet every time a deal went to Comark.

I still smiled when I put my check in the bank, but I was starting to wonder if the grass might be a little greener (or at least a little softer) somewhere else.

CHAPTER 14

"TO HELL WITH CIRCUMSTANCES; I CREATE OPPORTUNITIES." –BRUCE LEE

————

February 1996

One of the biggest lessons I learned from State Farm was the importance of taking the lead when it came to innovative new technologies. For example, they were pioneers in using barcode technology. Once it became obvious how important barcodes were to their operations, I made it my business to earn my stripes when it came to this new technology – not just how it worked, but why it was valuable to the company.

I quickly learned that State Farm was using these barcodes to streamline warehouse operations in its new IT distribution center in Las Vegas. That distribution center served a lot of people – more than 50,000 agents and employees spread across distribution centers and regional corporate hubs nationwide. The Las Vegas distribution center handled a staggering array of products. Just from Hartford alone, they purchased IBM ThinkPad notebooks, network adapters, and hundreds of different types of cables – printer cables, ethernet cables, ribbon cables, and token-ring cables, to name just a few. State Farm's vision was to use bar code technology to attain unprecedented levels of immediacy and inventory control, and they established procedures that are now standard operating procedure in almost every industry.

The key was in the information encoded on those labels. First, each product had to be labeled with its own individual State Farm barcode tag. That was then packed into a carton and labeled with a code that indicated the component type and manufacturer, as well as the product's State Farm-specific cross-reference number. This innovation controlled overhead, duplication, waste, and pilfering. It was huge.

State Farm put the onus of applying these individual and carton labels on the reseller, as part of the purchase order. Let's say State Farm ordered 900 IBM Token Ring network adapters. Before we shipped the goods, we had to apply the product's unique State Farm identifier label to each one. Then, per State Farm's detailed instructions, we packed 30 adapters into a customized State Farm carton and affixed a barcoded "part number/box of 30" label to the outside. We then loaded the 30 finished cartons onto pallet skids that (again per instructions) could be stacked no more than five feet tall and shipped them off to the State Farm distribution center in Vegas.

Within seconds of arrival in Bloomington or Las Vegas, the cartons would be scanned and received into State Farm's inventory, before even leaving the dock.. Any shipments that arrived without the mandatory barcode labels would be rejected and sent back. No exceptions.

On one level, State Farm was not asking for anything unusual. Any product we shipped would need some kind of label and would have to be shipped in an appropriately marked container. But the specificity of State Farm's barcode requirements opened an opportunity for me, and I fearlessly added a $10 per item labor charge on every quote we sent to them. So, sticking those barcodes on those 900 adapters cost them $9,000.

If you think it sounds like we were nickel and diming our customer, you've got it wrong. We were making a statement to State Farm about the value we put on the services we provided.

That $10 covered more than the cost of printing labels and sticking them on boxes. That $10 charge was a sign of our commitment to making sure that State Farm would get what they wanted, the way they wanted it. The reality is, our diligence in labeling those goods probably saved them at least that much, as compared to the labor costs of unboxing, labeling, and reboxing every product that came in the door.

To avoid any confusion, we added specific details about barcode labeling on every purchase order they placed with us. Our system worked so well that I was able to convince them to include this requirement in every Request for Quote (RFQ) they issued. That way, I said with a very straight face, State Farm could be sure of an "apples to apples" comparison as they reviewed the bids for goods and services. That this also protected me from being underbid by a competitor willing to eat the cost of barcode labeling never even crossed my mind.

Ten dollars may not sound like much, but when you consider that "State Farm multiplier," it added up fast. Take that $6 million purchase order for 34,163 mousepads, network adapter cards, and surge suppressors. The charge for labeling all those items was $341,630 – about 95% pure profit over the actual labor cost on our end, which represented 48.6% of the total direct profit Hartford made on the deal. (Of course, that doesn't count the 6% back-end rebate from IBM that went into the Tonys' pockets.)

State Farm took up much of my time, and deservedly so. But thanks to my excellent customer service team, which managed the day-to-day transactions and support, I was able to look for other opportunities. So, I reached out to my HP contacts and struck gold again, thanks to what I call a "reputation referral."

A Hewlett-Packard sales rep, whom I had never met, got my name from one of the local HP reps who worked with me during my days at Robec. After hearing good things, the sales rep passed my name along to the HP account manager covering Connecticut, who introduced me to Senior Procurement Manager Dawn Cox at General Electric.

When I first met Dawn in 1997, GE was the second-largest company in the world. They manufactured military and communications technology and a full range of consumer appliances – refrigerators, dishwashers, microwaves, etc. They owned NBC. They also oversaw the twenty-six GE Capital financial companies, which represented the bulk of GE's computer-related purchases.

After our short, early-morning introductory meeting in her office in Fairfield, Connecticut, Dawn picked up the phone and called Kim Giancaspro, who ran the procurement for GE Capital. Kim's brash confidence came through loud and clear through the speakerphone, and I loved her chewing gum-chomping New England accent. We hit it off immediately.

I was not wasting any time. From Dawn's office, I drove the 90 minutes to meet with Kim in person at GE Capital's headquarters in Stamford, Connecticut. To my surprise, Kim brought in Mark Allen, HP Global account manager for GE. My timing could not have been better. GE Capital was standardizing its HP servers, and they were looking for a vendor who could handle their anticipated volume.

The three of us went to lunch at Bennett's Restaurant, a steakhouse owned by a legendary former NBA referee, Bennett Salvatore. It was the easiest meeting of my life. Mark did most of the talking. He told Kim that, although he and I had never so much as talked on the phone before, it was the consensus option of all his fellow HP account managers across the United States that I was the absolute best person to work with her on the HP project.

I sat there quietly, almost blushing, causing me to get pinker than the inside of my steak, while Mark went on and on about my sterling reputation throughout Hewlett-Packard, my superior communication skills, and my all-around general wonderfulness. After all that praise, the least I could do was pick up the lunch check. Although it felt a little bit like listening to my own eulogy, that luncheon really brought home an important lesson: When you establish a good reputation based on trust and proven results, amazing things can happen.

The HP vendor reps' willingness to bring me to their largest customer gave me instant credibility with both Kim and Dawn. When you are hand-delivered to a customer by someone they already know and trust, it gets all those "first date" questions out of the way. By the time the meetings ended, Kim and Dawn saw me as a member of the HP team. After that, they just dealt with me directly, eliminating the middleman.

The HP reps were all on board with this because they knew I would respect their commissions. As soon as I got back home, I set up their accounts on our system. Within two days, the onslaught of orders from GE Capital began. Over the next three years, GE and GE Capital purchased over $28 million in HP servers and workstations.

Kim and Dawn added Hartford Computer Group to their special HP price letter. This allowed us to purchase products through our regular distribution partners at GE's special cost, which was generally fifty cents on the dollar. That showed the clout and buying power of GE.

Initially, GE Capital sent their purchase orders via fax. Those orders started coming in at 5:01 p.m. Eastern time, after phone rates dropped. So, every day at 4:01 Central time, I walked to the fax machine and waited to start grabbing pages.

Each fax took two minutes to transmit. The faxes were virtually all the same: the first page spelled out what the company wanted to order, and the next seven pages were full of boilerplate terms and conditions. I kept the first page and shredded the rest, with the cash register in my head quickly tabulating the totals on the fly. Every day, we received a dozen or so GE Capital purchase orders, averaging $60,000 a day, or $1.6 million per month. It was a great recurring business – for me, and for Hartford.

So, why was I so underappreciated by the Tonys? My reward for all the State Farm business I had brought in had been scrutiny and criticism. When I unleashed a tidal wave of business from GE and GE Capital, I barely got a pat on the back, let alone an "attaboy." Likely because it was HP, and all the back-end "funny money" came from IBM.

One day, I was in my office stuck on a call at 4 p.m., when the GE faxes started coming through. Tony Sr. happened to be passing by the fax machine at that time. Apparently, he intended to do me a favor by bringing me the faxed orders. But as he walked down the hallway, he started reading those boilerplate pages of terms and conditions, and he blew a fuse.

He walked into my office, waving the paperwork at me. "I never agreed to this!" he thundered.

"Gosh, Tony, it's GE, the second-largest company in the world," I said. "I'm not sure they care what you think." I laughed a bit to soften the snark, but I was not sure how he would respond. He surprised me by not saying another word. Instead, he just handed me the paperwork and left my office. If you cannot get the "attaboy" you deserve, I guess sometimes you must be satisfied with silence.

CHAPTER 15
MOVING THROUGH SOME CHANGES

———

June 1996

IBM and State Farm were making headlines, at least in our little corner of the world. IBM took over State Farm's procurement process.

This was part of a larger corporate trend, in which large leasing companies and hardware manufacturers, such as HP and IBM, began offering Procure-to-Pay (P2P) services to their larger customers. State Farm was essentially hiring IBM to take over its procurement department and manage its purchasing process.

On paper, this P2P arrangement was supposed to benefit both parties. IBM would have direct control over State Farm's spending, which would give them a line of sight into the pricing offered by HP and other rivals. They also would be empowered to route as much business as possible to themselves. State Farm would benefit by reducing headcount in the procurement department, perhaps by as much as 40%. State Farm also expected reduced equipment costs, because using your main hardware vendor to source your products should drive savings that would reduce prices.

Spoiler alert: Within a year, State Farm – with its state-of-the-art pricing and procurement procedures – would revert to its previous practices. But that outcome was far from obvious when the deal was announced. These were two rich and powerful companies that seemed to know what they were doing.

It was obvious that my business was about to undergo a massive change. Now more than ever, I needed to be on my toes, alert to opportunities to take customer service to higher levels with State Farm. Otherwise, with IBM's procurement arm available to purchase their ThinkPads for them directly, why would they need me?

I had always been a relationship seller; my reliability, my dependability, and my trustworthiness were qualities people valued in our dealings. But I had no relationship with IBM procurement, and I was not sure if State Farm would consider my good qualities in their quest for the lowest possible price.

I desperately began seeking new ways to increase my worth to their organization. I thought it was imperative for me to stay visible to the remaining State Farm procurement staff, so they would continue to recommend me within their new buying organization. So, I bumped up my visits to the Bloomington campus from once or twice a month to three times a week.

The State Farm procurement teams were worried about their job security, so I wanted them to see me as an ally and a friend as they navigated this change. I made a point of keeping them in the loop on upcoming IBM products and explaining how the new products and accessories worked together.

In a very short time, it became clear that, from our company's perspective, it was business as usual. We continued to receive purchase orders from State Farm for internal computer components – nothing in the eight-figure range, but always decent-sized orders that totaled $8 million or $9 million each. What mattered most was not the size of the orders, but that the orders kept coming. The oil might not have been gushing as it had been, but it never stopped flowing. It is odd that $9 million orders were not considered gushing. I was a little spoiled.

Significantly, the only orders we received in the first weeks of the new regime came directly from the State Farm purchasing team; nothing yet from the new IBM procurement arm.

Finally, three months after the new procurement program was announced, we received our first purchase order directly from IBM Computer Products. The order was "on the behalf of State Farm Insurance," and was sent to my personal attention at Hartford Computer Group. The order was for 16,000 IBM ThinkPad notebook computers, at a total purchase price of $45 million. What a way to make an entrance!

The massive size and scope of this purchase order required the signature of Louis Gerstner, then the chief executive officer at IBM. It was impressive to see that this internationally renowned executive had signed off on the order, but I was happiest to see my own name on it.

Just about a year later, on September 15, 1997, I received another purchase order sent directly to my attention at Hartford Computer Group. This time, the order came from State Farm – not IBM Procurement. The third-party procurement experiment was over.

This new order included just two lines: 20,000 IBM monitors and 20,000 IBM PCs, for a total of $39.5 million. That "two-item" order is also framed and hanging on my home office wall. Two line items requiring five internal signatures on the PO. I had never seen anything like it and never have since.

A month after this monumental deal, Hartford "promoted" me to sales manager. There was no question that I deserved a promotion; by any standard, I had been killing it for the previous couple of years. But no sooner was the word "promotion" off their lips than the real headline from the meeting was revealed: they were altering my compensation formula, and not in my favor. I would still earn the same base salary, almost half a million dollars, but the commission plan changed drastically. My "promotion" would cost me about $375,000 a year.

I stood there and tried not to roll my eyes at their "how this will better the company" bullshit. When Tony Jr. told me that State Farm had become a "house account," and that was one of the reasons they modified my comp plan, I just laughed, glad that I had paid off my house by then.

Perhaps they were hoping I would quit. I had been openly critical of the poor work ethic of those other so-called heavy hitters, and of the way management scrutinized my every move while letting the others get away with phoning it in. Maybe they thought one massive financial insult would send me and my complaints out the door. But I was not going to give them that satisfaction – at least not until I had my next move locked and loaded. My wife and our (now) three kids were more important than my ego.

There was really nothing to say; they had made their decision. My only option in the short term was to play the game and collect my paycheck while I quietly looked around. I made sure I did this outside of the building, and outside of company time. At that point, I had to assume they were tapping into my email, and possibly monitoring my office phone calls as well.

It felt like I was in purgatory. More than anything, I needed to fake it, which is not in my skill set. (Probably why I get invited to so many poker games.) So, I put on my not-very-convincing poker face and got on with the job of sales manager.

My new duties required me to hire some additional salespeople, which required me to know a little bit about golf. I was not much of a golfer. I only played with customers once or twice a year, and for me, that was less about golf and more about the chance to spend four hours building a customer relationship. But I was surrounded by avid golfers, from the Graffia family on down.

My first question for prospective hires was always the same: If they got the job, how many customers would they be able to bring with them on day one?

If they did not have a portable book of business, my next question focused on Hartford's annual event at Medinah Country Club for the company's top salespeople and their customers. Did they know about the annual event? If they had heard of it, I followed up by asking for their golf handicap. Many applicants would brighten up at that question, talking about their scores and the legendary courses they had played in the past.

Unfortunately for them, it was a trick question. I would never hire a candidate whose handicap was under ten. You need to play a lot of golf to achieve a single-digit handicap. If I hired great golfers, they would be playing on our dime, and without any short-term customer movement to offset the expense. So, I thanked them, wished them luck with their short games, and kept looking.

Things came to a head in the early spring of 1998, when Hartford hired Chris Froman as vice president of sales. Froman was an ex-director at IBM, and one of Tony Sr.'s golfing buddies. I would now be reporting to him.

At IBM, Chris had earned the nickname T-Rex, because he was notorious for biting people's heads off. On his first day at Hartford, he walked into my office, matter-of-factly said, "You're making too much money!" and walked back out. This was just 45 days after my comp plan had been downsized by 33%. Welcome to the company, Chris!

I called Joanne and told her what happened. She responded with a few choice expletives, directed towards him, not me. Then she said, "Hurry home!" (I love my wife.)

I probably should have thanked Chris Froman for the huge favor he did for me on his first day. Before Chris walked into my office and dropped the bomb about my pay levels, I had been angry at Hartford but unfocused on my next step. If Chris had been able to keep his mouth shut, I might not have sensed there was more unwelcome news coming my way until it was too late. Thankfully, Chris was an even worse poker player than I am. So, I started making my plan to walk away from that table, with a full stack of chips in hand.

CHAPTER 16
TIME IS ON MY SIDE

———

September 1998

I knew that Hartford was unlikely to fire me outright. They would have had to pay me severance, and they were too cheap to do that. My dismissal also would have prompted some uncomfortable conversations between the Tonys and two of their largest accounts, State Farm and GE.

But I did not want to run the risk of getting fired, which would have harmed my reputation with my customers. There are always questions when a guy is canned. I needed to leave the company on my terms. If I left voluntarily, the move would be perceived as part of a salesperson's normal career arc – a search for new horizons, a place where I was a better fit and could offer better services for my customers.

The hard part would be going into stealth bomber mode and keeping up a business-as-usual profile as I planned my getaway. Over the next two months, I made a show of focusing on my work, serving my customers, and hitting my numbers.

Pretty quickly, I discerned the key elements of what I wanted from my next job. Even though I was confident that I could have put a serious dent in Hartford's State Farm volume, I ruled out going to Comark, their closest competitor. I was not crazy about their corporate culture, and I did not want to jump from the frying pan into the fire.

Compensation was important, obviously, but with three children I was also focused on finding a job with a strong benefits package.

What was most crucial for me was maintaining the relationships I had built with my customers. Going back to my time at Tek-Aids, I had worked hard to build a reputation for responsiveness and trustworthiness. I felt a real connection with Dawn's team at GE, with Kim's team at GE Capital, and with all the HP account managers covering these accounts. Even though our paychecks came from different companies, I was considered a member of the HP team – the go-to guy who knew how to get things done.

At this point in my career, I had worked at two regional IT computer distributors, a name-brand retailer selling to corporate America, and now an independent reseller who was joined at the hip with their manufacturers' sales force. I had gained valuable, diverse experience within the corporate ecosystem, and I was ready for something new.

As I explored the job market, I started looking more closely at En Pointe Technologies. They were a national IT integrator – a reseller that integrated all the additional internal parts, such as memory, video cards, and hard drives, into the computer prior to shipment, as I had done during my short stint at BSSi. Based in El Segundo, California, En Pointe was a pioneer in business-to-business (B2B) distribution paperwork. Basically, they were taking the remote warehouse system, which had been so revolutionary when Ingram Micro and then Tech Data had introduced it a decade before, and raising it to a whole new level.

It brought me back to my early days at the Tek-Aids warehouse. Most people think of a warehouse as just a place to keep stuff. In fact, it is a crucial component of the sales operation. When you manage your own warehouse, the equation is simple: If you cannot find it, you cannot sell it. And if you do not have it, somebody must go out and get it – while the buyer finds a different place to shop.

Ingram Micro, with a chain of fourteen warehouses across the country, changed the equation. If a reseller or integrator did not have a product in stock, they could call Ingram Micro, (or later, their competitor Tech Data), which would drop ship the item to the client. That way, the customer got the product in a timely fashion and the distributor would still make the sale.

In my early days in sales, endowed with an "I can find anything!" mentality, I used to power through eight-inch-thick product catalogs to find something for a client if it was not in our warehouse. But once I was armed with Ingram Micro's warehouse management systems (internally referred to as CAPS, an acronym I never could decode), I had at my fingertips a countrywide dashboard showing where the stock was in any or all the Ingram warehouses, coast to coast. They also provided free freight, so the goods could travel more quickly *and* more cheaply to the end customer.

I became a power user. With that *Mission: Impossible* theme playing in my head, I could ship from the warehouse nearest to the client to reduce time in transit. Or if the East Coast warehouses had closed for the day, I could ship from out West, providing overnight shipments if their need were dire.

All distributors had access to the Ingram Micro system. But in the hands of someone born with a sense of urgency, magic happened. Like in *Jeopardy*, all the contestants might hear the question at the same time, and they all might even know the answer, but only one has the fastest thumb on the clicker. (Yes, the *Jeopardy* theme was on my internal soundtrack as well.)

I recall once telling a customer, "We have the inventory in our Harrisburg, Pennsylvania warehouse and it can still ship today." But apparently, I was not the only one who had mentioned a Harrisburg warehouse. She shot back, "What's with you and all the resellers with locations in Harrisburg?" Taken aback, I went into my 'Dad to the Dean" mode and produced a completely random response. "It's the Amish, ma'am! They are great workers! They can build a neighbor's barn in the morning and then come out and ship orders at the warehouse in the afternoon." She laughed, recognizing that I had pulled that explanation directly from my butt, but that quip became the foundation of a relationship that has stayed strong through multiple decades.

There was just one problem. When the product arrived, the customer who purchased an item from Elek-Tek would find himself looking at a box from Ingram Micro. The packing slip would have their name on it, but not his purchase order number. So, some of the time saved by a direct shipment was lost as customer and seller tried to match the product with the purchase order and straighten out all the paperwork.

That paperwork confusion caused delays in making payments. If the paperwork is clean, the client can easily enter it into their system. When your invoice hits the accounting department, it can get approved and forwarded for payment, likely within 30 days or so. But if something is missing on the paperwork, or if there is a wrong PO number, a wrong price, a wrong anything, the invoice gets put to the side. No matter when the invoice came in or how it was transmitted, it will be addressed later. Maybe months later, thus becoming an Accounts Receivable nightmare.

Which brings us to En Pointe. Its brilliant innovation was to develop a way to ship items from other companies' warehouses with En Pointe paperwork. Packing lists included their customer's shipping address and purchase order number, along with En Pointe's corporate verbiage, watermarks, everything! Even the shipping label showed En Pointe Technologies in the first line, with the actual address of the distributor's warehouse below. And the shipping was free!

It was genius. Today, 25 years later, it may seem ordinary. Look at Amazon. Everything you receive has their paper and packaging, even though they outsource more than 70% of their orders. But En Pointe Technologies was the pioneer.

Ellis Posner was the vice president of sales of En Pointe, based in their El Segundo headquarters. He and I started a conversation of "what ifs" in August 1998. I liked what I heard. I was fascinated with the company's ingenuity, not only for inventing the paperwork process, but also in the way they implemented it.

As it happened, En Pointe had a branch office in Oak Brook, Illinois, roughly 20 miles from my house. Through my trusted vendor network, I heard that the branch was poorly managed and underperforming, and they were about to cut bait with its manager.

The notion of returning to the role of branch manager excited me. I saw the opportunity as a combination of two worlds: the familiar world of managing a local branch, and the new world of seamless delivery engines. I would have visibility into live data in thirty distribution warehouses in the United States, and the proven ability to use data to my advantage as a selling tool.

The challenge was to make Ellis as enthusiastic as I was. During our phone calls, he seemed to respond to my confidence. So, rather than wait for him to send me an offer letter, I sent one to him. My terms were fair to both parties, yet radical. En Pointe would guarantee my current Hartford salary for the first two months of my employment (roughly $35,000 amonth). After those first 60 days, I would take zero salary. Instead, En Pointe would provide me with insurance coverage and a 50% commission of the gross profit on my sales.

Of course, I bounced this off Joanne first, and all she said was "You'll kill it!" I was unsure if it was based on trust or respect. It did not matter, as both only served to motivate me.

"I admire your boldness," Ellis responded, "but I worry you might have buyer's remorse after a few months and end up regretting it." I told him I was not worried that my commissions would fall short. My only risk, I said, was with them honoring the arrangement. That made him laugh, and we had a deal.

By late September, I was back running a branch and embarking on a new and exciting chapter in my career.

CHAPTER 17

BRANCHING OUT YET AGAIN

October 1998

On my first day at my new office in Oak Brook, I arrived around 8 a.m., about an hour before the company's official start time. My new teammates started showing up around 8:45. I hoped one of them would pop in to say hello, if only out of sheer curiosity. That did not happen. So, at 9:05 a.m., I took the initiative, moseyed into the central office area, and introduced myself to all at once.

Well, almost all. Just as I was finishing my introduction, the last of my new team members walked in. "Who are you?" he asked.

I smiled and responded, "What's your guess?" To his credit, he got it right.

Then I got down to business and talked to them about my expectations: Show up early, be disciplined, and do not criticize your teammates.

I reminded them that the Oak Brook branch was En Pointe's flagship location in the Midwest, the second-largest market (at the time) in the country. Yet they ranked near the bottom of the company's fourteen US sales branches. "If you trust me," I said, "we can all fix that." I only asked them to bring a sense of urgency to everything they did. "As trite as it may seem, that attitude will fill this office with positive energy and will guarantee success."

I closed by telling them that I needed one of them to be my

primary customer sales representative (CSR), the number two person in the office. I added that Mary, my primary CSR at my previous company, had a $30,000 base salary but tripled her income with commissions, earning $90,000 on her W-2 the previous year.

I spent the rest of the day meeting individually with six of my seven new employees. I gave them an abridged version of my resume and talked about how I had achieved success at all the places I had worked. My hope was to excite them, energize them, and convince them to follow my lead. Even if they did not like me, I thought they would be excited about the prospect of making more money.

Disappointingly, each one was less impressive than the one before. I had expected to encounter some skepticism; instead, their reactions ranged from indifference to outright resistance. "That is not how we used to do it," I heard multiple times. "Perhaps that is the reason the old manager was terminated," I replied in frustration.

Their body language made their lack of enthusiasm even more clear. No matter what I said, nothing clicked with any of them. I was mystified and my ego was a bit bruised, as I always thought I was a better salesperson than that.

But I was not ready to quit. My two-month clock was ticking, and I needed to stop wasting time trying to motivate unmotivated people and start selling.

I ended up finding my own CSR/office manager. Elizabeth was the sister of someone I knew in the industry. She had never worked in the industry before, but I had always admired her brother's work ethic. I was taking the chance that she shared his industriousness. Bloodlines, and all.

Besides, her inexperience was perfect for me. No baggage, none of the "that is not how we used to do it" bullshit. Although the folks at corporate headquarters were unhappy with her lack of history, I gently reminded them that I had two short months to get this branch set up for success – theirs and mine. "She'll work out, or she will not," I told them. "All I'm trying to do is force a quick resolution." They agreed, and we were off to the races.

I personally took charge of Elizabeth's training, emphasizing response times, message accuracy, setting customer expectations, and multitasking. Responses that included words like "soon," "today," and "later" were forbidden. To me, those words made me think of beauty; they were all in the eye of the beholder. I guarantee you, "soon" to you means nothing like what "soon" means to me. And "today?" How is that helping the customer? The request may have come at 9 a.m. Are you really going to make them wait until 5:30 p.m., or even 11:59 p.m.?

> **Telling a customer, "You'll have it within the hour" offers a lot more reassurance than a broad "You'll have it today." If you cannot respond that quickly, come back with, "I'm a bit swamped, so it may not get to you until 1 p.m. Will that work for you?" Being busy is a sign of strength; it shows that we are involved with our customers, not sitting around waiting for something to do.**

Odds are, the customer will understand your circumstances and come back with, "No worries, as long as I have it in my email box by 8 a.m. tomorrow, it's all good."

For the record, responding "You'll have it today" may have been perfectly satisfactory to the customer on many occasions, especially if you wound up solving the problem within an hour. The difference is the customer had no idea when to expect it. Setting an expectation, and then delivering on it, is one of those trivial things that makes you indispensable to the customer. For a salesperson, that is nirvana. It is the ultimate level of trust, and it is 100% in your control.

Elizabeth's training went well. Within the month, I put her in charge of the office, with everyone else reporting up through her. Within 60 days, all my inherited, lackluster employees were replaced by people with proactive attitudes and zero baggage. If only I could have said the same about the higher-ups who had brought me on board!

CHAPTER 18

GREED LOSES AGAIN

———

October 1999

When I joined En Pointe, I did not even hint at the possibility of bringing old clients with me. But of course, the thought was in my head, especially when it came to State Farm and their remarkable multiplier. Of the $300 million-plus in sales that I had accounted for during my 20-year IT career, almost half of it had gone to State Farm. Much of that was due to the mutual trust we shared. They knew I took their expectations seriously, and that gained me their respect. That trust and respect did not disappear when I moved over to En Pointe.

It took over a year to get up within State Farm's procurement system. I had no doubt Hartford and Comark were both pushing against it, thus slowing the process. My first "sale of substance" with State Farm was for 16,800 IBM 128MB memory models, a $2,674,952 purchase order. That represented more than half a million dollars of profit to En Pointe, even after my fifty-three thousand dollar commission. Most importantly, thanks to these efforts, En Pointe became an authorized vendor to State Farm, a status that normally takes most companies months, if not years, to earn. Talk about hand-delivering a customer on a red carpet into a company. The sky was the limit. Or it could have been, anyway.

State Farm was so important for IBM that IBM-badged system

engineers were embedded at the Bloomington campus. When the order arrived a few weeks later, one of those engineers called me first thing in the morning. "We did not receive IBM memory," he reported. I didn't know what to say. "I do not know what happened," the engineer went on. "All I know is the memory we received was not IBM-branded memory."

I told him I would investigate it immediately, with the caution that El Segundo was two hours behind us, so maybe I might need up to three hours to get back with the answer. (Even in an emergency, setting a customer's expectation of response always takes priority.) "Some wires must have crossed," I told him. "I will uncross them by end-of-day."

It was the longest two hours of my life. When California finally woke up and I was able to get hold of the procurement manager, he told me to speak with Bob, the president. I sensed that meant I was going to get some news I was not going to like; if there was a simple explanation, the procurement manager would not have handed me off to the boss. With the needle on my internal gauge pointing into the red, I called Bob and left a message to call me immediately. I do not even think I said please. I was growing angrier by the minute. I did not know what the hell En Pointe thought it was doing, but whatever it was, they were treading on my reputation.

After a second message to Bob roughly 20 minutes later, he called me. He thanked me for bringing in the deal and then started to praise his operations team for tripling the margin by finding the "exact same" memory available as a clone of the IBM memory from Kingston Technology. "It's 100% compatible with the IBM version," he assured me.

"Are you out of your fucking mind, you greedy fuck?" I replied. "There are IBM engineers on site to install the memory. The memory you sent would void the system warranty. It will never be accepted. I will drive down there tomorrow, pick up that cloned crap that you subbed in, and get it out of there immediately. We do not want word of this to spread any further than it already may have."

I was too furious to care that I was talking with the CEO, and I did not mince my words. "Bob, you need to have the exact IBM memory that the customer ordered purchased from IBM, as stated on their purchase order. I need that new purchase order number that is being issued to IBM by tomorrow morning, so I can share the number with the IBM engineering contact. I need him to see that it was properly ordered, so he can attempt to accelerate this information within his own company's procurement department. We need to stop the negative communication about En Pointe immediately. Bob, do you understand and confirm this?"

I knew that it was imperative to get a mistake off the customer's site as quickly as possible. Even if you are waiting on a Return Merchandise Authorization (RMA) from a third-party vendor for return approval, you need to arrange to have the goods off that site and delivered back to you.

A return approval can take up to two weeks. You do not want that blotch on your reputation taking up space at your customer's site, where it will serve as a constant reminder of your fuck-up. It does not matter why it happened; the only thing they care about is "who." And in this case, I was that who.

The next day, with a copy of the new, correct PO in hand, I drove the company van to Bloomington to get that memory out of there as fast as I could. As you can imagine, 16,000 memory pieces filled the van, including the passenger seat. Once the truck was loaded and secured, I spoke at length to the engineer and his team members, apologizing for the screw-up, and assuring them, face-to-face, that it would never happen again.

Their response set my mind at ease. They told me, "We knew it could not have been your doing. We did not doubt your credibility. We know each other too well." They never even asked to see the replacement PO. That credibility comment alone almost made the whole thing worth it. Well, almost.

On the way home with my memory-laden van, I made a point of rewarding myself with a drive-thru lunch of two steakburgers and a vanilla shake from the original Steak 'N' Shake on Veterans Parkway – the flagship location of a legendary hamburger chain that is positively revered in Central Illinois. That had always been Jeff's "Happy Meal," but none had ever felt quite so happy as the meal enjoyed that day! (Joanne shared my love of Steak 'N' Shake, thanks to her years at the University of Illinois. Sometimes, I would bring home a "happy meal" for her as well. The hamburgers had to be microwaved.)

CHAPTER 19

TAKING STOCK

September 1999

The brazenness of En Pointe's under-the-table switcheroo offended me. I did not see how they thought they could have pulled it off. The stunt showed a complete lack of respect for me, for IBM, and for State Farm. This was not a mistake by some inattentive shipping clerk, or a junior salesman's bright idea gone wrong. This went all the way up to the top. Were they stupid, or did they think I was? Either way, the answer was not good.

Randomly flipping that much product without communication led me to suspect that these types of shenanigans were not limited to procurement. What else had they gotten away with over the past year?

I began digging, and it soon became clear that En Pointe was adding a 3-5% "load" to the true product purchase costs across the board on the system. Of course, they spun it six ways to Sunday as to why the company needed to offset their expenses.

Now, En Pointe was neither the first nor last company to add surcharges and fees to the listed price. I get that; a seller can do that from the top by increasing the sell price, or from the bottom by reducing costs from vendors. Or both. But En Pointe had chosen to increase its take by shaving commissionable dollars from its sales staff. We were paid a commission based on gross profit; En Pointe was fabricating these additional costs to reduce the deal profit and screw its sales employees.

Once I realized that, it was obvious why neither the CEO nor any of his staff reached out to me to discuss the possibility of substituting the Kingston memory. The company was planning to pocket the additional margin, without having to pay my commission on it. I had given them my best effort and delivered a blue-chip client that they had been light years away from securing. And this was my reward.

I have always considered myself somewhat of a Teflon man, as things usually slide off me. As the saying goes, "If you never heal from what hurts you, you will end up bleeding on those who did not cut you." But the En Pointe product switch devastated me. This was insult *and* injury. It was a harsh lesson that, regardless of my success and the success I brought to the company, none of that really mattered at the top. I had already learned everything I wanted to know about storing inventory on someone else's nickel, and about shipping from remote locations with your company's own paperwork. Now it was time to remove myself from these unreliable people.

But where to go? I was at a crossroads in my career. I knew the computer industry was where I belonged, so why was I not feeling happy and respected? Was I expecting too much? Was I naïve? Maybe the chicanery I saw at En Pointe was more the norm rather than the exception. Did I miss something at Tek-Aids, or Robec, or Elek-Tek, or Hartford?

I knew I could get another job in sales and be successful. But all my jobs ended unhappily. Was this what the rest of my career was going to look like? Great heights followed by bumpy landings?

Looking back on my experiences, I could see that I was always at my happiest when I was running a branch. Even though I still reported to someone in Corporate, my kingdom was often hundreds of miles away from HQ. I thrived in that scenario at three different companies. In many ways, I was running my own company within a company.

So why not cut out the middleman? Why not run my own show?

That question could inspire an endless list of *what if?* scenarios that could drive a man crazy. Fortunately, I still had a day job that needed my attention. While I was considering my career options, my top priority was breaking the bank at En Pointe for the remaining three weeks, until I found my next destiny.

Throughout my career, I had prided myself on being the guy who could find the hardware you needed, fast. If I did not have it on hand, you could rely on me to find it. I knew where to look, and I knew how to put a hold on it right away so nobody could snatch it out from under me. To make sure I had what I needed when someone needed it, I often worked proactively, to secure products before the customers even knew they needed them.

Every day, Ingram Micro published a list of hot products, and every day I would grab my coffee and check to see how many of those items they had in stock, and how many I could scoop up. So, imagine my excitement when I saw that they had just received fifty impossible-to-find IBM corporate ThinkPads – the corporate models, not the consumer ones. The cream of the corporate crop!

I did not have an order for any ThinkPads, but I saw the opportunity. I immediately called and had them put on hold for me. Once I had them locked up, I reached out to the Midwest IBM regional sales manager to alert him that I had these high-demand machines "in stock." My goal was to get him to route his laptop-hungry customers to me, to let them know I was the guy to go to when you needed something scarce, and you needed it right away.

The IBM rep referred me to the buyer at Comark. She wanted to buy thirty-two of those fifty, to fill an order for one of her customers.

Was there any way I was going to give Comark this cache of gold? Not at any price. These machines were my ticket into new accounts. She kept calling me two to three times a day and asking for them. Finally, she caved. "I cannot take this bitch anymore," she said. "She is yours. You call her." Then she gave up the name and phone number for Nancy, the senior buyer at Takeda Pharmaceuticals, a billion-dollar company with headquarters in Lincolnshire, just two suburbs away from my hometown. Incredible.

I have always gone by the axiom that "first impressions are lasting impressions." This was an excellent opportunity to make a great first impression. I called Nancy and informed her that I was the one who had the thirty-two IBM ThinkPad notebooks she needed. "I'll take your entire stock," she responded. "I will take a few hundred more, if you have them. We need them for a sales rollout for our pharmaceutical sales force. Please do not lose those units."

I immediately reassured her. "Nancy, these notebooks have your name on them, and your name only. I know it will take you a day or so to get us set up in your system, but they'll be waiting for you." Within a day and a half, I got her PO. I did not have a couple hundred more, but I had 18, which she also snapped up.

Because her office was not far from mine, I arranged to pick up those eighteen units at Ingram's distribution center in Carol Stream, a 20-minute drive from my home, and deliver them to her in Lincolnshire.

I just wanted to meet her, give her my thanks and my card, and get my 30 seconds of fame to tell her who we were, what we were, and why IBM came to us when they could not find their own product. It was a rather happy story. When I was finished, she said, "You're my hero." If you ever need a favor, call me." I knew that I would be taking her up on that offer, and soon.

I now had my next mission: Find a few hundred more, in the next couple of weeks. Overall, Nancy purchased 177 of these units from me in a month's time. I flashed back to one of my earliest Hartford experiences, when I sold $2.7 million worth of IBM Token Ring network modules to State Farm. I was getting the feeling that this deal could be almost as valuable. It felt like déjà vu all over again! Only this time, I did it all singlehandedly.

But was I ready to leap out on my own? That was the question.

One thing was clear: I could not stay at En Pointe. I had invested too much in building a reputation for integrity to let these losers drag me into their ethical vortex. I decided to leave quietly, without throwing any more fits. But I must admit, it brought a smile to my face two decades later when I saw that the Justice Department had fined them almost $6 million for misrepresenting themselves as a small business to secure government contracts.

PART TWO

THE COMPANY

CHAPTER 20

TAKING CHARGE

November 1999

Throughout my career, I had been a salesman and a good one. But when it came to opening my own business, I needed to think like both seller and buyer.

> **A good salesman needs confidence. He may know that the product has some drawbacks, but he does not let them become obstacles. (The paragon of this way of thinking is Rudy Russo, the relentless, fast-talking salesman in Used Cars.). But a good buyer needs a healthy dose of skepticism. I had both. The question was whether I was ready to put those attributes to work in my own company.**

I knew the industry. I knew the ins and outs of stocking inventory, proper volumes, cash liabilities, stock rotations, ensuring price protection – all the hurdles that had crashed other start-ups. My 20-year journey along the IT highway had taught me far more than I could ever have learned in business school. I had seen it all.

Of course, I knew about salesmanship. I could have recited the fundamentals in my sleep: "Know your customer. Know your competition. Respond with urgency. Relieve your customer's pain points." I also had learned valuable and sometimes hard lessons about leadership – the approaches I wanted to emulate, and the ones I wanted to avoid.

The boss I most wanted to emulate was Bruce Weinberg from Business Systems Solutions, Inc. (BSSi). Although he was an accountant, at heart he was a salesperson who just happened to own the company, which was what I had in mind for myself. He was a hands-on CEO, working out front with his customers while a strong back-end engine took care of accounting and support services. I really admired the way he set up his infrastructure to allow him to do what he did best, and I hoped Bruce's model would do the same for me.

I learned valuable lessons from some other CEOs over the years as well. At my first stop at Tek-Aids, Jud Beamsley taught me how to think through situations, to be creative, and to seize opportunity. Hal Goldman at Elek-Tek trusted his employees to do their jobs, which had made it possible for me to expand his business within Elek-Tek.

As for the CEOs at the other companies where I worked? They gave me confidence in a separate way. Honestly, they were not that impressive. I concluded that if these guys could run a company, I surely could, too.

As I got ready for this next big step, I reached out for advice from the vendor account managers at IBM and HP. I knew I could trust them, so I told them my plans and asked if they would deal with me in this new company in the same way they would deal with any other authorized reseller. They both assured me they would. I mean, why would they not? I had established a reputation for performance, which benefited us all. But still, I needed to hear them say so.

I was starting to realize that it was a bit naïve to think that running a company was just like running a branch, only on steroids. While I was confident in the skills I had honed over the years, the boss went beyond overseeing the sales and warehouse operations. I had to figure out how to oversee all the foundational elements of setting up a business – legal, accounting, insurance, and leasing the space. Being the boss means taking responsibility for everything, even the stuff you once considered boring or trivial.

Fortunately, I had some great connections to a group of professionals who could help me set up this new business. Through my cousin, Rick Hiton, I could reach into his network of University of Illinois fraternity brothers from ZBT – unofficially known at the time as "Zion Banking and Trust." Rick was just two years older than I was, and he had always seemed more like a brother to me. He put me in touch with one of his frat brothers, Rick Patinkin, who was a well-established business attorney. The two Ricks and I walked through the process of starting up a business in Illinois. Both assured me that we could be up and running within thirty days.

As always, Joanne and I carefully weighed the pros and cons. Being the CEO – let's face it – would be great. If I believed in something, I would have the unilateral authority to make it so. Plus, being CEO would give me even more leverage with customers. They would know they were not dealing with just a salesperson, however trusted, but with the owner of the company.

Overall, the risks were small. The buy-in would be minimal. All I needed was one customer, and I already had ten in mind. My cousin Rick would guide me through the internal financial and corporate setup. I was confident that I could gain the support of my biggest and best customers, the manufacturing sales reps. And I was confident that I could sign up the key manufacturers, especially HP and IBM. That was crucial, since those two companies were where those manufacturing sales reps would come from.

Most importantly, I had Joanne's full backing. She is smart, savvy, and extremely protective of me. It meant everything to me that she liked the idea, that she was proud of me, that she believed in me. Not as a wife, but as a mother of three children under the age of twelve, whose welfare she would never leave to chance.

The more we talked, the clearer the choice became. The only

thing missing was my balls, but they were not missing for long. On the fourth day of doing all this pro-and-con research, Joanne and I both realized that we had wasted four days. We would never be more ready than we were at that moment. It was time to open my own company – MY business within a business!

The next few weeks passed in a blur. Rick Patinkin filed papers for us to become Burgess Computer Decisions (BCD), an Illinois corporation. Rick Hiton secured a whopping eight hundred square feet of office space above the Ron of Japan restaurant in the Northbrook, roughly five easy miles from my home. Joanne and I walked through it with him. I could see Joanne already mentally decorating it.

From En Pointe, I brought Elizabeth, whom I had hired and trained, to be my operations manager. Then I hired her brother, whom I had known since my Elek-Tek days, to be a salesperson. Elizabeth got busy making the place functional – renting the office furniture, setting up the phones, getting business cards and letterhead, and other necessities – while Joanne helped add special touches to warm up the space. We also contracted with another of Rick's ZBT frat brothers, Hal Roseth, to be our accountant. Now I needed to make sure he had something to track.

My most valuable assets were my relationships with HP and IBM. I had already been assured by the vendor account managers that they would be receptive to doing business. The problem was with their company policy. Each one had an Authorization Program that required that a reseller be in business for one full calendar year before he could be approved as an authorized vendor. Until I received this designation, I would not be able to buy products from their authorized distributors. I understood why; this protected their brands. But I could not afford to wait a year. Moreover, I knew I would not have to. Instead, I felt this rule gave me the upper hand.

I reached out independently to the regional territory reps for HP and IBM with whom I had worked so long. I made it clear that I could not wait a year for authorization. I would likely be out of business before then. But I did have one alternative. There were subterranean markets where their product could be procured. I certainly did not want to go there; those companies were generally considered grey market and using them could have stained my reputation. But not-so-subtly, I let the territory reps know that if I did go there, they would be the ones who would lose out.

"You cannot expect me to stand still for a year," I told them. "I have a wife and three kids." I pointed out that I could buy the hardware anywhere; if I weren't authorized, I would not need to submit any point-of-sale reports. That would mean millions of dollars of goods would be landing in their territory, and they would get no revenue credit, all because I had not yet been authorized.

I made it all about them. It was the only play I had, but it turned out to be a great one. When you can steer the messaging to being all about them, to help them (especially helping them hit their quota numbers), business friendships and trust are forged.

Miraculously (but not surprisingly), Hewlett-Packard and IBM both granted my company Authorized Reseller status in less than 30 days of our incorporation. All these years later that "one-year rule" remains in effect at both companies, with BCD remaining the lone exception.

On Tuesday, Nov. 2, 1999, we received our Illinois corporation status. We took a few days to get the office in order. That Saturday, Joanne and I celebrated with a dinner at our favorite Tavern restaurant, which the Wyse team introduced us to. We had a wonderful time and shared a bottle of champagne. Her pride in me was bursting through her sparkling eyes and her smile. I was a happy man. Sunday was just another quiet football Sunday. Monday morning could not come quickly enough.

But Sunday night, I tossed and turned. A seed of doubt entered my psyche.

What made me think I could do this? Why was I putting my family's lifestyle at risk? Was I jeopardizing my reputation in the industry? What the hell was I thinking?

By 3 a.m., I was sitting at the kitchen table with a blank sheet of paper and a pen, ready to list the pros and cons of my decision. But after an hour of staring at the still-blank page, I realized I was looking at the answer. The future was a blank canvas, and it would be up to me to fill it.

And just like that, everything became clear. I saw what I had liked about the businesses I had been at – and more importantly, what I had not. I realized that as much as I admired and respected the way Bruce ran BSSi, the CEO whom I most wanted to emulate was my father.

Dad had to leave the University of Illinois after his sophomore year; his father had died, and my dad had to take over his company. Dad molded a diverse group of employees into a happy, productive team, and he gave all of them the opportunity to gain experience within the company. More importantly, he was my first exposure to a "salesperson running a company." Those three hours being "stuck" in his office after he fired me provided the greatest sales education I had ever received.

Now it was my turn. My company would be founded on two simple fundamental principles that I had learned from my father: Trust your people and earn the trust of your customers and business partners. With that solid basis, my company would reflect my personality – my expectations of proactiveness and my ability to pirouette on a moment's notice.

I wished that I could hear Dad's thoughts about my fears and anxieties, as well as my confidence. But sadly, his Parkinson's had progressed to the point that he could no longer talk. I had arranged for him to receive 24-hour nursing care in my childhood home. Over the next year and a half, just knowing he was alive and close by became my rock. While he may have been unable to speak, I knew he heard me. I was determined to build the kind of company he would have built, and one that would make him proud. I was now ready for day one.

On Monday, Burgess Computer Decisions opened for business. We were selling hardware, but our most important product was our sense of urgency – urgency about serving our customers and urgency about everything we touched. Our initial tagline was "Proactive Response. Personal Service." Immediacy pretty much summed up our value-add, and I am proud to say that it always has.

CHAPTER 21

"ONE HELL OF A MARKER!"

———

December 1999

Getting authorized by HP and IBM was a critically necessary first step. Next came getting control of my cost infrastructure.

IT sales companies are not a level playing field. (That may be true for all industries.) Newcomers are welcome, but small players do not necessarily get room to grow. The biggest customers leverage their volume of sales to get the best prices, which enables them to grow even more and squeeze out new competitors.

The two top IT computer distributors – the companies from which I would be getting most of the products – were Ingram Micro, based in Santa Ana, California, and Tech Data, with headquarters in Clearwater, Florida. Their biggest customer – heck, everybody's biggest customer – was CDW, a "computer superstore." They had been my customer more than a decade earlier when they were still known as MPK Consulting, so I was well-acquainted with them.

CDW had multiple paths to market: sales directly to the end customer, sales to the reseller, and sales to government agencies. They also established purchasing relationships with all the computer manufacturers and with all the distributors, including Ingram Micro and Tech Data. CDW was the 800-pound gorilla in the room, and it was the company I would be competing against. Go big or go home.

When CDW wanted products from Ingram Micro and Tech Data, it could rely on getting the best prices. They had earned that status. Other established resellers could get lower prices as well, just not as low as CDW's. When Burgess Computer Decisions, the new kid on the block, placed an order, we expected to pay 10% to 15% more than any of the established resellers. Obviously, we would be at a huge competitive disadvantage, no matter how great our customer service was.

What was not obvious was why we would have to pay more. I was a known commodity, a guy with a proven reputation. Moreover, we already had our HP and IBM authorizations. These were not merely the Good Housekeeping Seals of Approval; these authorizations would not have been given unless HP and IBM had approved of them, and Ingram Micro and Tech Data were both aware of this status. These special pricing approvals had been made by the CEOs of Ingram Micro and Tech Data themselves. If they had already authorized me to be a vendor, why handicap me with higher costs, especially considering my reputation?

I knew those CEOs. Kevin Murai from Ingram Micro and Steve Richmond from Tech Data were good guys. We had done a lot of business together. I had spoken to each of them before I decided to open my own shop. Each of them wished me luck and added, *"If you ever need a favor...."* I am not sure if they expected me to call in those favors, but I did. I had little choice.

I reached out to each of them, reminded them of their offered favor, and very respectfully asked to be able to purchase goods from them at the same cost charged to CDW. I did not ask for less, as that would have set precedent, and I was uncertain they would go there. But I saw no risk to them; if they were already giving that price to one, what was the harm in giving it to another, especially one who had a proven history? The bigger risk, from their point of view, was that if one said no and the other said yes, I would take all my business to the other distributor.

It was a ballsy ask on my part. But I had driven hundreds of millions of dollars' worth of business through both those distributors, and they knew me. Nothing made them think I would not do it again. Both agreed to my request the same day I made it.

Then, figuring that as the door was already slightly ajar – or more properly, that two separate doors were ajar – I pushed for an additional concession. I asked for free ground freight on everything leaving one of their distribution hubs.

Free freight was going to enable me to compete with CDW. I knew that, even as I was having these conversations with Kevin and Steve, five 53-foot trucks, fully loaded with products, were on their way from Ingram Micro's distribution hub in suburban Carol Stream to CDW's location in Vernon Hills, about forty-five miles away. There the items would be repackaged in CDW-branded boxes and stocked or reshipped from there. Two shipping charges would be attached to every one of those products, freight in and freight out, and those charges would likely get passed on to CDW's customers.

That was the opening that would allow me to beat CDW. That was the chink in Goliath's armor. I was never going to win merely on price, but I had eliminated CDW's price edge by calling in those CEOs' favors. Now I could use free freight as my competitive edge. I would apply what I learned at En Pointe: Attach our information, logo, verbiage, watermark, etc., at the warehouse, and ship the cargo from there directly to the customer – for free.

I told each of them the same thing: the free freight would help me close more deals, which would lead me to buy more from them. Each of them had distribution warehouses close to my office; they likely figured the cost of providing free freight to me would have been, at most, 1.5% against their profits on my purchases – likely less than $50,000 on $4 million of purchases. At that point, with so many parts of the arrangement in place, why let freight charges hold things up? I am still unsure why Ingram Micro and Tech Data went for it. I assume they just wanted my business.

This was a huge win for a brand-new company. And now, with the authorizations from HP and IBM in hand, and with the cost infrastructure in place, it was time to climb to the next summit. It was time to go to the bank.

CHAPTER 22
FUNDING THE ENTERPRISE

———

December 1999

Credit is the lubricant that keeps the economy running. You can buy and sell things all day, but without money, you cannot complete the transaction, and as everyone knows, the money is not always there exactly when you need it. Credit lets the deal go through.

This is as true for large businesses as for small ones. All my customers were credit-worthy. Takeda, GE, and GE Capital were all billion-dollar customers, but they would not have been worth my time if poor credit references or cash flow prevented them from establishing a credit line. We had very few COD or pay-in-advance customers. But there were times, with GE for instance, where we would receive a million-dollar purchase order. At a 20% margin, this single order would cost $800,000 to fulfill, which could hamper our credit lines.

To keep that outstanding deal from having a negative impact on our credit line, we would initiate a new bank loan based solely on that PO, referred to as a one-off purchase order. The payment remit address would be the bank's lockbox, not our lockbox at the bank. The bank would wire our "cut" upon receipt of payment. This would prevent the one-time deal from strapping our credit lines with our key distribution partners.

The point is that credit was a balancing act. We needed credit – credit to run our business, credit to fund our purchases so that we would have goods to resell, and credit to extend to our customers until they had funds available to complete the deal. Having good credit makes the world go round.

Armed with the IBM and HP authorizations, and with the cost-controlling arrangements I had made with Ingram Micro and Tech Data, I sought to establish a credit line. My attorney and new friend, Rick Patinkin, got us set up with a $250,000 loan at a local community bank. (I should add that I did not use our family home as collateral. Our home was intentionally in Joanne's name and set up as a trust, and I promised her the home would never become a lien against the business.)

With the loan in place, we set up relationships with the local Ingram Micro and Tech Data account teams. Within two weeks, we obtained a $35,000 line of credit from Ingram Micro and a $25,000 line of credit from Tech Data. I'm sure my history with those companies helped.

But those credit lines were challenging. Clouds are essential, but you do not want them hanging around every day. The same is true of debt. From the very start, we worked to pay down these 30-day credit lines as quickly as possible. Our top priority was always covering payroll; paying down the open credit lines was a close second. Early payments showed good cash flow; even more importantly, they showed good faith.

Credit managers generally only see black and white (preferably never red!) numbers and payment trends, but I tried to bring technicolor into the conversation. At least once a quarter, I would reach out to the credit managers at these companies and give them the big picture – what we were working on, which customers were growing, whom we were targeting, and what each of us could do better. This transparency brought another level of trust into the relationship. Some of my best relationships in the industry have been with the credit managers at our key distribution partners, first at Ingram and Tech Data, and later at Synnex, D&H Distributing, and Dell Technologies.

These relationships supported my belief that, at some level, everyone you speak to is a customer, one way or another, and you are trying to sell them on what you are discussing. To make all four of these credit managers "fans" of BCD was a significant accomplishment for the company. It made them feel a part of our success. So, when our credit lines were stretched, as they often were, a phone call to the credit manager released the order. In return, we gave a promissory date for the next payment, which we always honored. Trust builds more trust.

We had to earn higher credit lines, and we did just that. Within six months, that combined sixty-thousand-dollar credit line from Tech Data and Ingram Micro had increased to $250,000. The stairs we had been climbing turned into an escalator. (Now, of course, our credit lines are in the millions. But we had to earn our way there, which made it even more appreciated.)

For some reason, I always migrated to Ingram Micro as my primary distributor. Tech Data was incredibly good, too. They even had my favorite credit manager at the time, Jennifer Griffin. But even now, off the top of my head two decades later, the only account number I remember is our account number at Ingram, 40-350206. (And this is from the person with the near-photographic memory!) Year after year, Ingram was our number-one distribution partner.

Ingram was always my comfort zone, perhaps from being so reliant on their Ingram CAPS product locator system in the past. But more likely, my reliance was based on the consistent excellence of our Ingram account managers. The Ingram team was always top-notch – Michelle, Tina, Derek, and Sue. Our first account manager, Daryl Klube, went on to Hewlett-Packard as Ingram's relationship manager. Kelly Nagel, who was on Daryl's team, took over as BCD's primary contact at Ingram and set the table for our accelerated growth within the Ingram Micro ecosystem. Kelly recently retired after five years as the president at Jabra, the headphone and speakerphone company. So, it seems clear that having BCD as your customer launches you to new heights!

While I was happily getting the business on its feet, I was also an active and involved father. I was spending my springs coaching both sons in Deerfield baseball leagues and looking ahead to Lizzie's start in Deerfield softball. I welcomed every minute of coaching all the kids on these teams, especially mine. I relished their innocence, and it was one hundred and eight degrees away from the office for me. Great therapy!

CHAPTER 23

ESTABLISHING OUR DNA

January 2000

With the banking and credit lines set up, it was time to make new deals. The first call I made was to Nancy Lubecker from Takeda Pharmaceuticals. We had first connected when I managed to source those "impossible to find" ThinkPads for her. "Do you remember me?" I asked.

"How could I forget you?" she replied. "You are my hero. You saved my project." I could not have asked for more.

I wanted to present myself to Nancy as something familiar, yet different. The familiarity part was easy. I knew that CDW was her primary vendor, so I started off by making it clear to her that we had a distribution model and cost structure remarkably like CDW's. This enabled her to visualize my company through her CDW lens, to see that buying from us would be just like buying from them. That left me free to focus on what made us unique.

I was the first differentiator. I had made a difference to her business, and to her success. But the past can only take you so far. So, I needed to offer something else to set us apart.

Around this time, the chemical company BASF was running a brilliant advertising campaign. Because the chemicals BASF produced were sold as ingredients and not as end products, most people did not know who they were. So, the BASF campaign was built on variations on the tagline, "We do not make the product; we make it better." Or stronger, or more colorful, or more durable. I wanted to position BCD as the BASF of the computer industry. We took the product, the service, the anything, and we made it better.

Following the precept of "Know Thy Competition," I knew that CDW charged freight to their customers. In fact, I had Nancy in mind when I negotiated for free freight from Tech Data and Ingram Micro.

"Nancy, let's assume that CDW and BCD offer you the same price. How is the product going to get to you? CDW's price does not include shipping. Ours does. We call it 'Landed Cost.' That means no invoice surprises negatively affecting your budget."

I knew I had her attention, so I went for it. "Can you do me a favor?" I continued. "Look up your freight charges from CDW over the past 12 months. I am estimating that your freight costs will be in six figures. At the very least, my company will save you that."

Nancy called back the next day. "When can we meet?" she asked.

We met for lunch that following Friday. (This was in late January of 2000, forty-five days after I opened my business.) I gave Nancy a hard-copy tabletop presentation on what we are all about.

When I finished walking her through what we did, how we did it, and how we could take care of corporate America, she said, "I will make you one of my three vendors, along with CDW and Comark." I was juiced! (Comark, of course, was that other big IBM shop I competed against when I was at Hartford Computer Group, during my State Farm days. Comark also led to that first deal with Nancy.)

As I walked back to my car from the restaurant, I felt jubilant. I called Joanne from my cell phone. "We are going to own this account!" I crowed. "I can feel it already." She was as excited as I was, and I could feel her pride over the airwaves.

Within nine months, BCD was the primary vendor at Takeda Pharmaceuticals. Takeda ended up purchasing five-million-dollars from us in that first calendar year, which represented half of the company's first-year revenues. Nancy gave me my shot, and that was all I ever asked for.

Over the next months, I forged a tremendous relationship with Takeda's young and fun IT team. We fed off each other's energy. I arranged monthly lunch-and-learn product training sessions with the local vendor reps at HP, IBM, and other manufacturers. We brought in food and gave the Takeda team lunch while the manufacturers' reps walked us through their product roadmaps and dug deeper into the technology within those products.

My value-add was being the one that brought them in, the conductor of the orchestra.

These product trainings did not just spotlight generational changes in the product platform. They also strengthened communication and connection between all the players in the room. By bringing in various manufacturer sales reps, the customer could see that we had strong authorized relationships, while the reps could see how tight I was with the customer.

My primary relationships were with Takeda's two IT leaders, John Witham and Dennis Jensen, who reported to IT Director Frank Alvino. Frank gave me carte blanche to meet with his team, which had ten additional staff members. Within a short time, I was presented with a guest pass that gave me access to the IT floor. No more buzzing in for Jeff! I was at the site two or three times per week, and I made a point of always showing up close to lunchtime, so we could run across the street for "extended" team lunches.

All these years later, it is amazing that this entire relationship started because I found Nancy with those laptops that "no one could find." She put the word out with the local IBM reps, who became my unofficial free sales force.

That became our reputation. We could find anything, even before the Internet. Maintaining that reputation AFTER the Internet only made me work harder. When it came down to the Internet versus Jeff Burgess, the Internet lost almost every time.

CHAPTER 24

POSITIVE CHAOS

February 2002

I have made a lot of customer visits over the years. One of my favorite places to go was always the GE corporate headquarters in Fairfield, Connecticut. The facility's landscaping was incredible – a botanical garden combined with a park. The second place had to be PepsiCo in Purchase, New York. It had a long circular driveway that ascended to their front entrance, which became the eighth floor because the building was tucked into the side of a hill. Crazy.

In 2002, two critical business developments occurred – critical for me, anyway. First, in a deal that was one of the largest in technology history, HP purchased Compaq Computer in a $25 billion stock swap. Many skeptics predicted that the two companies would have trouble integrating. From where I stood in the sales trenches, that certainly seemed possible; the HP field sales team had always looked down on their noses at Compaq, which were inferior products.

As the HP team soon discovered, however, Compaq products were cheaper and had higher consumer awareness than the HP line, which made them much easier to sell. Salespeople adapt easily when they see commission opportunities; once the HP people began to receive revenue credit for those sales, they became huge fans. Soon the Compaq product line became the HP sales rep's best friend – next to me, of course!

In the second critical business development (business life-changing), Mike Gholson contacted me. I wrongly assumed that he got my name from his local HP sales rep, since I seemed to be near the top of the HP reps' Rolodex whenever someone needed hardware. Only later did I learn that Mike had gotten my name from Bruce Budnek, a systems engineer at Vicon Industries, an early participant in the security marketplace. I was unfamiliar with Bruce, and uncertain as to how he knew of me.

Mike was the operations manager at Interlogix, a relatively new company that was born through a merger between two technology companies. My knowledge about Interlogix was basic; I knew they used servers, and that a lot of their clients were banks and financial institutions.

In 2002, computer servers were having a transformative effect across global commerce, yet if you asked most people, they had no idea what they were.

Servers were computers that enabled other computers to work together internally within a company. There were generally PCs and desktop workstations connected to the server via the network.

Before the advent of server technology, companies and staff members were connected via CRT monitors, reading, and writing data to and from the mainframe. This was more or less the state of the art back in Austin in the early 1980s with the State of Texas contract.

Multi-user computer servers were not introduced until 1986, when Hewlett-Packard brought out the HP 3000. That machine was marketed as a "minicomputer" capable of supporting up to fifty-six users, with a whopping (joking!) 8MB of system memory and less than 5MB of storage. To put that in perspective, today's servers can support thousands of local and remote approved connected users and can house terabytes (1,000 gigabytes) of system memory and petabytes (1,000 terabytes) of storage.

With the start of the new century, servers were becoming part of nearly every major company's IT backbone. New, powerful servers offered scalability, system integrity, and reliability. This allowed massive commercial applications, such as Customer Relationship Management (CRM), and Microsoft Excel, to be spread across the network.

When I opened BCD, I had a feeling that server sales would be a key part of my business model. Servers accounted for more than half of Takeda Pharmaceuticals' $5 million in purchases that first year. All told, Hewlett-Packard servers – the only brand we sold at the time – represented over one half of our first-year sales.

Thus, BCD was pretty server-savvy by 2002, when Mike first reached out to me. As he explained, Interlogix's intention was to develop a computer application that would enable the customer to capture video surveillance at a business or residence while simultaneously managing access control and fire detection.

His Salem, Oregon-based company was a pioneer in developing software that detected the presence of people, indoors and outdoors, within the facility or corporate campus. But their application required a high-availability server – always on and always up and running. For instance, if surveillance video was not captured during an incident in a retail store because the server was down, the perpetrator could get released, or the insurance company could refuse to honor the theft claim. Even worse, if the software were being used for access control, a server failure could mean that no one could get in or out of the building. Imagine this happening during a fire! (That may sound overly dramatic, but it was a real possibility.)

Mike told me that several people inside and outside of Hewlett-Packard knew that Interlogix wanted to start building a catalog of specialized servers for their customers, and that they had referred him to me. I will not lie; it was very flattering that HP thought enough of us to recommend us to another HP customer. The ultimate of trust.

Mike's issue was that Interlogix was a small company and lacked the capability to build the servers. They also needed help customizing the designs and testing the performance of the servers, on a per-customer order basis. That is where he wanted to involve us: He wanted us to build and performance-test his servers, while simultaneously building out a catalog for them.

This was somewhat of déjà vu for me. In my first job at Tek-Aids, I shared space in the warehouse with guys who assembled the components of the machines customers had purchased, and I never forgot the value of that service. From the moment I opened my company, we committed ourselves to installing everything inside a unit and testing it before shipping, instead of sending customers pieces and parts and letting them figure it out.

At first, I thought of pre-installation mostly as a basic quality-control exercise that would cut down returns for bad or incorrect parts. But it turned out to be another one of our differentiators. Even Fortune 500 companies with deep IT departments appreciated the service because it freed up their team members to handle other projects.

Working under Mike's direction, BCD helped engineer Interlogix's innovative systems. It was an interesting project, and it would become the playbook for BCD going forward.

At the onset, we had none of the components he specified in stock. It took us roughly three weeks to gather all the parts, and we grew more anxious by the day. We were so eager to start this new opportunity! Once everything arrived, we wasted no time getting the system and parts on the bench. It took us about an hour to build the first prototype and to start running Mike's performance tests. Within an hour, we had the server running at peak performance. At that point, we packed it up and overnighted it to Mike in Oregon.

Mike was impressed by our work. Just that quickly, Phase I of the project was over, and we were on to Phase 2. That entailed creating a customer catalog with several different models, each one based on recording criteria that Mike had mapped out – the number of recording cameras, their density, the number of days holding the storage, and even the environment in which the cameras would be deployed.

Mike had unique criteria for every one of their systems, be it for a school, a business, a hospital, or government agency. Case in point: Schools generally start at 8:30 a.m. and end at 3 p.m. Therefore, they have some motion at 8:10 a.m., more motion at 8:20 a.m., and even more at 8:29 a.m. Yet, at 3 p.m., you have 100% motion, as the kids cannot get out of school fast enough!

Depending on the usage and location, some Interlogix customers could need larger amounts of memory to run their software programs. Others would require faster hard drives to run their applications, and others needed none. These systems were the equivalent of buying a custom suit. We were absorbing all this on the fly.

We spent the next week pricing quotes for each different model. Roughly ten days after the catalog was finished, we received our first official order to drop ship the completed system of choice to an Interlogix customer. Within the first year, we shipped just under one hundred Interlogix systems to their customers. I had walked into a goldmine. Or, giving credit where credit is due, the goldmine had walked into me.

The crazy thing was that we were building these servers in 100% office space. When Interlogix first reached out to us, we had 5,250 square feet of office space. Thanks primarily to this influx of orders, we outgrew that space within three months and added an additional 5,200 square feet of space next door. This was better, but still not ideal. We carved out desktop build areas in some of the open offices, sometimes using actual office desks as tech benches. At times, space got so tight that we had to line up systems down the hallways and through random offices. Not the ideal conditions for an anti-static environment!

The space had no dock, just a front and back door. It was a bit clunky with UPS pick-ups and drop-offs, and even tougher when the larger trucks were delivering new shipments.

Our offices were next door to our landlord, David Berkson, who headed one of the area's largest, best-established real estate companies. He was less than enthused about the traffic. Before long, he banned freight trucks from the parking lot, leaving us to collect most large deliveries and palletized orders on the side street parallel to the parking lot. We did this rain, snow, or shine. Our discarded shipping cartons consistently overwhelmed the outside dumpsters, leaving us to stack empty boxes in the hall until the next morning. Eventually we had to hire a nighttime clean-up crew and retain our own daily carting service.

Somehow, we made it work. We soon occupied three of the facility's four office suites, in a maze of more than 15,000 oddly connected square feet of space.

They were glorious times. It felt electric! My favorite part of being at work was hanging around our techs and watching them build products. They never seemed to mind all the questions I asked them (unless they were just being nice because I was the boss) and I had too much respect for what they did to screw things up.

This was especially true when we were building the first couple of units. Mike from Interlogix was on the phone, 2,100 miles away, using our eyes as his eyes on the first versions of each of the dozen or so systems. (This was decades before Zoom or Teams was invented.) Mike worked from a basic script, asking questions like, "How much memory is showing?" We would answer with either "64MB," "128MB," or "256MB," depending on the model, as all models had different capacities.

He would also ask questions about the drives and video cards. At the onset, I was the one who fed Mike this information from the tech benches. It was exciting to be a hands-on member of the team. It also escalated my learning curve on the insides of computers – what went with what and, most importantly, the "why," which always fascinated me. Once each system passed the long-distance verbal checklist, we packed it up and overnighted it to Mike in Salem.

Even as we were building the catalog models, Mike kept us plenty busy devising new variations. Every time HP or Compaq launched upgraded server families, we tested those next-generation units using Interlogix's standards. My entire company was buzzing, as were our distributor and vendor partners since we all shared in the benefits of this account.

I could not believe how smoothly this process had gone, especially considering we were utilizing office desks as tech benches. I started thinking of other markets where we could launch this "system builder" model. We would be able to use what we had learned to serve other customers. Very quickly, we evolved from that initial business plan into an actual, thriving business.

During that time, Interlogix was purchased by GE Capital and renamed as GE Security. Since GE Capital was a financial organization, I assumed these systems were now ending up in banks and financial institutions. In time, I would learn that I could not have been more wrong.

CHAPTER 25
POSITIVE MAYHEM

———

October 2003

After just over three years of busting through walls, adjusting, and improvising, we finally broke down and rented another of David Berkson's spaces. It was a 5,000-square-foot sales office about a mile away on Doolittle Avenue, also in Northbrook. Of course, we turned this additional space into our dedicated build center, moving the techs and rerouting all the UPS and Federal Express deliveries and pickups there. Renting additional space always chills things out with a landlord, and moving noisy, space-eating operations away from his headquarters made David not necessarily happy, but at least happier. He did have larger office/warehouse space available, but I was not sure we were ready to absorb the rent on 50,000 square feet, with a three-year lease. At that point, we were occupying a total of more than 20,000 square feet, with twenty employees.

We kept on expanding our business offerings. More and more, we noticed that when customers bought servers, they ended up housing them in racks. Often, they bought the racks from us, and we would simply drop ship them to the customers' location of choice. These were six-foot-tall shelving units, weighing five hundred pounds and capable of holding as many as 15 servers, along with all the power needed to drive those servers. Those were known as power distribution units, or PDUs. The racks were usually mounted on locking casters, making for easy movement, and were typically kept in server rooms, or data centers. All the servers were connected to the company's internal computer network.

Not all our customers had the IT staff on hand to build out these racks. So, with Doolittle space, we could offer our customers free rack-building services. These finished racks would ship directly to the customer's site, ready to deploy. I saw it as another way to lock in the customer. If they were buying all these rack parts from us, as well as all the computer servers, power units, and accessories that went within it, why would I not make it a free service? By offering the service at no charge, we could capture all their server business, and all those additional rack options generally combined to equal three times the average server price. At that point, the labor was basically free for us, as our techs were already salaried employees.

I began using "server math" as a business formula, looking for other creative variables that we could use to draw customers to BCD. In the end, offering these services for free may have meant that I left some money on the table; on the other hand, I am not positive that I would have gotten all those server sales without it.

For building servers, the single Doolittle facility was an upgrade over our original Northbrook offices. For building racks, however, it still left a lot to be desired. The space had no dock, so the truck driver would need to lower the back plate of his truck to street level in the business unit's parking lot. He then used a pallet jack to move this six-foot-high, 200-pound empty metal rack to a covered, shared area just outside our office.

Often, our office was so full of racks and servers that we had to leave the palletized racks in the canvas-covered, semi-secured area overnight. This was usually safe to do, but if the weather called for storms with high winds, we had to cram the cartons into the building, which the techs had to crawl over to reach their areas.

The standard 42U rack was six feet tall, but occasionally, a project would call for a 48U rack, which was almost seven feet tall. Then there were times when we had to work with custom, extra-large racks that would not even fit through the doors, so we had to build them outside in the canvas-covered space.

We were often so jammed up that we had to synchronize the pickups and deliveries. The trucks would back up to each other with their lift gates at ground level, and we could transfer these large, now-finished racks from truck to truck. It was "rack ballet!"

While all this sounds like pure chaos, for us it was magic. We fed off the mayhem. It was revolutionary! We were fearless. Our tech team embraced every challenge.

During those early years, our dedicated team chose to work through the day after Thanksgiving and over the Christmas holidays to complete shipments. And it was a true team effort, not limited to the techs. I was always there, generally helping by staying out of their way (and paying overtime.) I also remember once, during that first year in Doolittle, when we needed to get two large orders out before the end of the month in November. One of our salespeople, Tracey, helped during Thanksgiving Wednesday until 9 or 10 p.m. before heading to his parents' farm for the holiday. Without his help, we would have missed the deadline. OTFD was always the name of the game.

Despite the growth in our server-building operation, sales remained our focus. While we enjoyed selling fully stuffed servers, and while we especially enjoyed selling a fully stuffed rack with a bunch of those fully stuffed servers, we were still committed to selling whatever IT product the customer was looking for.

Our "we can find anything" mentality never changed. Even if it was merely a $50 order, we did not care. We wanted to be that one-stop IT shop. We practiced "live another day" selling. Sell them what they want today, and you are in. Turning down the opportunity just sends the customer to another company. Once you are out, you are scratching on the door hoping to get back in. Why would anyone want to do that?

Soon after we opened on Doolittle Avenue, one of our recently hired salespeople, a young man named Frank, landed a new account: Matrix Systems in Dayton, OH. Matrix was purchasing only one item from us – Serial ATA (SATA) drives – but they were buying lots of them. In those days, most server customers preferred SCSI-based drives, which were faster but more expensive. The hard drives that Matrix purchased had larger storage capacities but ran at half the speed. That was the trade-off.

After a few months, I realized Matrix was not paying their bills. This new account had roughly $50,000 open, which was 60 days over on their net thirty terms. We were still a newish company with a tight cash flow, and $50,000 was a lot of money to be owed to us. I reached out to the salesperson and asked what the situation was with the account. "I called them," Frank said, "but nobody gets back to me." I asked him the last time he tried, and he told me it had been a few weeks. I was not happy to hear that, but I figured I would deal with him later. First things first. I called the customer directly. Instead of asking for accounts payable, or even the owner, I asked for the buyer, whose name was Darlann.

We had a lovely and informative 10-minute conversation. I knew she was buying stand-alone internal hard drives, so I asked her how she was incorporating them. She indicated that she needed them for the systems they built for their Dayton-area customers – systems, it turned out, that we carried ourselves. "Oh, I did not know you sold those systems," she said when I informed her. (Another step closer to OTFD for my salesperson.)

"Let me ask you a question," I said. "If you're buying all the other goods elsewhere, why are you buying the hard drives from me?" She did not hesitate. "You are the only ones who can get them."

I responded: "Darlann, you seem to be a very nice lady and all, but that is going to become an issue for you if your company is not going to pay our invoices." As nicely as possible, I told her that we were going to have to cut off her supply.

She seemed sincerely horrified to hear this news. "I had no idea!" she said.

All the overdue bills were paid the following week. It turned out their accounts payable team had been asking Frank for BCD's Federal Tax ID to process our invoices, and he had not responded. Not good.

I could have left matters there, but I was willing to make the five-hour drive to Dayton to follow up on a hunch and meet Darlann in person. She was in her mid-thirties and seemed very connected to the pulse of Matrix Systems, not just her procurement department. As she guided me through the company's entire operation—a 30,000-square-foot facility—she introduced me to her teammates, most of whom seemed ardent fans of the University of Dayton Flyers; their signage was everywhere. I loved visiting the warehouse and seeing all the brands of hardware they had. It was eye candy to me!

Before I left for my next stop in Toledo, I almost felt guilty for driving five hours for a "collection call." But there was tremendous benefit in speaking with someone eye-to-eye. It built trust. Darlann even treated me to lunch at The Upper Crust, where we both had combo pastrami and corned beef sandwiches on rye piled with coleslaw. At $10, I was a cheap date!

When I got back to our office in Northbrook, I proactively sent her our product price list for all those brands I saw in her warehouse, along with some cross-product solutions for brands we did not carry. (Thank goodness for the photographic memory.) Darlann soon began buying all she could from us, and we never had a payment problem going forward.

After I sent her the price list, I asked Frank to come into my office. I did not want to drag things out, for both our sakes. I liked hiring people, especially salespeople; I blindly tended to fall in business love with them, and Frank had shown promise. By the same token, I hated firing people, but I had no choice. Frank had really fired himself. Six times, their finance people emailed him requesting our Federal ID number so they could pay us, and six times they got dead air. He did not even bother to forward the request to Elizabeth, our operations manager. I had spoken to him multiple times about the importance of follow-ups, but I guess the message did not connect. Laziness never worked for me. Urgency worked.

In hindsight, however, I can see Frank did the company a favor. His inaction got me in front of the customer, who turned into one of our largest customers on multiple products, and not just a single hard-drive SKU. Frank did not know that Matrix was installing that hard drive in a machine we carried. Why? Because he never asked.

It was unfortunate that this business relationship started with a negative—an overdue payment. But honestly, in my case, the negative situations tend to get my heart rate up. Things do not always go as planned, and negative situations do happen. If you prepare for that possibility, you are rarely caught off-guard, and you can use that moment to shine. And I have always loved being in the "hero business."

CHAPTER 26
REALITY CHECK

January 2004

During the company's first four years, I was guided by the theme of the movie *Field of Dreams*: "If you build it, they will come," I built it, and yes, they came.

The first to arrive were the vendors—HP, IBM, Ingram Micro, Tech Data. Then came the customers, who seemed attracted to our fair pricing and the unique additional free services we offered. But then, after a while, came the reseller copycats and wannabees, who told customers that they were "just like BCD." I did not know whether to be flattered or sue them for defamation, as no one was like BCD.

On paper, they were not wrong. They carried the same brands, and they were price-competitive. They all had people on staff who could put a server on the bench, open it, install the parts, test it, and ship it. We had blazed a path, and now they were following . . . closely.

The competition was hurting us. In the second half of 2003, sales were down some 17% year, over year. My experience told me that these measurements were snapshots of one moment, not proof of a trend, and that I was always one sale or one new customer away from charting an upswing. But although I had lost no faith in my selling ability, I began to have doubts about whether the business I built had staying power. I could not, and would not, reinvent myself, as all the successes I'd had in the past had brought me to this point. But what if I had already reached my peak?

Joanne and I had plenty of friends—close friends. (She always had more friends than I did.) But I had no mentors I could talk to about the business. I needed to find new paths to markets that would value our product offerings. Properly building computer servers is an art form, and I needed to find new customers who could see the value our skills would bring to their organization.

Maybe my situation would not have seemed so important to me if it had not appeared to be such a big deal to Northside Bank, who controlled our credit line. Noticing general patterns, they began to oversee us more closely and began asking for monthly and sometimes even bi-weekly financial reports. I hated the scrutiny. Did they not trust us anymore?

I did not like being micro-managed. I had always believed in being a hands-off manager, more like a mentor—the same kind of mentor I was quietly but desperately looking for.

But I did not have the time to dwell on these problems. As 2004 began, we had thirty-four employees, roughly 15 more than we had at the start of the previous year, distributed across finance, administration, warehouse, and sales. Our expenses were up roughly 45% over 2003. I had a company to lead and employees who counted on me and trusted me to come up with the right answers. I made sure there was never panic in my voice or on my face.

While we were not necessarily losing money, we certainly were not making money either. When I opened BCD, my aim had been to "be my own boss, earn enough to keep our heads above water, and hope to break even." But while breaking even may have sounded like a win when I was founding the company, it is never looked upon fondly by the people on whom you rely for credit. I may have been a hands-off manager, but I never kidded myself about the numbers, and what they showed was that the competition was eating away at our revenues and margin.

We were also beginning to feel heat from another source. By this point, our largest customer was not actually a customer at all. Instead, it was HP, a company that never bought anything from us, but with whom I had been working for more than a decade. Their four hundred account managers, from Maine to California, had us locked and loaded on speed dial with the IT and procurement departments of more than 30% of the Fortune 500 companies in America. All of them had accounts with BCD.

But what had been a strength was turning into a vulnerability. A new player had arrived. Dell was already a buzzword in the computer industry and was making inroads into HP's business. Dell's products were as good as HP's, and they were less expensive. Conservatively assuming a Dell product cost 10% less than the equivalent HP item, a corporate IT director with a strict $2 million IT budget would have an additional $200,000 to spend if they went with Dell. Or better yet, $200,000 saved. Coming in under budget is everything in corporate America. Dell was eating HP's lunch, and ours along with it.

Many colleagues and friends urged me to start offering Dell products to our customers. I refused. At that time, bringing in Dell would have been company suicide. Even offering Dell as a fallback for HP's customers would have seriously damaged my relationship with HP, and by extension, with those one-hundred-and-fifty Fortune 500 companies that HP brought to us. HP would have feared that sooner or later—probably sooner—one of those companies would balk at paying the HP price and ask for the Dell equivalent, and that we would cave into their pressure and switch. HP's whole price structure would have cracked, along with HP's dominant position within the industry.

For the record, we never would have caved. We were loyal to a fault. Somewhat blindly loyal. But gossip burns through vendor sales reps like a brushfire in California. I knew that if I sold one Dell product to a customer I had met through HP, within 48 hours, every HP rep from coast to coast would have heard about it. With one sale, I would have risked a reputation that took over a decade to build. Unfortunately, many of my competitors did not face this conflict. They did not have my relationships, so they had no relationships at risk.

We were not getting any breaks from the economy, either. We had fallen a couple thousand dollars short of breaking even in the first quarter of 2004. Always looking at the bright side, had we been able to count the orders that arrived in March but were unable to ship until April due to availability, we would have been profitable. Nothing worth doing cartwheels over, but the ink would have been black, rather than barely black. On the other hand, if it had not been for a few grand slam orders in February, the ink might have been much redder. I hated being in that precarious position. I had always survived by depending on my ingenuity and my urgency, not by wearing a catcher's mitt and hoping something would come my way. That is no way to run a business when you are responsible for protecting 40-some team members who have put their trust in you.

This was new terrain for me. Was I feeling pressure? Absolutely. But did that pressure lead to doubt? Not really. I knew that somehow, some way, I always landed on my feet. I was confident that I would again. Hard work and confidence had always paid off in the past. Why should that change now? But that mantra would not necessarily convince my employees, who could see that things were down.

Joanne and I talked about our situation over dinner—a lot. She was always looking out for me, and she did not share my "blind eye" when it came to my employees. She took umbrage with those who, in her opinion, were not working as hard as I was, and she was not afraid to share those feelings with me. As much as I did not want to hear it, I was listening to her.

The second quarter began as the first quarter had ended, a little slow. I remained confident that we would turn things around, but I was starting to struggle with the how. Cutting expenses with layoffs would ease the squeeze, but I thought that would be counterproductive. It made no sense to terminate struggling salespeople without having the replacements on board. I could see that they were trying; they just were not closing. With everything going on around me, I stopped taking my $15,000 monthly salary, only keeping my Blue Cross health benefits.

In April, I made a very tough move. Mark, our director of sales, made $175,000 a year (roughly worth $290,000 in 2024.) By cutting his $14,500 a month and my own salary, we could save almost $90,000 for the quarter. Mark was a business friend of mine within the computer industry when I hired him, and I liked him, but he was unable to move the numbers. So, I had to let him go. He understood, and he took it as well as anyone can take such hard news.

Two days later, still feeling bad about releasing Mark, I got a visit from our banker, Bill Kivit. We had "the talk." Bill told me that Jim and Patty, the bank's owners, were concerned about our negative turn. He reminded me that things had been softening since the previous year (as if I was not already aware of that!) He shared that the bank was seriously considering cutting my line of credit from the current $1 million to $750,000, or perhaps even $500,000. That was hard enough news to swallow. Then came the second part of this one-two punch: with the smaller bank line, the interest rate would be higher.

"Hold on," I argued. We were being squeezed between two payment cycles. We had to pay our vendors, most notably Ingram Micro and Tech Data, within 30 days, while our major customers did not have to pay us for 60 days. We had roughly $4.5 million in open invoices from March and the first half of April, all due to be paid by June 15th. That did not even count all we would sell between then and the end of the second quarter, which could be a lot.

The Japanese business year ends on June 30, so we were now in the sweet spot for Takeda. Moreover, one of the IT guys from Takeda had just moved over to Astellas Pharmaceuticals, and he had been pushing them to move some of their business from CDW to us. Walking a fine line between asking and begging, I asked Bill to please give it until June 30ᵗʰ before cutting the credit line. He agreed. Six weeks of grace.

I was happy to have Bill's foot off our Adam's apple, but the relief did not last long. A few days later, I met with our accountant, Hal. I asked him—just in case worse came to worst—what bales of hay could be thrown off the boat to keep it afloat. This was not me being negative. On the contrary, this was me putting my big boy pants on and acting like the CEO of the company. Still, the Pollyanna in me was hoping he would pat me on the head and say, "Don't worry, everything will be alright."

That is not what happened. Instead, Hal told me there was no alternative; the bales of hay were all in the Selling, General, and Administrative (SGA) expenses. I would have to let more people go, likely five more employees. I politely and passionately told him I could not do that. These people trusted me, they came to work for and with me. Letting them go would have to be a last resort.

Fortunately, we got some breathing room. As I expected, over the last week of April and the first half of May, Takeda and Astellas came in with combined purchases close to $1.8 million. Still, it did not relieve all the pressure. Banker Bill was still lurking. Accountant Hal was still recommending layoffs.

I was in a tough place, and I did not have much time to alter the flow. I started jotting down some names—a draft shortlist if you will. Every day, I was crossing one name off and adding another, based upon the circumstances of the day. Wrongly, I tried keeping everything from Joanne. But she knew me too well, and I had to let her know what was going on.

I told her I was merely being internally tested, and she reminded me that I always land on my feet, somehow, some way. I knew she believed in me, but that did not necessarily mean she slept any more easily.

In the meantime, I had to prepare for the worst while keeping a positive outlook and my game face on. I rallied the sales team, which had grown to six salespeople. I challenged them to win every deal, not with price but with their sales ability. I also told them to take any new deal north of 10 points profit, whereas fifteen points had always been the minimum. In the meantime, I instructed them to go back to their open sales quotes and follow up with the customers to see how the opportunity was progressing. In other words, stop waiting around for the phone to ring.

A few days later, we caught a break. Back in January, I had quoted a project for servers on what was figured to be a million-dollar deal from General Electric. Now, five months later, the order magically came through. "Fuck, yes!" I screamed and almost broke my arm trying to high-five myself. I immediately forwarded a copy of the GE purchase order to Bill at Northside, if only for him to have something to share with Jim and Patty. I heaved a sigh of relief. There were not going to be any layoffs. Not that quarter, anyway.

Soon something else remarkable would happen. ``Stop waiting around for the phone to ring," I had told my sales team. But one day the phone rang, and that phone call changed my life.

CHAPTER 27
CASHING THAT REALITY CHECK

———

April 2004

Roughly a week later, after finishing our weekly Monday morning sales meeting, I was about to head off to Anton's Fruit Ranch for my daily salad bar and soup-to-go fix when Nick, one of our salespeople, popped his head in and said there was a Carol Heyward on the phone looking for me.

Considering all that had gone on during the past four months, my first thought was, *Shit, now what?* Instead, I replied, "Who's Carol Heyward? Did she say what she wanted?"

Nick shrugged. "Just somebody from GE Capital." I told him to transfer her over.

Carol introduced herself. "I am a procurement specialist. I got your name from Mark Allen." I knew Mark well. He was the HP Global account manager assigned to GE. Mark got all that revenue credit on my sales to General Electric and the twenty-two GE Capital companies. "Mark says you are the guy. I hope so."

If ever you want my full attention, just tell me, "You're the guy." Seriously, at that point Carol owned me. I would have climbed the Matterhorn for her. Instead, she had something more interesting in mind. "I'm looking for help in fulfilling a GE Capital customer order," she said.

The main item she was seeking was the HP D3000, an external

storage device. I knew that product. We had sold them to Interlogix when their server systems maxed out on the drive bays.

Data storage requirements were getting larger and larger, but the space inside servers was constricted. Customers needed external drives to increase capacity, and the D3000 could hold 786TB, which was a huge number in those days. *I guess there is a shortage,* I thought. With my heart racing and that damn *Mission: Impossible* theme playing in my head, I jumped onto my dashboard connected to US distribution centers.

There was no shortage. There were hundreds in stock. Everybody had them. *WTF?* I thought. *She couldn't find these?*

But who was I to question? I just grabbed the opportunity. ``There is inventory available," I told her blandly.

"Can you send one to me?" she asked. I do not believe a customer has ever asked me that question. "Wish I could," I chuckled. "Tell you what . . . how about you send me the list of the parts that you will need to go with this device, and I will get right back to you with a quote using the special bid pricing from Hewlett-Packard that we have exclusively for General Electric, with the proper parts pricing and the availability?"

I made sure I responded to Carol with that exact verbiage, so she knew that I was not only "the guy," but that I could also speak HP like a second language and knew that part was merely an empty chassis. After all, Mark could have told her that I was "the guy" just because we were drinking buddies or golf friends (which we were neither.)

I banged out the quote (with that blasted *Mission: Impossible* theme still permeating my brain) and forwarded it to her. "Everything is in stock," I reassured her, still somewhat in awe that HP could not find their own goods.

Then came the real life-changing moment. Roughly ten minutes later, my quote came emailed back to me, attached to an email from a guy named Ron Pope that said, "Approved, please ship." Wow! That was easy! Seconds later, reality set in. Who was going to pay me?

Ron's email address had an HP domain. I replied to both him and Carol, asking if this was going to be a PO from GE, where I was already an established vendor, or from HP? Ron replied quickly that it would be from HP, but to please be patient while he got my company set up in the system. He asked me to hold the goods under lock and key for him while he arranged to send me HP's vendor set-up form.

Within minutes, he sent me another email. "In the meantime, do you have these?" It was a list of parts for GE Capital Appliances. Joanne and I had a GE refrigerator in our home, but GE Capital Appliances was one of the few GE Capital companies I had not penetrated. I saw this as an opening to finally get into GE Appliances, just as they had gotten into my home. Fair is fair, right? I immediately started surfing my dashboard for those units.

While I was busy doing that product search, Ron sent me another request, for roughly $400,000 of goods going to Home Depot. As you can imagine, my heart rate was running high, and yes, of course, that damn *Mission: Impossible* theme was playing—no, scratch that—*blasting* in my head. I scrolled through his shopping list, and everything was creatively available, one way or the other.

I sent the first two quotes back. Ron emailed back that he was still working on sending me the vendor form so they could issue Purchase Orders, and to please not lose any of the held goods. Then, astonishingly, he sent me yet another opportunity, this time for $270,000 of goods needed at Johns Hopkins University in Maryland by Saturday, which was just three days away. I was getting dizzy.

Within half an hour, orders worth more than a million dollars had just appeared on my screen, from a complete stranger. Who the hell was this guy? I wrote back, stating, "I'm calling you."

I called the number at the bottom of his email and opened with, "Who are you?"

"My name is Ron Pope," he responded, in a pure Texas twang. "I run the HP Global Customer First program and report directly to Carly Fiorina." She was then the president of HP.

As we were working through the nuts and bolts of filling out the vendor form, we began to chitchat. I love chitchat; you can learn a lot in a relaxed conversation. Ron talked about how he played freshman football as a fullback at Texas A&M University, and about the 14-plus knee operations he had undergone since. Then he started venting. He was very frustrated that it took so long to get his POs cut, but that was a process that was recently moved to India, and bureaucracies moved at their own pace.

Even worse, HP was amid changing their existing internal enterprise application system to the System Analysis Program (SAP), which entailed migrating all the old data to the new one, much of it manually, line by line.

"We are 60 days behind on our orders because I cannot find them in our SAP system," Ron said. "Carly is getting ready to meet some of these customers, and I need to take care of their orders before Carly goes to visit them and gets an earful about our incompetence." Ron may have managed to work a few profanities into his explanation.

Ron was in full scrambling mode. He already had 60 days' worth of orders that he could not either find or fill—*or both*—with more coming daily. His boss was impatient, and he was looking for a hero. By this point, I already loved the guy. And like I said, *I am in the hero business.*

To me, sales has always been about understanding the customer's dilemma, recognizing an opportunity, visualizing the potential outcome, knowing what you can offer that a potential competitor may not, and having faith in yourself and your ability to make something happen. A winning formula.

I knew Ron had options, but I also knew that none of them were very good. He could buy what he needed through regular IT distribution channels like Ingram Micro or Tech Data, just like I did. But they certainly did not move very quickly.

He also could have found this HP hardware on his distribution dashboard, just as I had, but that would have meant shipping the systems and accessory parts back to the factory, where the items would have to be built to the order specifications. It would likely be a three-week turnaround to ship those finished goods. Ron did not have three weeks. He did not have three days.

He could have bought the items through CDW, but they did not offer the same instantaneous response times as we did. Nor were they known for their multi-tasking capabilities, and it was obvious that this opportunity called for superior multi-tasking. Moreover, CDW was at the time a public company and was forbidden under SEC regulations from shipping anything before receiving the customer's purchase order. I had no such guidelines.

I laid out the scenario to the best of my ability with full transparency. "Ron, it looks like our biggest constraint is that I cannot hold inventory for more than two days. I could if the goods were in my inventory, but they are not. I am just holding them on your behalf at distributors such as Tech Data and Ingram Micro. Once I get your order, I then need to bring those goods to our build center, build the system to your specification, and get it out the door via overnight freight within two days, max."

I was ready to close the deal. As the saying goes, "No balls, no glory!" In this case, I knew Ron could not wait days or weeks to get the order placed from India, or from CDW with their SEC limitations, so I went for it.

"Ron, how about this for an action plan?" I said. "As the delay seems to be getting purchase orders issued fast enough from India, what if my company were to build and overnight ship your requests off of your 'Approved, please ship' email response? I will not wait for the PO. Instead, we will fill your orders all week, and then every Monday, you and I can reconcile the last week's orders and you can send me the purchase orders then."

To that, Ron replied, verbatim: "I will never fuck you. You have my word." Things do not get any more official than that, do they? And he never did.

There was still one major hurdle. How was I going to fund these purchases? By this time, we had roughly a $1 million combined credit line with the distributors, and a $1 million line with the bank, although that was shaky. I needed to make sure I had the necessary credit to make this happen.

The next morning, I met Bill Kivit of the Northside Community Bank for breakfast and told him about the Ron Pope opportunity. He was excited to hear it but not surprised. "I do not know how you do it, but you always seem to come up with an answer!" I really appreciated hearing that; in fact, I almost *needed* to hear that.

Yet Bill just could not grasp why Ron Pope needed me. Bill's a very smart guy, but even after numerous attempts to walk him through Ron's role and the HP process, he did not see how I fit in. "Why can't they buy it themselves?" he would ask. "And why do they need *you* again?"

This uncertainty was going to kill the deal. I needed the credit line bumped up at least fivefold, and I needed it done yesterday. To make that happen, I needed Bill.

"Look," I said, "How about I fly you to Houston and you can hear it from Ron Pope himself?" He agreed. I called Ron and explained the situation. Once again, this was not a show of weakness, but a show of strength and transparency. It became obvious to Ron that I was not just going to wing this.

The following Thursday, Bill and I flew to Houston and met Ron for a tour of Building Ten, which housed the factory on the HP campus. As we walked around the second-floor sales mezzanine, Ron pointed out the different production lines on the factory floor below. It was a very cool site.

Then Ron iced the cake. "See that man down there?" he asked Bill, pointing to one of the production stations. "That is Pedro. He is the build manager, in charge of making sure the products have everything that is specified in the order. Before I found Jeff, I would need to go down to the floor every day, find Pedro, and ask, 'What job are you building today?' And on many days, regardless of what he told me, I would give him new order paperwork and tell him to build this order next instead. There were problems every day. But since we found Jeff, I no longer need to do that."

The instant credibility Ron had just bestowed upon me, right in front of my banker, was literally money in the bank! After the tour, as we were in Ron's office, Bill asked Ron, "How much do you think you will need to buy monthly from Jeff?"

Ron replied, "I am not sure when this SAP nightmare will be over, but, until then, likely $3 million a month."

I looked over my shoulder at Bill behind me and asked, "Do you get it now?"

"Oh yeah, I get it," Bill replied.

Mission accomplished. I even bought Bill a George Bush Intercontinental Airport shoeshine on the way out of Houston.

Over the next six months—starting just three weeks after those initial bank and accounting meetings about potential workforce reduction—we navigated through 443 HP Big Deal Customer special pricing letters, which equated to 443 orders processed, for a total of $15,400,000. This made up 70% of our $22 million year.

I was lucky and fortunate to catch Ron when I did. And vice versa. Ours was a marriage made in heaven. I was feeling a lot of pressure to find business. Ron was facing a remorseless enemy: time. His customers needed their products, but somewhere in HP's botched migration their products had disappeared.

I have always felt that the most important quality I could offer customers was a sense of urgency. I could solve his problem. I could be his hero. Once Ron pulled the trigger, we made things happen.

Finished goods were landing at customer sites no more than four days after Ron requested them. Indeed, for some government customers located at sensitive sites, we delivered the goods within 24 hours. We used what is called Hot Shot freight, a secure freight method using two drivers who alternate shifts driving and sleeping. The trucks' bays were locked and then wax-sealed, not to be opened until they reached their destinations. One rack-built system, which was custom-made for a US military base, was delivered just eight hours after leaving our dock.

By recognizing that HP opportunity and creating the workaround to solve the customer's problem while locking out any potential competitor, we increased BCD's revenues by 192.5%, from $8 million in 2003 to $23.4 million in 2004. Because of that percentage growth, we were ranked second on the *Computer Reseller News* Top 25 Rising Stars in the IT Industry list in 2005. Per the magazine, "BCD continued to grow its sales through the recent recession and IT spending slump by sticking to its model of offering high-volume IT products." All because of one customer named HP. And one hero. Nope, not me. Ron Pope.

That $15.4 million we sold to HP directly was just the tip of the iceberg for us, as it truly became the "gift that kept on giving." That is why, even to this day, I laugh when I hear people say someone is such a good salesperson, they could even sell ice to an Eskimo! Forgive me, but that person is a rookie. I sold over $15 million of HP servers to HP themselves!

As great as 2004 had been, things began to change for Ron's Customer First program in 2005. Carly Fiorina, who had given him carte blanche and who had signed off on all his expenditures, was removed from her CEO position. The problems caused by the SAP migration also began to diminish. As a result, in March 2005, Ron's Customer First program was reassigned to HP's new Omaha procurement team.

This was a predictable development. Hewlett-Packard was and is a fiscally responsible company, where methodical, responsible, prudent decision-makers have been known to take up to eight months to finalize the next year's budget. Ron operated in hyperdrive, an urgent response to an urgent crisis. Everything his team did was in full company compliance; there was no overcharging, nothing renegade. But none of the $14 million Ron spent in 2004 hit anyone's budget, except Carly Fiorina's. When you add to it all the sales commission paid to the territory and account reps where those servers landed, Ron's purchases probably added a $20 million hit to HP's non-forecasted budget. Quite a shock to the corporate culture.

With the emergency caused by the SAP migration cooling, Omaha could not take control of Ron's program fast enough. As it turned out, that was about the only thing they did fast. Deals that Ron and I would close in seven minutes now took seven days. The Omaha group had its requirements: check stock availability, get three quotes, etc. We adjusted to them, but the excitement was gone, and they became just another customer. The relationship went from buzzy to boring, just like that.

Ron still ran Customer First until he retired from HP in 2023. He could still place orders on his own authority, if they did not cost more than $10,000. And his team continued to call on us to find parts that no one else could find. While it was nothing near the same volume, their respect was my reward.

The year before Ron retired, I brought a customer to HP for a factory tour. As we were walking down that same second-floor mezzanine in Building Ten where Ron had taken Bill the Banker and me, I heard a familiar Texas twang behind me. "Are you showing these folks all those things I showed you?" It was Ron, who'd had no prior warning of my pending visit. With 10,000 HP employees in that massive facility, there was Ron, walking the mezzanine right behind me.

What were the odds? Easy. 100%!

PART THREE

THE BRAND

CHAPTER 28
THE TIMES ARE A-CHANGIN'

January 2008

By the beginning of 2008, we had been working with Mike Gholson at GE Security for a solid six years. Over the last four of those years, we helped them perfect their systems by testing their components and evaluating their performance. In the process, we helped them develop their customer catalog. All their products had the GE Security logo affixed to the front bezel, but they were joint builds between GE Security and BCD.

I did not realize it at the time, but this was BCD's first foray into becoming an Original Equipment Manufacturer (OEM). OEMs create products for other companies that carry those companies' logos. This practice is not limited to the computer industry; it is done in virtually every marketplace. Take the Kirkland brand at Costco. Fisher nuts, Huggies diapers, Starbucks coffee, and Duracell batteries are all products sold under the Kirkland brand. This amounts to a fifty-six-billion annual business for Costco.

I was more than happy being the person behind the scenes. It did not matter whether the BCD logo was on the product or not. If customers were buying my servers, I did not care how they did it. I laughed all the way to the bank!

This collaboration allowed us to diversify our paths within the marketplace. Soon, we were also able to offer online product catalogs for our key customers Takeda, Astellas, Fortis Benefits, and Pepsi-Cola. The catalogs made it easier to buy from us, which is a valuable feature. The easier it is for a customer to buy from someone, the more likely they are to buy again, and again.

> **Nothing is better than repeat business. It's gold, a statement from the customer attesting to his satisfaction. I know many vendors who focus on new business, often to the detriment of their existing customers. I always felt that was the wrong way to grow. Instead, pay attention to your existing base, even as you try to add to it. Some people think that swapping one customer for another is breaking even. In fact, it's a loss. There is a cost associated with bringing in a new customer, even if that only cost is time. If you keep your customers happy, they become excellent referrals. That is how reputations are formed.**

One Friday in March, at exactly nine in the morning, I received a call from Rick Taylor, the local GE rep for the Midwest territory. I had heard Rick's name within the territory, but since most of our dealings with GE Security were with their server building management team in Oregon, our paths had never crossed.

Rick was calling to let me know there was an issue with the system we had just sent over to the Illinois State Toll Highway Authority, about twenty miles west of Chicago in Downers Grove. "The system just stopped working," he told me. "The person on-site tried a few times to cold-boot it"—unplug it and plug it back in—"but with no success. The power came back on, but he couldn't get a home screen."

Rick's tone was casual and calm, but I still put on my corporate game face. After all, I was dealing with a division of the second-largest company in the world (at that time). Even before I knew what was wrong, I wanted to project confidence that we could fix anything. Because I could fix anything. After all, I had always been able to fix State Farm, which meant that I had already been to the mountaintop and lived to tell about it.

The very first thing I did was get in front of the problem. When there's a problem in corporate America, the first task is to determine who is at fault. But until that happens, the proper response is to assume ownership of the issue. "That is unusual for us, Rick," I responded. "I think we both know that we're better than that. I'm not sure how this could have happened. I am disappointed, as something must have been flawed within our quality assurance process on this one."

In doing this, I made it clear that this was a unique, one-off situation. I brought him into the circle with "We both know we're better than that." I reminded him that we had a quality assurance process in place, and I neither admitted a mistake nor denied that it was possible. I have always been able to initially defuse situations with that approach. This does not mean it always had a positive outcome, but it certainly lowered the temperature from the start.

As it turned out, in this case, my soothing approach was appreciated but unnecessary. I had barely finished the *"my bad"* when Rick indicated that it was not a BCD issue. The third-party contractor on-site, Ray, wanted to see what would happen if he pulled a spinning hard drive out of a server during a RAID reboot. This changed the conversation for me by one-hundred-and-eighty-degrees! I was back on home court.

"I'm not a technician, Rick, I just play one on TV," I said, cribbing a line from a legendary Vicks Formula 44 cough syrup commercial. It was a self-deprecating quip that customers enjoyed, and that I continue to use effectively to this day. (Similarly, when the tech talk gets over my head and I need to bring in my CTO, I will say, "Let's hear it from the horse's mouth, as opposed to the other end." Just another soft way to indicate my ego is not important here.) "I am guessing that yanking the disk crashed the system," I replied.

In those few short minutes, I had acquired leverage. The case of "Whose fault is it?" was solved! Instead of being back on my heels taking a pummeling, as happened so often in my State Farm days, here was another chance to be the proactive hero. I saw the opportunity to add Rick Taylor to my fan club.

I asked Rick where the system was now. He said, "Tollbooth 99.". That was a big help . . . NOT. "For us laymen out there," I asked, "where would Tollbooth 99 be?" He gave me the address, which was about ten miles from our office. I went for it. "If you can get the system packed up within the hour, I'll have my messenger pick it up at 10 a.m. He'll bring it back to my lab, we'll reinstate it as new out of the box, and we'll get it back to the site by 4 p.m. today."

It was all very matter-of-fact, as if we had done it a hundred times; this is how you deal with corporate America. It is having confidence in your ability without overselling it, then displaying a sense of urgency.

Rick even offered to pay for it, which was certainly a rarity. I thanked him but refused, telling him, "You are GE, a great customer who has been even greater for my family, and I am just happy to help. I'm even happier knowing the problem was not caused by us."

By bringing my family into it, I was subliminally connecting us to the greater extended GE family. For me, the key was to end it with the gentle, subtle reminder that it was not a BCD issue, but it was a BCD fix. As I write this, I can almost hear that same cavalry bugle charge playing in my head, just as it did almost two decades earlier when it happened in real time. So many soundtracks in my head, so little time, and so few brain cells left.

Once I arranged for the fix to happen, I never really gave the problem any more thought. I just knew things would work out. I had that much confidence in my team. Checking back with Rick and Ray to see if it had been picked up and returned would have sent a message to the contrary. So, I went home after work Friday and returned to the office Monday. Just business as usual. Or was it?

Again, promptly at nine, I received a call from Rick. I must admit, my first thought was *Now what?* But this time, Rick had a different GE Capital-related person on the phone with him. They were looking for a local enterprise systems builder for a security system project at Chicago's massive Merchandise Mart. Now *that* got my attention. I went off the defensive and listened to them with open ears.

It turned out that most of their customers, who were generally computer resellers, had been buying Dell computer servers for their projects. They did not always work correctly right out of the box. Rick was calling because they were impressed with the same-day turnaround on the fix and the "business as usual" attitude with which we had conducted ourselves.

I told them I appreciated that they noticed it. "It's what we do for any customer," I added. The other guy on the phone with Rick said Dell would not even support the server once they learned it was being used for video surveillance. I really liked where this was going.

This seemed to be a double win—get formally introduced into the security market and displace Dell-based servers with HP-based ones. It smelled like burgers on the grill to me, which is always my happy place.

I had gained a reputation in the IT industry as the "Dell Antichrist" ever since Michael Dell came up with his late 1980s build-to-order computer model. Under that model, holding inventory turned from an asset into a liability, sending convulsions through many of the businesses where I had worked at the start of my career. Additionally, HP had purchased over sixty-million-dollars million from me over the years, which made me more than a bit partial.

I asked them to send me the Dell system build that was not working. We had never worked with this kind of company, but I was confident that any Dell products could be matched with HP versions. There were so many sounds playing from the jukebox in my head, from *Mission: Impossible* to a cash register ringing up a sale. Within a few minutes, they faxed me over the Dell build, and I was able to match the hardware specification with an HP version. The system and components were in stock. I told them the project would be no problem.

As I waited to hear back from them, my thoughts surged ahead. What they wanted was not some server that was unfamiliar to us. We used this same server model for many orders from many companies, including those we had built for GE Security. The realization dawned on me: BCD had been building video surveillance systems since 2002. It was certainly a "Hello, McFly!" moment for me. We were not merely an IT company. *This* was our marketplace.

Apparently, despite our seven years of working with Interlogix/ GE Capital, our fading brain cells had never stored the fact that they were security-based companies. In all fairness to those brain cells, we had always considered ourselves IT server builders. We also had always thought that, since GE Security was a division of GE Capital, the products were for financial security, not physical security. Of course, had we seen the entire GE Security catalog, we would have noticed that it also offered video cameras and access control devices. But GE Security had only sent us the BCD section for final proofing, which gave us tunnel vision.

Sometimes when we assume something, our minds do not accept new data neutrally but instead adjust it to fit the assumption. In 2006, GE Security ordered twelve servers from us to ship to the Pan American games in Brazil. I do remember raising an eyebrow, but then we remembered that a lot of illegal banking activities were alleged to be taking place in South America. So, we were able to reconcile this purchase with our assumption that the servers were being used to provide financial security. And for two more years, we kept building and shipping GE Security products that we thought were being used in finance. Major brain cramp.

But at long last, the GE light bulb over my head was illuminated. Now I could make the connection that the systems we were selling to them were designed to record video, not IT data.

I suppose a different person might have felt embarrassed to realize that, for six years, he had been completely ignorant about what he had been doing all day long. Not me; I was enthralled. This was an eye-opening opportunity!

We had yet to hear back from our first official security client, but I was already six steps ahead. This could be the rarest thing in business: a new, growing market in which we already had six years' experience. BCD could bring to the video surveillance market the competitive pricing and zealous service that we provided to Fortune 500 and other large organizations for years.

We could also start bringing surveillance recorders to our existing customers. They were already using our IT servers; why couldn't they use our security video servers? For all I knew, they were already using our servers to store their surveillance data. My head was spinning.

I knew right there and then that we could maintain our IT identity while morphing into a whole new vertical that was seemingly desperate for our enterprise server-building expertise— the CCTV video surveillance marketplace. There was no reason to drop one for the other, especially since the video surveillance market needed an IT builder. The earliest video surveillance systems had no-name servers without much functionality running the cameras. (Think of those grainy video footages at a convenience store.) Those were merely boxes to record the camera data.

I was already visualizing BCD building systems that could allow for more cameras to send recording data over off-the-shelf Dell servers, or even HP servers. Once we started testing them on our bench with cameras, we could offer systems that managed that camera footage, not just recorded it. Our systems could support more cameras per server, using high-resolution cameras recording pristine video frames. And thanks to GE Security, we were already six-year veterans of designing and building such systems, and apparently we were pretty good at it, since they stayed with us.

If we had built all these systems with me being oblivious to what the real market was, imagine the havoc we could cause in this market segment now that we were aware of what we were doing! My adrenaline was off the charts. It was too good to be true.

Then came the hiccup. The $3,500 Dell quote to the customer was $1,000 less than our $4,500 cost for the HP equivalent, and that was before I added my markup. However, I recognized that the thousand-dollar write-off was our buy-in to a lucrative new opportunity. "I know you're in a tough spot here, so I'll match the price," I said. Knowing that the customer had trouble with Dell support, I added a sweetener: "Please tell your customer that I'll have one of my local technicians follow the system to the site and personally install it." That clinched the deal, and we received the PO almost immediately.

I was so excited that I called Joanne and told her we were having dinner out, and that I had some great news to share. Luckily, Alexander was old enough to babysit Max and Lizzie.

Joanne and I dashed off to our favorite local Italian restaurant, and I told her about the incredible new business opportunity that came to us just because of the guy who fucked up our system at the Tollway. Joanne is a very smart person, smarter than me, but I needed to walk us both through it a couple more times because, as usual, you just couldn't make this stuff up!

We toasted the new opportunity with our wine glasses and enjoyed our pasta dinners. She had the toasted ravioli, and I had the penne Bolognese. Bolognese is my go-to pasta sauce, but I will settle for Ragu, should Bolognese not be on the menu. I'm all about compromise!

The Merchandise Mart system worked flawlessly from the get-go, and a whole new market opened for BCD to bring our IT-savvy solutions. Thus, BCDVideo was (unofficially) born. In a very short time, BCDVideo added a half-million dollars of this new security business to our top-line revenue. We also learned a lot, most crucially that we weren't just building solutions for this newly emerging marketplace, but supporting it! That was something, apparently, that even Dell did not do. Now I know their Achilles' heel, and how to capitalize on it.

CHAPTER 29

EVOLUTION HAPPENS

May 2008

I think of myself as a lucky man. I know I've caught lightning in a bottle more times than most people catch a bus. State Farm, Ron Pope, Carol Heyward, the Illinois Tollway blunder that led to the call from Rick Taylor—I have frequently found myself in the right place at the right time. But I viewed this opening to the security world as *a* once-in-a-lifetime opportunity for my company and my career.

This sector was taking off. In the aftermath of the 9/11 attacks seven years earlier, private-sector businesses had woken up to the need for security. Previously, most businesses primarily viewed security in terms of loss prevention. But after 9/11, companies woke up to their vulnerabilities and the need to be consistently on guard. About eighty-five-percent of the nation's critical infrastructure, such as power plants, data storage centers, hospitals, and chemical facilities, was privately owned and operated. Even private companies that weren't in critical industries began to recognize that they were subject to attack, simply for being symbols of our American way of life.

Just as I had been around at the beginning of the PC revolution and the development of the Internet, now I paddled my surfboard in the water as the next new wave of opportunity rolled in. We were more than ready for this new challenge. I did not just want to enter the security market. I wanted to reinvent it.

We had years of experience in building IT-ready computer servers. We were accustomed to leading with trusted hardware. *Our* hardware. Customers who purchased a system from BCD knew it would work from the moment they plugged it in, and that it would continue to perform for years, usually long after the five-year warranty period.

We had seen how companies spent their money elsewhere to save a few bucks, and we saw why and where they were dissatisfied.

At this point, customers usually guessed how much storage the project would require. Often, they overestimated or underestimated, with serious cost exposures either way. But if we knew the number of cameras they'd be deploying, the resolution of those cameras (measured in megapixels), and the number of days the video footage would be retained, we could calculate with some precision just how much memory and storage they would need.

To eliminate the guesswork for our customers, BCDVideo began offering purpose-built video recorders. For us, it was a natural transition, taking those same IT servers that corporate America had trusted and retrofitting them to capture the density of the video data. That one proactive move eventually led to close to a quarter-million BCDVideo purpose-built video servers capturing surveillance in ninety-one countries over the next 15 years.

As expected, we had some bumps and bruises along the way. The first involved navigating through the legal departments of our key manufacturers, especially Hewlett-Packard. HP was always laser-focused (no pun intended) on how their products reached the market. They had a phobia that every reseller or value-added distributor was looking to dump their goods into the grey-market channel. This would undermine HP's ability to control prices and where their product landed. People on the outside even referred to HP's legal department as "grey market Nazis."

Ordinarily, it took just two or three touches for an HP product to reach a customer. Either the goods went right to an end user, as we had done for Ron Pope's customers, or they went through a distributor to an approved HP reseller, such as Ingram Micro or Tech Data, and then to the end user. The more touches involved, the more demanding HP legal became. Our plan involved up to six touches, including the security integrator passing it to the end customer. More than likely, that integrator was not HP-authorized. Thus, the issue.

Based on our long relationship, we had every reason to believe HP would approve. But maybe they would not. And as an OTFD company, we were more than anxious to get started.

While we were waiting for HP's decision, we pushed ahead. We began testing other platforms currently in use in the market, brands like NEC, Supermicro, and Promise. Thanks to this awakening by Rick Taylor at GE Capital, we increased our security work by one-hundred-percent on projects throughout the Midwest.

Simultaneously, we began testing HP's products for surveillance usage. I was confident that it was only a matter of time until we received the legal department's blessing, and we wanted to be ready to offer HP products, once approved, as part of our solutions.

We wanted to maximize our exposure to the marketplace, so we decided to meet with billion-dollar security distributor Anixter, Inc. The Anixter brothers founded the company in 1957, the year I was born, as an industrial supplier buying wire and cable by the 5,000-foot spool and selling it by the foot. Over the next thirty years, they expanded their offerings to include security cameras, network switches, and other components of the security ecosystem, except network video recorders (NVRs).

We saw this as a major opportunity. Anixter was more than a multi-billion-dollar distributor; the company was the world's largest seller of Axis cameras, somewhere north of $400 million a year. When a customer bought a security system, the industry standard for estimating storage costs were 30% of the camera costs. Based on this math and their camera sales, Anixter had the potential to sell $133 million in servers a year.

But would they see this opportunity the way we did? During the last week of March, we met with Anixter's senior vice president of global product marketing, Steve Leatherwood. The company was nearby. Anixter's global headquarters was in Glenview, just one town over from our offices.

Steve knew the GE Capital team who introduced me to this market, so we were able to shortcut the small talk and get right to telling him about BCD's history and our grand plan to bring an IT mentality into the surveillance market. Steve was very receptive and confirmed that such an approach would be welcome. I believe his exact quote was, "There's a lot of unstable shit out there."

We spent two and a half hours describing how our products complemented theirs, and how mutually beneficial we could be for one another. As the meeting was winding down, Steve realized it was close to lunchtime, and mentioned a burger place close by. I had him at *mutually beneficial*. He had me at *burger*.

Shortly afterward, we were contacted by NEC about a systems integrator looking to install six NEC-branded 400-terabyte systems to support video surveillance at ESPN headquarters in Bristol, Connecticut. ESPN was a marquee name, and what a fantastic entry into this "new" market! It was likely not as good as being featured on SportsCenter's Top Ten Plays, but we were still walking on air about it. The integrator did not have a strong enough credit history for the size and scope of the project. He was, however, an Anixter customer, so we floated the deal through Anixter. It was not the last time that Anixter's financial clout helped make good things happen. The Bank of Anixter was officially open for business, as were we.

CHAPTER 30
CRISIS AVERTED

———

June 2008

Late in June 2008, HP finally granted us the authorizations we had been seeking. This meant a lot to me, especially considering it only took their legal less than a month! I knew we were already in the security business: making deals, signing contracts, installing systems—all the things we wanted and needed to do. But at some level, I just did not have the same confidence in the non-HP brands we were using. Getting the HP certification changed the way I felt. Now we were legit!

With HP locked and loaded, we got down to work. We spent almost a month deep-diving into the HP server and workstation product portfolio, calling up HP's "Quickspecs," the complete DNA they provide so wonderfully for every platform. These gave us an inside-out look at the components available in each model and helped us identify the proper and authorized processor, memory chips, hard drives, and other options. This would allow us to build the correct video surveillance server on paper.

Of course, how it looks on paper is just the blueprint. We used HP's demo program to bring in those units that best fit our build expectations and took them for a "test drive" on our benches. What's most important in video surveillance servers is the throughput, which is the speed at which data can move through the network (as opposed to bandwidth, which is the amount of data that can move through the network.) Every video software company has its own way of maximizing performance; regardless, most video servers require the maximum number of hard-drive bays for internal storage expansion.

From the beginning, we wanted to do both things better than anyone else. We also sought to maximize the number of high-resolution cameras running pristine video footage that could connect to a single server. The key word was always "pristine." I was determined to make our systems Fortune 500 worthy, and I had enough history selling IT servers to those companies to know their expectations. Generally, Fortune 500 companies spent the most to get the best. Every system we built was constructed with that expectation in mind. Just treat them all as mission-critical, and excellence will follow.

Using HP as our build server enabled us to achieve those goals. Importantly, HP servers were also scalable. If a customer wanted to add more cameras or replace existing cameras with higher-resolution ones, our HP-based solution could easily handle the upgrade. This attribute became critical as we embarked on this video adventure, as camera densities kept increasing. When we started, 720p was the default camera resolution. This was quickly replaced by the 1080p standard, followed by 2GB and then 5GB. Today, the most important metric is frames per second (fps), and the upper-echelon cameras record at 25-30fps. Three-dimensional (3D) cameras will be the new industry standard in no time.

From the beginning, I was determined to build a video surveillance server company brand that would be synonymous with availability, scalability, and most importantly, reliability. To achieve this lofty reputation, I knew BCD had to design quick-to-deliver video storage solutions, purpose-built for the site—whether it was a school, a commercial enterprise, or a government facility—based upon the total number of cameras, the recording density of each camera. the video software being used, and the number of days of storage retention required.

This was even more challenging than it might sound. First, we needed to standardize the products we offered. This meant we had to pre-certify them and guarantee their performance capabilities. If companies were going to look to us as trusted advisors, we needed to offer customers solutions we could wholeheartedly recommend. We wanted to avoid falling into the trap of blindly selling the customer the server he requested, then getting blamed when it did not meet the needs of his project.

Having our own tested systems gave us the ability to stock accordingly. Instead of ordering a server chosen by the customer, we could build from proven servers in stock. This allowed us to right-size the server to the project need, including any other idiosyncrasies pertinent to his project.

These were big objectives, but we were getting the job done. By Labor Day, we had integrated our HP video surveillance portfolio into the Anixter catalog, while dropping the NEC and Supermicro products from our line. I was vendor-loyal to a fault, and HP was my partner. But by Halloween, all hell had broken loose.

After months of declining stock prices and bank failures, calamity struck in September. Lehman Brothers, the venerable financial services firm, filed for bankruptcy. This set off a chain reaction that pushed the global credit market close to collapse, a catastrophe that was prevented only through massive governmental intervention.

The impact was devastating. Housing markets shrank and unemployment soared, resulting in massive evictions and fore-closures. Household consumption declined, as did business investment. Between the fourth quarter of 2007 and the fourth quarter of 2008, the US GDP declined by 8.4%. It was a brutal time for almost everyone. If you had not lost your job already, you woke up every day wondering when the ax might fall.

My habit had been to watch Brian Williams and the NBC Nightly News while I worked out in the basement after work. Every night, I watched as another one of my current or former customers—Merck, Home Depot, Abbott Labs, GE, AstraZeneca—was getting whacked by layoffs with 1,000-plus body counts. I remember being hit particularly hard when I heard about layoffs at General Growth Properties, which years earlier had acquired Homart Development. I wondered about the fate of Shelly, my customer contact from my Elek-Tek days, whom I had wooed with so many bi-weekly lunches at Italian Village, especially after the email I had sent to her bounced back to me.. Where were these hundreds of thousands of people going to find work? I had to give up watching the news; I couldn't take it anymore.

During the financial crisis and the recession that followed, about 1.8 million small businesses went under. We did not. We were blessed. I do not use that term easily. Video may have "killed the radio star," but it sure as hell saved us. Our HP reseller revenue bucket was empty unless you counted the loose change in there. But we had been lucky; with just four months to spare, we had fallen headfirst into the video surveillance market. If that had not happened, we would have been just another IT tragedy. I can hear it now: "Who were those guys again? BCD? Oh yeah, I remember them. Too bad."

While the economy suffered, the threat from terrorism remained strong. Every few months, it seemed, an attack was launched or a plot thwarted. Companies had to remain vigilant against terror, and with so many people suffering unemployment, they had to prevent theft as well.

So, while IT spending faltered, corporate spending on security remained strong. I always relate this period during the financial crisis to an action movie in which people are jumping out of the building just before it blows up. BCD's rebirth into BCDVideo felt like that action movie, and security was the hero. The economy may have been collapsing, but our numbers in 2008 kept pace with 2007, with $27 million in revenue. Of the $35 million in revenue we earned in 2009, $33M of of it was video-related.

No disrespect to Lou Gehrig, but I felt like the "luckiest man on the face of the Earth!" And to think we skated through it all because some contractor named Ray wanted to see what would happen if he pulled out a hard drive during a RAID reset. He's my other hero.

CHAPTER 31
ACCOUNTABILITY MATTERS

December 2009

As the housing market crisis slowly came to an end, our long-term plan was simple: build on our relationship with Anixter to sell our servers to the major global integrators like Convergint, Johnson Controls International, Tyco, and Stanley Security. These companies needed cameras for the security systems they were installing, and they bought thousands of them from Anixter.

Obviously, the huge volumes of data those cameras were recording needed to be stored on servers. Systems that protected sporting arenas, for example, required petabytes of storage. We envisioned scenarios where Anixter was discussing various projects with major security integrators. When Anixter finished quoting their cameras, we expected the reps to go on and ask, "What are you planning to use for storage?" and then quote our products to them. It seems simple, doesn't it? It was not.

For the first months of the relationship, Anixter's main contribution to BCD was financial. We had a lot of companies ready and willing to do business with us. More than a hundred security integrators called us directly to get project quotes. The problem was that handfuls of these newer customers lacked the credit references we needed for any deal greater than a $5,000 sale.

That is where the Bank of Anixter came in. Many customers

who were new to us had already done business with Anixter. If they had, we would send our quote to the customer, pricing the system with Anixter's twelve-point profit margin factored into the price. We would instruct them to order the system through Anixter, and to make sure to include a copy of our quote with their Anixter purchase order. All told, we drove over $10 million of our server sales through Anixter this way.

But while using the Bank of Anixter certainly helped, it was hardly the same as having Anixter's sales force proactively positioning BCD video servers. That just was not happening. Anixter's sales team seemed to have a difficult time navigating through our product offerings and understanding which storage solution to use when, and we had a hard time understanding why.

In fairness to their sales reps, Anixter carries thousands of products, with each of those manufacturers trying to get the reps' attention. Still, we worked very hard to train Anixter's sales teams. We arranged numerous training sessions, "lunch 'n learns" where we presented situations and solutions. We even created a script that was like a product flow chart; the salesperson would ask yes or no questions and use the customers' answers to arrive at the best answer. But even after all those training sessions, the bump in sales was far less than we had hoped for.

We thought it must have been our fault. We were used to working with IT resellers. Now we were learning that the sales cycle of a security integrator was one-hundred-and-eighty degrees apart from the IT reseller. If an IT reseller requested a quote, you could expect a Purchase Order within a day or two. If there is no PO within five days, they likely bought it elsewhere.

A security integrator is a whole different beast. They work on large projects that can be years in the making. In many cases, they need to submit their budgets to contractors well before the buildings are even under construction. The project installations have many components: high-voltage wiring, low-voltage wiring, trenching, network switches, cameras, storage, just to name a few. By the time work begins on the project—and a two-year gap between bid and build is not uncommon—the equipment might cost more, or worse, it might be obsolete.

The Anixter sales team was reluctant to push products that might become obsolete, even ours. But our products were not obsolete, in the sense that they were out of date and no longer useful. The only risk was that, during the two-year lag, new and improved servers would hit the market. Intel was always announcing faster processors, for instance, and hard-drive manufacturers would continually announce new, larger storage densities. But that did not mean that the servers initially quoted would not do the job.

The fact was that Anixter's sales force was just not confident enough about our products to push them. Camera-wise, Anixter's customers knew what they wanted and where to find it. If the customer wanted to buy one-hundred Axis high-definition cameras, the Anixter rep had no problem fulfilling the order. If a customer knew what kind of server he wanted, the sales rep would be happy to take that order too. But customers seldom were as well-versed in the intricacies of video servers, the brains of the installation. Recommending a server, which is what we wanted the sales rep to do, was a riskier venture. If the server did not perform as stated, if it was too small, too slow, or not scalable, it would be the rep's fault. The Anixter sales reps thought it was safer to just keep their mouths shut.

It was obvious what BCD had to do next. We knew the capabilities of our servers; we had confidence in them. We needed to convey the same confidence to the Anixter sales force so they could have the same hop in their footsteps that we did when selling our video servers. We had to physically remove their fear of failure.

Out of the blue, I came up with the idea of a Performance Guarantee. If BCD had calculated the proper system and storage, based upon the parameters provided, and the customer bought the server as quoted, BCD would guarantee that the system would work to spec. If the system was not running quite right, we would recalculate the requirements and send any necessary parts or additional servers at no charge to make up any deficiency, at no charge to the customer. If it still did not work, we would take it back for full credit.

This would take one-hundred-percent of the risk out of the Anixter salesperson. All they had to do was send us the camera counts and the recording parameters, and we would quote the proper system and guarantee it would perform at full capacity at the project site.

We ended up rolling out our Performance Guarantee to all our customers. I'm happy to report that customers only invoked the guarantee four times in our existence, and two of those were swapped for goodwill. Pretty good, considering we have close to 200,000 systems out there recording video surveillance. There's nothing like a .0001% failure rate as a show of quality.

The Performance Guarantee began to have the desired effect. The Anixter sales reps began asking the magic question: "What are you planning to use for storage?" The desired results started to follow.

But then came the event that took the relationship to a higher stratosphere. Like most companies in the tech business, including BCD, Anixter was a major customer of the gigantic distributor, Ingram Micro. If Anixter needed network gear or other products, they could purchase the stuff from Ingram as easily as we could, perhaps even more cheaply.

Ingram had been slowly venturing into the video surveillance market, adding cameras and other security products to their product portfolio. In November 2009, the company took the plunge: Ingram Micro announced a Security Division, naming Tom Burns as the security director. *Computer Reseller News*, a major magazine that nobody in our industry ever missed, quoted Tom as saying, "Anixter is an outstanding competitor in the security market."

This may not seem like a very controversial statement, but it had an impact. The reason? Anixter did not buy from their competitors. And Ingram was now a direct competitor.

The next morning, Don Hoffman, Anixter's procurement manager, called me. Without mentioning Tom's comment, he posed a simple question: "If Anixter was to drop Ingram, could BCD handle that spend?"

I did not even blink. I said yes. We were still new to the security field, and being approached by Anixter in this way was valuable recognition from a major player, a testament that we belonged in the game, Hesitation would have been poison; dickering about a price would have been insane. Had I shown even a minute of concern about potential pricing issues, the opportunity would likely have been pulled. While I paused, somebody at Anixter would have said, "Let's think about this. Let us mull it over. There is no rush." I never, ever want to be on the back burner. Maybe I was overreaching but fuck it—this was Anixter and a no-brainer.

By Monday morning, Anixter had changed their internal system. Anything labeled with Ingram as the main vendor was changed to BCD.

The floodgates opened. By the end of that first month, Anixter's monthly purchases went to $28,000, tripling their spending from BCD. We soon extended our reach to Anixter hubs in the United Kingdom, continental Europe, and the Middle East. Almost immediately, BCD's monthly purchases from Anixter increased to over $100,000. The largest spend was going to their Dubai office, which was procuring tens of thousands of dollars of Cisco network switches at a time.

CHAPTER 32
GAINING RECOGNITION

February 2010

In addition to the Anixter business, there were many other exciting developments—mostly good ones. Less than a year after receiving our HP North American OEM certification, HP named us as a Global OEM partner. That opened the doors to international business with HP's servers.

We also landed our first two direct security opportunities. The first was the MGM Grand Detroit Casino, where Johnson Controls supported four-hundred-fifty cameras with multiple Supermicro servers acquired from us. (We had quoted that project almost a year earlier before we received our Hewlett-Packard authorization.) The other project was at the Palazzo Hotel and Casino at the Venetian Resort Las Vegas. National integrator North American Video installed eight of our fully loaded servers to support the site's four-thousand-cameras. This time, those eight systems were HP-based, and upgraded for video usage by BCD.

We also developed relationships with two important systems integrators. We became an Authorized Partner of Milestone Systems, a Copenhagen-based software company who is a global industry leader in open platform IP-centric video management software. This authorization gave us access to their software for our internal testing of bandwidth capabilities. In turn, we shared our results with them.

We also signed up as a vendor with one of the country's largest security integrators, Vermont-based SimplexGrinnell. We began this relationship at the International Security Conference & Exhibition in Las Vegas—also known as ISC West—the physical security industry's largest US event. From the moment we got there, we were immersed in a whirlwind of meetings and greetings. One of the people we connected with immediately was Stephen Vowels, a SimplexGrinnell sales manager. He liked our story, and he especially appreciated our IT mentality. "I'm so tired of installing crap that never works!" he said at one point.

Right in my wheelhouse! Stephan utilized us for a few small projects, which got us into the SG procurement system. From there, we were off and running. We met remotely with Stephen's regional sales manager, Kevin Fady, who began bringing us into all his projects. Within a month, we were journeying to Westminster, Massachusetts, to meet with Kurt Butterbaugh. Everyone in security reported to him.

Westminster is just forty-six miles from Boston, but the further we put Logan Airport behind us, the denser the forest around us became. With twenty miles left to travel, our Wi-Fi signal disappeared. When at last we reached what we had assumed would be a modern technology hub, we discovered an office that was a throwback to the 1950s, a haven of wood paneling, metal desks, and old pictures. I found it both fascinating and ironic that their address was 50 Technology Drive. Kurt could not have been nicer or more welcoming as he laid out the "rules of the road" for working with SimplexGrinnell. We were officially part of the security industry! (Since that time, SimplexGrinnell has been purchased by Tyco, which is now part of JCI. Pac-Man is alive, well, and still gobbling in the security industry.)

But even after all these positive developments, we were somehow still a worry to our local community bank. From where they sat, they could see that we were bringing in revenue, but they couldn't see a lot of profit. Our sales margins were healthy enough, but we were spending money as fast as we got it. We brought in video cards, hard drives, and other items for stress testing, and we did a poor job of managing that demo inventory. We acquired items for testing and then held onto them even after testing showed they made little or no impact. The graveyard of one-and-done parts in the tech room amounted to tens of thousands of dollars, and that was something I should have been watching.

But I had never been a bottom-line CEO. I kept on hiring new salespeople and acquiring new technologies, which meant we were basically breaking even on our financial statements.

Then the problem with the bank at work suddenly morphed into a problem with the bank at home. The year prior, Joanne and I had begun planning to build a new home. We found a wonderful five-acre lot about a mile north of our current house and bought the home site with financing from those new friends at Private Bank. I had kicked Northside Bank to the curb six months prior.

Our architectural designs had to be approved by the then-stringent Village of Bannockburn Architectural Review Committee (or as I referred to them at the time, the Unwelcome Committee.) They demanded multiple changes to the design, and those architect's fees for the new home added up in a hurry. At that time, the technology was not available to make a simple cut, paste, and replace. They had to spend hours redrawing the blueprints to reflect the changes. After a few months of this, the bank got nervous.

We were just about to begin demolition of the original 1932 farmhouse on the site when I got a phone call from the bank. The bank was getting anxious about covering both the business and the home and that they had decided to pull out of the home financing. It was a rude wake-up call.

I sucked up the gut punch—actually, it was more of a kick a little lower—and called Joanne. As it so happened, she was at that moment serving coffee and donuts to the excavators. I tried to be the voice of reason. I told her what had transpired, but that it should not take more than a week to find a new bank. In the meantime, we would have to stop the process.

Crying on the phone, Joanne told me, "Do not come home!" Jesus, that hit me hard. But I did not listen. Instead, I went home and let her cry and scream and get it out of her system. I felt like crying and screaming myself. It had taken months to get our plans approved by the village, allowing us a giant exhale. Now, with demolition about to begin, the rug got pulled out from under us by the cowardly bank.

It took five days, but we found a new bank, MB Financial, in Chicago. They became my company bank as well. Years later, MB Financial was purchased by Fifth Third Bank, causing a mass exodus of the staff. My bankers landed at BMO Financial, and BCD (as well as Joanne and Jeff), followed them.

CHAPTER 33

STRETCHING OUR LEGS

February 2010

Private Bank's decision to pull our home loan was a very upsetting event, one that injected a lot of unnecessary stress into the life of the Burgess family. Even more unforgivably, they made my wife cry. Joanne is the strongest woman I know, and she does not cry easily. Joanne's voice telling me not to come home still haunts me all these years later.

I was furious with the bank. They never even offered me the chance to walk them through our finances. Nothing could excuse their decision to bail on us just as we were about to pour the concrete. I thought they were cowards, and that is why I never thought twice about pulling my business.

But the truth is, the bank was not entirely wrong. This was mostly a timing issue—of course, at the shittiest time possible. At that point, all they could see was a CEO who was seemingly content to break even. That had to change. BCD had to get back into the black, that black being breaking even. It was time to put on my big boy pants and focus more on the bottom line.

Once that disaster was behind us, I needed to start looking harder at our bottom line. It was either to lower our costs or raise our margins; perhaps a little of each. It's an Iron Law of Business: the bigger you are, the less you pay. You and I might pay $4.99

for a box of Cheerios, but the guy who walks in ready to buy a thousand boxes is going to negotiate a lower price per unit. From the beginning of our existence, BCD had operated within a certain range that enabled us to enjoy certain pricing benefits.

But when Anixter, a behemoth by any measure, started buying through BCD, we could for the first time see the lower price point that Ingram Micro was giving to Anixter. And boy, was it lower! It was a revelation. The network switches that used to cost $18,000 now came to us at $16,200. Even HP hard drives were roughly 10% lower across the board.

By this time in BCD's decade-old history, I had established a business relationship with Kirk Robinson, who was then Ingram's VP of sales. As I was certain that any special pricing request would land on his desk anyway, it seemed best to cut out the middleman and reach out to Kirk directly. Kirk understood I wore Ingram Micro like a badge of honor on my sleeve, and that I was always ready to talk about how our partnership with his company benefited my company.

I called Kirk and his secretary patched me right in, which I thought was cool. But I needed to be careful here, as I was playing on both sides of the fence with him.

Certainly, gloating about how we took over the Anixter account from Ingram would not be the best way to open the conversation. My plan was to tread lightly and gauge his interpretation of the overall situation first.

I started the call with a harmless comment: "Ingram is sure in the news these days, Kirk!"

He took it from there. Knowing that BCD had morphed into video surveillance the year before, he excitedly told me about Ingram's move into the security market. "Hopefully this will give us a chance to grow our business together," he said.

"Glad you feel that way," I replied. Now things were going to get tricky. I needed to find a way to excite him, rather than burst his bubble. I did not want to let him know that I had already cut my deal with Anixter; I could hear my mentor Jud Beamsley telling me, "First, get the deal, then worry about it." At the same time, I did not want to lie to him.

So, treading lightly, I told him that since our move into the security market, Anixter had become a large customer of ours. We were positioning ourselves to be their video recorder vendor, although that was still a work in process. Kirk was very excited to hear that; he knew that we bought most of our HP servers through Ingram Micro.

I paused to see if he would use the Anixter opening to tell me his own news. He did not. When the pause became pregnant enough to produce octuplets, I asked if he had heard anything about Anixter since the *Computer Reseller News* article had come out a few days before. "Oh," he said coyly, "I did hear that they weren't too happy about us moving into their market."

I had run out of room. I dived into the deep end.

"So, I got a call from Don Hoffman at Anixter," I said. "He reached out to me about Anixter buying all their Cisco switches from us, and not you guys, going forward. The good news is we buy all our Cisco switches from you anyway, so you should see minimal, if any, degradation in the sales volume."

I let the shock and awe of the message dissipate for a few seconds, and then I went for it. "We're going to need your help with pricing, or else this will never work."

I told him we did not need pricing help upfront. That would have resulted in all goods being shipped together, causing a logistical nightmare in our warehouse as we tried to separate the regular Cisco stock from the Anixter Cisco stock. Instead, I told him, "Kurt, I have enough trust in our mutual relationship after all these years that I am willing to sell Anixter the switches from regular stock at their current Ingram purchase price, whatever that is."

I did not have to spell it out; Kirk knew this meant I would be selling at a loss, since whatever Big Dog Anixter had been paying Ingram was certainly less than Ingram would charge me. I went to the bottom line. "I'm going to need you to give me a rebate," I told him. "Monthly, quarterly, whatever works for you. But it must be big enough not only to offset this loss, but to factor in a profit for us."

I went for the close. "Kirk," I said, "I am willing to do this through Ingram because I trust Ingram, and I trust you. We have had an incredible ten-year business lovefest. I think this is the best way to ensure that Ingram continues to fulfill Anixter's massive Cisco spend. Only now, it will go through us."

Kurt thought it over for a moment. He knew I could walk over to Tech Data and buy Cisco switches, and that Tech Data would almost certainly charge less than I was currently paying Ingram. He also knew that there was value in maintaining our relationship. "Well, that is fine," he said. "I do not think a monthly rebate would be an issue. How much were you expecting?"

I was ready for that question. I knew what Anixter paid Ingram for Cisco switches because Don Hoffman had sent me copies of Ingram's invoices. I needed eight percentage points back on the rebate, so I asked him for eleven. I knew I would not get it, but hoped he would knock it off by two points and offer me nine. That one extra point would add $10,000 for every million dollars spent.

Kirk got back to me a few hours later, thanked me again for being such a loyal Ingram customer, and for offering Ingram this opportunity, yada yada yada... I thought for sure they were not going to offer the rebate. But he finished by telling me the best they could do was an eight-point rebate on all Anixter Cisco products purchased by BCD through Ingram Micro.

Silently saying farewell to that extra $10,000 per million, I said: "Kirk, we have come to terms. Thank you for allowing us to grow the partnership with you."

Of course, there were still some fine points to iron out. I knew there would be an immediate ramp-up, so I used that to negotiate even more favorable terms based on hitting specified purchasing volumes. Within three months, the accelerated pace of our combined Anixter and non-Anixter purchases brought our cost structure from Ingram slightly below what Anixter had been paying for them. And that was *without* that 8% rebate, which represented another quarter-million dollars of profit. We started to include rebate negotiation in every new vendor contract going forward.

BCD's climb with Anixter was meteoric. Anixter went from $910,000 in purchases in 2008 to $2.4 million in 2009. After the Ingram deal, they almost quadrupled their 2010 number to $9.7 million, then soared to $16 million in 2011. As our purchases increased and we hit new plateaus, we kept benefiting from revised lower pricing, so the margins for all other non-Anixter sales rose as well. Another stable revenue source for BCD! Hindsight is perfect, but it's clear that if Northside Bank had been patient with us for just three more months, they would have joined us on this ride, and saved the Burgess family a lot of stress.

Much of this exponential growth came from Anixter's branch in Dubai. It was one of the world's hottest markets, and Anixter's Middle East group was insatiably purchasing as many Cisco network switches as possible. The saying that "Sunday is Monday in the Middle East" was absolutely true. We relished this sixth day of the workweek, as they buried us with quote requests that turned into instant orders, shipping from the States directly to their Dubai warehouse and sales operations center. I was thrilled that we were enlarging our presence abroad.

But beneath all that excitement, buzz, and revenue, there was still a problem with Anixter. We were making a lot of money from them by replacing Ingram Micro, but their sales team was still reluctant to push our storage devices. Even after the time we spent training them and offering spiff money (a bonus for selling certain specific products), all they were sending us were odds-and-ends sales orders for entry-level systems supporting four to eight cameras. We were nowhere closer to getting in front of more customers the size of Simplex Grinnell, who had been doing one-million dollars per year directly with us.

As wonderful as the revenue bump had been, I did not think we could sustain the Anixter relationship if it never amounted to more. I felt that our being a fulfillment house for their orders diverted their focus from promoting our video servers to their largest customers. I had bigger dreams.

It certainly was a conundrum. Something would have to give.

CHAPTER 34

THE GARDEN

———

March 2011

We were riding the wave. But as much as you try to prepare, there are some situations that completely blindside you, becoming a test of your mettle and intestinal fortitude.

In the fall of 2010, Madison Square Garden was looking to upgrade its security system. SimplexGrinnell had installed the original system and was again bidding on the upgrade. To our immense delight, they invited us to join their team. This would be the most famous marquee-named project BCD had worked on. At last, we were putting on our big boy pants! I remember being a 13-year-old kid in 1970, watching the Knicks' Willis Reed hobble back into that arena for the first half of Game seven of the NBA Finals. It was likely the most inspirational four points and three rebounds in NBA history. Talk about "Must-See TV."

SimplexGrinnell's Northeast regional manager, Kevin Fady, whose team had installed BCD's initial video surveillance system at Madison Square Garden, introduced us to his account managers covering New York City. In turn, they introduced us to the decision managers at MSG. In no time, we were considered part of the SimplexGrinnell team and began speaking with the MSG team directly on a weekly basis.

We studied the arena. We absorbed Simplex's plans. We learned the details of the cameras and their coverage, the Genetec Security Center software being installed, and all the other parameters of the work. Among the project goals was to replace MSG's analog security cameras with newly released digital cameras. This would allow them to store the footage for a longer period, primarily for insurance purposes.

In the end, we proposed that the project employ thirty-two BCDVideo servers, each equipped with two external HP X1000G2 Network-Attached Storage (NAS) devices. That would mean that each server would have 11TB of storage, or roughly 350TB of total video storage, enabling MSG to store the video data for six months before moving it to long-term storage offsite. That was the easy part.

The hard part would be getting all those massive video streams through the network cabling. In a video surveillance system, data—the images being recorded—are separated into smaller segments, called "packets," of roughly 64 thousand before being sent over the network. This is done to prevent the network from being overwhelmed with one massive lump of data.

The Garden already had hundreds of Cisco unicast switches installed, and they planned to employ those for the project. We strenuously warned that those unicast switches would not work. Unicast switches are fine for IT purposes since IT data is sent via one user keystroke at a time. Those types of switches send data packets from one sender to a single receiver across a network.

By contrast, a multicast does one-to-many communication, and those large blocks of video data would congest the standard pipe. There would not be enough Liquid-Plumr in the world to unclog that much video stream coming through MSG's unicast network.

When we met with the MSG team, we stressed the benefit of multicast. We explained that the unicast network sends data in multiple streams, which can cause a network traffic jam, just the way New York's Long Island Expressway gets backed up during rush hour. In a multicast network, however, data flows in a single stream, like the express lane of a highway. Data in those multicast express lanes arrive sooner, with pristine video images. And there is less road rage!

We truly believed we had turned them into believers. While we weren't counting any chickens yet, we were feeling good about where we stood. Anytime you have a customer who is happy with the first installation and willing to use the same security integrator for the upgrade, you must believe the customer has a sense of trust that others will find difficult to break.

At that point, we were working with a popular incumbent on what would be one of our largest jobs since moving into the video surveillance space, bringing in $500,000-plus into the company. We thought we were just waiting for the purchase order.

Think again. And, welcome to the world of sales channel conflict. As we were getting ready to pop the champagne corks, we learned there was a new last-minute proposal, directly from HP. This was odd, since our proposal used HP servers and would have been a big win for HP's New York City server team and their external hard-drive storage groups covering both MSG and New York.

But much to our surprise, HP's tape division got wind of the deal and pitched MSG directly. They offered a solution based on its StorageWorks system, an external LTO–5 tape system that used magnetic tape data storage technology for backup, data archiving, and data transfer. Since each system supports up to 16TB of captured footage, the tape could be used for extremely long data retention, opening drives for more current data.

Suddenly, one division of HP was competing with another. This SimplexGrinnell plan to use HP servers had looked like a home run, but it meant nothing to the StorageWorks team. The StorageWorks team proposal initially involved HP servers, but when they learned that their solution was more expensive than SimplexGrinnell's plan, they revised the proposal and eliminated the servers altogether. They dropped their own HP servers! Instead, the cameras would record directly to the units via the existing Cisco network. This must have made for some awkward moments at the HP water cooler.

MSG was intrigued by their proposal. Who could blame them? By eliminating the servers and using the existing Cisco switches, the StorageWorks quote was $600,000 less than the one from Simplex.

But the big difference between the two plans was not the servers, the switches, or the cost. The big difference was that our plan would work, and theirs would not.

As part of their proposal, the StorageWorks team included a video backup solution that was geared around their HP Data Protector software. Their plan was to automatically back up the entire Genetec surveillance software system on a nightly basis, starting about midnight and getting the backup completed by 6 a.m.

Sounds reasonable. The problem was that Cisco's unicast infrastructure was too slow. The backup would not be finished by 6 a.m. Meanwhile, the Genetec system would continue to record, writing over the existing data and compromising the backups. Since the whole point of the upgrade was to create video records for insurance purposes, what good was saving $600,000 if the whole job was worthless?

What's more, the backup was redundant and unnecessary. The Genetec Security Center software had backup capabilities built into their software. Failure to understand this basic spec should have made it even more evident that the HP LTO tape team was video surveillance-challenged and simply trying to sell as much as they could to the customer while the checkbook was open.

We told SimplexGrinnell and MSG that the tape solution would not work. We backed that up with data from third parties. We told the MSG team matter-of-factly that recording from the cameras directly to the tape via the not-ready-for-video existing network without the horsepower provided by the servers would be security surveillance suicide.

Far from yielding, MSG dug in its heels. So enamored did they seem to be with the tape solution that a new bidder jumped in.

Our friends at Anixter worked up a version of StorageWorks' tape solution. Anixter had been part of the SimplexGrinnell team; once they realized that they would get nothing if the contract was awarded to HP's StorageWorks, they decided to try to play both sides against the middle. They reached out to us, wanting us to get involved with their effort. The only thing anyone seemed to care about was getting the sale credit.

I wanted to think that rationality would be the victor here. I also wanted to believe that all of us would act in the best interests of the client. I hoped the Anixter team would use its relationship with MSG to convince them that we had a vast amount of video surveillance expertise and that we knew what we were talking about. But even though Anixter's team leader in the region, Severin Mulligan, swore to me that they pushed hard on our deal, we received a disappointing answer about a week later.

I got a call from Chris Haltek, the procurement manager at Anixter. He said he had good news and bad news. The bad news was that the deal was going to StorageWorks. The good news was that he had convinced MSG to procure the HP tape solution through Anixter. As they did not have HP set up as a vendor in their system, would they be able to process the $400,000 order for the tape system through us?

I was frustrated with Anixter. It seemed like they had caved, which had helped make StorageWorks' alternate solution seem credible. But I had copied them on all the communications. They had been told that this system was not going to meet the Garden's expectations.

I vented to Chris and Jim Ricker, who managed the channel at Anixter. I was likely less than professional, although no foul language was used. I went off on what a crappy partner they had been—that BCD had originally come to them to represent our video recording systems, but even after all the trainings, promos, and everything else possible to get their sales reps to even quote one of our recorders when they sold cameras, we were still scratching at the door.

"In the meantime," I finished, "We have been working on a deal with your partner, who buys all their equipment from you." But did we ever try to cut you out? We could have cut $100,000 off the price by selling around you. But we never did that because we would never *do* that. Instead, you guys took the coward's way out."

I guess I was left weakened after all that venting. I do not know if I wanted something for our time, and a $400,000 transaction was better than nothing, or if I was just tired of fucking with it over the past thirty days and wanted to be done with it. Either way, I took the deal and figured it was HP's problem after that. We got the PO and processed the order for the tape systems through HP. $400,000 was $400,000, after all. Or was it?

CHAPTER 35

NO GARDEN OF EDEN

April 2011

The equipment was delivered within three weeks, and the troubles began almost immediately. The Garden had 1,200 cameras sending data through the network, which included 50 Cisco 24-port network unicast switches that had been installed more than a year earlier. These switches were not equipped to handle the 76MB of data the Garden's 1,200 cameras were continuously pumping out.

We knew from the outset that this system was flawed, but never had we predicted the level of failure that was occurring.

The security integrator, SimplexGrinnell, spent days on the site trying to troubleshoot the system. Then days turned into weeks.

HP blamed the Cisco network design and the network speeds, but that would not fly; the network was already in place at the site. HP should have listened when we said that no unicast network could handle a backup process that involved 1,200 cameras and a six- to eight-hour backup window. They just had the wrong switches. We had told them the same upfront and had backed our argument with data. But neither HP nor MSG chose to listen. I do not know whether HP even investigated the network before they quoted their solution. They were too focused on selling a tape system to a marquee customer and garnering brand recognition.

Anixter was our customer, so we tried to help. At our own expense, we flew a video streaming expert, Jay Bartlett, from San Diego to the Garden. Jay had a long history working with Hollywood on video streaming technology in movies, and he also had experience in the surveillance industry.

Once at the site, Jay saw that the backup process would start off as scheduled each night. But 20 to 25 minutes into the process—a period that the MSG team did not initially want to analyze—he saw that the sheer volume of video data from those 1,200 surveillance cameras was overloading the network. The system started "dropping packets" almost immediately. Engineers who were monitoring the network on large monitors could see port after port on the camera streams literally drop to zero. As a result, the video data couldn't move to LTO storage within the overnight time window. In essence, almost nothing was being recorded, and what was being recorded was erasing itself within minutes. The backup process failed, putting the whole system so far behind it could never catch up.

The "smoking gun" was found. Jay and the BCD team showed Anixter, HP, and MSG teams what was happening. We proposed various solutions. The most obvious and direct answer, of course, was to replace the network switches. That would have cost MSG $150,000.

But the players involved were less interested in exploring alternatives than in blaming one another for why the plan failed. They were more concerned about how they looked than about taking care of the customer. This was an expensive lesson.

We sent SimplexGrinnell, through Anixter, a quote on our recommended switches. We quoted them at our cost. We thought we were good partners. We also thought we were doing Anixter a favor by not sticking it to them in a "we told you so" moment.

At this point, we were the only ones absorbing any costs here. Bringing Jay to New York cost us close to $10,000. (Not that they appreciated it.) But I did not care, as I knew I was doing the right thing. I was holding our company, and myself, accountable. *Fuck what they think*, I thought. *Not my concern.* My only regret is that we did not just give them the damn switches. It would have been a cheaper solution for us.

Looking back at it all these years later and wondering what we could have done differently, only one thing comes to mind: Since we were so cocksure that the unicast switches would not work, we should have drawn a line in the sand and refused to do the deal without the multicast switches. That is how sure we were that the Cisco switches would fail disastrously.

In the end, Anixter did buy the switches from us. Unfortunately, it took them over three long months to get them all deployed, and that was not the end of the troubles. As Michael Corleone said in *The Godfather Part 3*, "Just when I thought I was out, they pull me back in!"

After the initial installation, SimplexGrinnell engineers made hundreds of visits to MSG to troubleshoot the problems. Unbeknownst to us, SimplexGrinnell had been invoicing Anixter for each visit, a total of $1.2 million worth of time and material. One day, Chris Haltek from Anixter called and dropped the hammer: According to our contract, Anixter was going to pass those expenses along to us. Their position was that we had sold them stuff that did not work.

I told Chris I needed a week to absorb this news, and to think about our response. Once again, it was time to go into scramble mode. (I was always a pretty good scrambler; I should have been, considering how much practice I'd had scrambling.)

My mind went through a lot of scenarios, and I bounced off alternative solutions to Joanne during that week of family dinners.

I really did not want to have to borrow on our bank line to cover the $1.2 million, let alone pay the interest on that loan. But we had some money to play with. And as angry as I was with Anixter (as was Joanne, because of what they did to me), the relationship we had with them was still valuable—very valuable. After a few days, I came up with a plan. Joanne liked it well enough to tell me to "Go for it!" Of course, she added, "Fuck them!" That is why I love my wife! She's so passionate about what she believes in.

Instead of responding directly to Chris, I spoke to Jim Ricker at Corporate Anixter, who was the main overseer of our account. I used the conversation to reestablish our Anixter relationship. "We would find this situation much easier to swallow if we had more of a proactive relationship with Anixter's salesforce," I told him. "Nothing personal, but we've worked with Anixter for two years. After all that time, we use you as a credit source for customers more than anything else. Frankly, it's disappointing."

I reiterated that these costs at MSG were not our fault. "You came to us to get the HP equipment," I reminded him. "We're being penalized only because we did you a favor and sold you the goods you wanted." Anixter had skin in the game as well. "Anixter knew the deal shifted any potential liability on our plate, not yours," I said. "Chris should have made that clearer when he asked us to process it, especially since we told both you and them it would not work from day one."

Still, under the contract (which I know I should have read more carefully), the responsibility was ours, so I offered him a deal. BCD would pay Anixter $600,000 upfront and offer a 3% rebate on their future purchases, reconciled monthly, until the remaining $600,000 was settled. "The idea has promise," Jim replied. "I need to kick it upstairs." Apparently, the kick was good, and they agreed.

Thanks to our cash flow, primarily from Anixter, this kept me from having to dip into the bank line. My lawyer, Rick, reminded me that we had an Errors & Omissions insurance policy, which we had bought to protect us if a client sued for negligent acts, errors, or omissions that resulted in a loss. Good job, Rick! Chubb to the rescue! Cash flow is king, and Chubb kept that $600,000 in our coffers. Granted, our premium in 2012 would go up by 1.8%, but that was no more—maybe less—than the $11,400 of interest I would have paid the bank over the year simply to cover that $600,000 paydown.

The best part of the deal was that it prevented Anixter from getting their $1.2 million upfront and then dumping us. By paying them with the rebate, we forced Anixter to continue to buy from us to get the balance of their settlement. At their run rate, this gave us at least another two years to see if they could get their collective shit together by quoting our video servers to their customers and introducing us to their mega-customers like Johnson Controls and Stanley Security. If they stopped buying, well, they would be the losers; 3% of zero is, after all, zero.

Not immediately, but within the first three weeks, we quietly raised the fixed prices on the system by that same 3%. In essence, that rebate was now coming out of one of their pockets and going into the other.

Over the next four years, Anixter was BCD's top annual customer, purchasing another $55 million from BCD. That is $55 million of profitable sales revenue we would never have realized had I dropped them because of the mess at the Garden. Willis Reed's got nothing on me!

They did end up bringing us many new customers buying small-to-medium video servers for up to 16 cameras, but they did not deliver any of the big nationals. That was okay. We went around them and signed Siemens and Johnson Controls to three-year contracts directly. We also picked up regional integrators ordering directly from us in the Northeast.

Granted, the Anixter/MSG fiasco had absorbed a great deal of my time, let alone my emotions. Meanwhile, half a world away, an incredible tragedy occurred that had a big impact on BCD, as well as the entire IT industry.

Thailand was second only to China in hard disk drive production. Combined, Seagate Technology and Western Digital were a 30% share of the over 660 million hard disk drives manufactured in Thailand annually.

Most notably, they were both Hewlett-Packard's standard drives, albeit remanufactured to HP's specifications and branding. As much respect as I had for all the people missing as a result of the 2004 tsunami, I also saw a small window of opportunity to capitalize on any existing hard disk drive inventory in the United

States.

HP arguably had enough stock on hand in their Houston production to cover the short term. That helped them, but did not do too much for us.

As a judge once told me, "Possession is nine-tenths of the law." Right after the New Year, we started placing orders with HP for as many of the standard drives as we installed into our IT customers' standard server specifications—Astellas, GE, Takeda, and yes, even HP. In addition, we also stocked up on those drives we used for the video security servers.

To keep under the radar, we placed an order every third day in a mix-and-match mode for less than seventy-five IT drives. As this was going on in "stealth-bomber" mode, we continued to openly order our standard video surveillance drives by the hundreds.

As anticipated, just after the new year, the Thailand supply of Seagate and Western Digital to the United States had dwindled to zero. Other than in our facility, of course.

Around the middle of the month, HP's sales reps began to receive pressure from their customers about delayed lead times on their server, workstation, and even PC orders.

When HP investigated the cause, they saw that BCD had purchased most of their stocked drives.

We now had over $900,000 in these IT drives stuffed in offices and closets throughout the facility. By now, HP had officially closed the window for sales of loose hard disk drives, Instead, all hard disk drives had to be installed into systems.

Talk about power! HP sales reps were calling us from all over the country, asking me if we could "help their customer out of a jam". Of course, I was happy to oblige if those hard drives left the facility installed in a server . . . or three.

Over our first dozen years, BCD had survived events that happened thousands of miles away from us yet had a local impact: silicone-factory fires in Japan which led to Dynamic Random Access Memory (DRAM) shortages, and the Indian Ocean tsunami which reached as far as Japan, disrupting their supply chain, coincidentally in Southeast Asia where many Japanese companies had manufacturing operations. This led to temporary production slowdowns due to disruptions in raw material imports.

And yet, we survived. How? Because BCD always survived, and somehow, some way, we always came out better for it as well.

I found it amazing how we were able to influence change in such large corporations. It always brought me back to General Zod in the original *Superman* movie, with his "You will kneel before Zod!" declaration.

Something had to be done with Anixter. And they were nothing compared to what I dealt with over the past decade. In fact, I had Anixter right where I wanted them. And as Anixter would learn very soon at one of their national sales meetings, our patience was wearing very thin.

CHAPTER 36

CONTROLLING OUR DESTINY

January 2012

It was not easy for me to shake off the whole Anixter fiasco. I am not saying we were perfect, but we saw what was coming. We were fortune tellers, or in this case, misfortune tellers. Everything that we warned them would happen, did happen.

I guess I take accountability to heart more than others. Granted, with the Chubb claim, we not only lost nothing, but we came out ahead. But I saw no moral victory in it. Instead, I saw the absolute worst in those people. They acted without accountability. They behaved like cowards, afraid to let their bosses know they had made a mistake. It's a good thing I reported to myself; I had to answer to no one but myself, which made it easier to manipulate the fix in our favor. In the end, however, it was still whipped cream on poop.

I knew myself, and I knew that if I did not get the Anixter "thing" out of my psyche, I would never let it go. Once again, I reached out to Jim Ricker, not to vent, but to walk through the entire Anixter/MSG process together, and, as I told him, "purge it from our souls." I did not want the call to turn into a blame game, but I did want to hear his take on how things went down. Jim was willing, so he walked me through the events as he knew them, although as he acknowledged, much of his version was second-

or third-hand information. He told the story calmly and directly, even admitting that Anixter "could have been a better partner here," without declaring fault.

The conversation with Jim gave me this weird sense of inner peace. We were still struggling with Anixter's reluctance to promote BCD's video storage solutions, but they were who they were. I was never going to change them. I would either accept that or move on. For the time being, I decided to continue to use them to our advantage, even if that was just like a bank, and all those Cisco switches!

We were still selling IT servers non-stop to our two pharmaceutical customers, Astellas and Takeda. That amounted to roughly $12.1 million over the past two years. Add to that the $5 million we received from HP—yes, seven years later, we were still selling HP goods back to HP. But while this IT channel remained strong, I could see rough waters ahead. A few years earlier, TAP Pharmaceuticals had been formed by a joint venture between Takeda and Abbott Laboratories; now we were hearing that TAP would soon gobble up the rest of Takeda. History taught me that buyouts defaulted on the procurement arm of the buyer, not the vendor partner.

I had numerous meetings with TAP's lead buyer, Miki. She was spending a lot of time at Takeda's facility—too much time for my liking. She repeatedly questioned me about our pricing model at Takeda. Frank Alvino, the IT director, understood the value we brought to the Takeda organization and supported that to Miki. But Miki seemed to see little value in relationships and instead put more emphasis on costs.

One thing Miki never seemed to grasp was that buying from us saved the Takeda IT engineers dozens of man-hours per server. We explained that our systems arrived set up to Takeda's specifications, with all current Microsoft updates preloaded, ready to "rack and stack." Unfortunately, that did not show up on a price list. Since Miki's bonus was likely based on her ability to cut costs, that value would not factor into her equation.

It was clear that we needed to get while the getting was good. The good news was that it took Miki over three years to finally weed us out of Takeda. This spoke to the value that Takeda's IT team saw in BCD, and I have maintained ongoing relationships with the Takeda IT team ever since.

As 2011 ended, BCD was living at the intersection of IT and security. Whatever we were doing was working. Our messaging to both markets was resonating. Most importantly, we felt good about ourselves and the ability to juggle two markets with similar products. Double your pleasure, double your fun.

It gave us a lot of momentum heading into 2012, so much so that we were able to move into a 14,000-square-foot office/warehouse in Northbrook. We converted an 800-square-foot room within the warehouse into our system building center, with plenty of power to build the servers, and a double-wide door through which to ship them.

If it weren't for the BCDVideo shipping tape on the resealed cartons, by 4 p.m. you would not be able to tell which cartons were incoming and which were outgoing from the tech room. All these years later, it still fascinates me that we benched, built, packed, and shipped 9,600 systems from that room in our first year there.

It had a real dock, shared with our neighbor, Carol's Cookies. It was always fun to take a customer or vendor on a guest tour of the building. When we entered the warehouse, I could tell they smelled cookies. I would take a deep breath and say, "Smells like snickerdoodle day!" That always got a laugh.

We had a lot of adrenaline working in our favor, and we were making a name for ourselves. Much of that was due to our new IT director.

When Sharon, one of our salespeople, heard we had an IT position to fill, she recommended a friend, Eugene Kozlovitser. Eugene had a strong background in building both Microsoft and UNIX-based server solutions, and with numerous other technologies as well. Best of all, he was a communicator. Ever since my Tek-Aids days, I loved going back into the tech room, if only to watch, listen, and learn. Eugene was always most welcoming. And he really knew his shit. A major upgrade in our IT leadership!

One day shortly after we hired Eugene, we were hit by a crisis: our domain server had blown up. This meant none of us could access our emails, and any incoming emails were bounced back to the sender as "domain not found." It turned out that the previous IT manager, whom Eugene replaced, did not leave well; he blew out our domain server on his way out.

The mess was more than a one-man-fix. Between everyone's email accounts, the team email boxes, and the internal domains containing documents, well over a hundred domains were out of commission. Eugene could only reinstate about three domains per day—five at most.

We needed access immediately, so Eugene reached out to Netrix Global, a technology company in Bannockburn, less than 10 miles away. They specialized in enterprise infrastructure, which was where the breach began.

They arrived that afternoon and had us up and running by the end of the next morning. We were completely back to normal the following day. We were so impressed with them that we continued to use them for specialized customer projects.

In the spring, the US Patent and Trademark Office approved our trademark for the name BCDVideo, which gave us even greater credibility with our surveillance customers. Being a trademarked brand was a decisive moment.

Our IT business was slowly shrinking, and our security division was growing. With the trademark approved, it was time for us to realize our destiny and fully commit ourselves to the security marketplace. After all, the IT marketplace was full of server builders, whereas the video surveillance space was desperately in need of BCDVideo. We just needed everyone to realize it.

Joanne and I were always big on giving back and helping those who merely needed an opportunity. Around this time, we began working with College Bound Opportunities (CBO), a local non-profit organization whose mission is to help low-income, first-generation students fulfill their college dreams. The majority were DACA (Deferred Action for Childhood Arrival) kids, who had been brought to this country as very young children by undocumented immigrant parents. I began a program to hire CBO students who were studying electrical engineering. They worked on our benches as paid interns, building servers for customers during summer and winter breaks. I saw it as a win/win.

We were giving them the opportunity to take what they had learned in class and turn it into real-time expertise in computer server technology. I never understood companies that did not pay their interns, as if working for free at their prestigious company was compensation enough. Try being in college and buying a late-night pizza with that! Within a few years, we were almost certainly CBO's largest part-time employer.

By 2013, after TAP Pharmaceuticals' acquisition of Takeda had come to fruition, HP and Astellas were the only two IT-based customers in our top 10; the rest were all security-based. Anixter accounted for 30% of our total company revenues, and they were finally starting to bring more of their customers to BCD. Regardless, most of that Anixter business involved peripheral products, mainly Cisco switches, large-screen monitors, and other items they had formerly routed through Ingram Micro. We still were not getting many video storage opportunities through Anixter.

The security industry's project basic storage formula, embedded long before I came into this market, held that storage needed to run the project should equal 30% of the video camera costs. Based upon that formula, should the project call for 200 cameras at a total cost of $200,000, they should expect to pay $60,000 for the proper storage, whether server-based or external.

Anixter generally sold $420 million a year in cameras and is the largest distributor in the world of Axis Communications camera products. Using that same formula, that $420 million should have translated into $126 million of storage to properly house that video data. However, their strongest storage year with us was $3 million in 2013. That is $3 million out of a potential $126 million in storage sales—less than one-quarter of 1%.

Since the MSG debacle, Anixter had purchased enough goods from us to cover the remaining $600,000 rebate settlement. Once our debt was satisfied, I had had enough.

I suppose I could have offered a quiet goodbye. A note. A voicemail message. "Good luck in all your future endeavors." Calm. Cool. Dignified.

But that was not really what I was feeling. So, I invited myself to their 2015 January national sales meeting, offering to make a 20-minute presentation. They accepted.

For my presentation, I created three PowerPoint slides. That would be enough to get the message across. The first slide proudly displayed Anixter's prowess in selling $420 million of video surveillance cameras a year, noting they were industry-leading Axis camera's largest customer.

The audience cheered!

The second slide showed the formula I described above, showing that a video camera system should be supported by storage costing about 30% of the camera system total. By that measure, $420 million of cameras should be supported by $126 million worth of video storage devices.

The audience looked puzzled, perhaps suspecting where this was heading.

The last slide showed the $3 million of video storage BCD sold through Anixter. I added, "We sold five times that to security integrators directly last year, and many of those were Anixter customers. We just cannot wait and hope today is the day Anixter finally quotes, and even sells, our products. We wasted too much time with you. We are going after all the nationals directly."

Then I clicked my presenter remote once again: superimposed on that last slide was a cartoon of two humanized peanuts standing next to each other, with one peanut kicking the other peanut in the crotch.

I finished with, "That is a real kick in the nuts, don't you think?"

At first the audience was quiet, perhaps stunned. Not so much by the data, but because I had the "nuts" to present it.

As I made my way out of the presentation room, I got several dirty looks, and more than a couple "What the fuck was that about?" I just kept walking. I was hoping they would discuss it when I was gone.

I was wrong. I heard from a few in the crowd that the senior vice presidents felt insulted, but beyond that, they just went on with their meeting. I was glad they felt insulted, though. They should have been embarrassed, more than anything.

The following Monday, I phoned Jim Ricker and let him know that in the three years since the MSG disaster, we had yet to see the overall year-over-year growth for which we had budgeted. Therefore, we were invoking the six-month termination clause in our contract.

It seemed my actions served as a wake-up call. Over those last six months, Anixter purchased another $17 million worth of goods. That did not change my mind. Where had that $17 million six-month spending spree been all our lives? That is a $34 million per year run rate. All it proved was that we were right. Had they applied themselves to simply adding our storage device to every camera quote, it could have been historic.

Instead, it was a historic waste.

Some friends and colleagues thought I was making a poor decision, the equivalent of jumping out of the plane without a parachute. But this was like going out with someone who would not commit to the relationship. However much you get, you're still being held back. I was sure I had made the right call.

Despite our focus on all-things-video, *Computer Reseller News* once again included BCD on their 2013 list of the top solution provider organizations in North America. Ironically, *Computer Reseller News* got it right. We remained an IT solution provider. We were just building those IT solutions for the video surveillance marketplace. We were in a great place.

CHAPTER 37
STRETCHING OUR LEGS

April 2013

In 2012, just a few years after we entered the surveillance field, Milestone Systems named us their Global Technology Partner of the Year. As Milestone stated in a press release, "BCDVideo deserved this award for their innovative work in developing systems specifically optimized for Milestone XProtect® video management software, with a streamlined process and website to deliver quotes and receive orders, coordinating with the Milestone partner channel."

That award had everything to do with Eugene, and brought us a lot of notice, and certainly a lot of confidence. Now, as we doubled down on surveillance, we decided to reap the benefits of that recognition more systematically. We began a concerted effort to reach out and directly introduce ourselves to every one of the sixty Milestone-authorized security distributors in the United States and Canada.

The Milestone award increased our visibility, but few companies were aware of what we uniquely brought into the security market, and fewer knew about our Performance Guarantee. We were the industry's only system-builder guaranteeing its builds. Customers were impressed when they found out how that guarantee protected their business.

This was also the time when we began using the term "purpose-built solutions." To us, this was not a slogan; it was truth in advertising.

Our competitors churned out vanilla, one-size-fits-all systems. Not us. We sold nothing off the shelf. Each server was built explicitly around the parameters of a particular project. The BCDVideo servers recording at the US Capitol were completely different from those recording at Westminster Abbey, all because of their individual parameters.

We factored in the number of cameras, the type of cameras, their resolution, the expected days of retaining the data, and the video software being used, among other criteria. We considered shipping a unit without that information as a liability. We learned the hard way; such deals were a return waiting to happen. We challenged any customer wanting to purchase a server without giving us the camera information.

We guaranteed the system would deliver maximum performance. If the system integrator used our quote to win the deal and there was an error in our calculations that led to the deal, then we would supply whatever products were required to make the system work—at no additional cost to the customer. After telling customers about the guarantee, the usual question they asked was: "How can you afford to do that?"

We also got used to hearing, "I can get that server for less." But early on, we learned that the product that cost the most was the product that did not work properly once it was installed. The security market is flooded with those broken systems. Fortunately, none of those were BCD-branded. This was because, from the onset, we committed ourselves to building a better mousetrap. The truth is that our servers rarely fail. Many have been working at sites for more than 10 years, double the system warranty.

Our best customers turned out to be those who bought elsewhere for the first time, even after getting a price proposal from us. We were confident that they would come back. And they did.

Some rivals pointed out that our costs are higher. That was true. But most security integrators did not care. We cost less to maintain in the long run.

Typically, a security integrator offers his customer a three-year warranty. If a problem arises at the site, the security integrator sends a technician in a van to the site to fix it. The industry term for this is "roll a truck." Rolling that truck generally costs the security integrator $600 an hour.

It's a choice: The integrator can pay us for a guarantee, or they can gamble that they will not have problems. Most integrators do not think it's a tough decision. They would prefer to pay $1,000 more upfront for our guaranteed product, rather than buy the cheaper option and bite their nails for three years, hoping they do not have to pay $600 an hour every time there's an issue with the server at the site. Let me assist with the math. After just five one-hour truck rolls over a three-year period, the integrator is already out $3,000 more than they would have paid us in the first place. Not to mention the priceless potential stain on their reputation.

The next time you are driving down a highway and you pass a white van with a Siemens, Convergint, or Johnson Controls logo on the side, you can be sure that they are on their way to a site because something went wrong. It could be a camera outage, a door that will not open, or any number of things. But the odds are it will not be because their BCDVideo server was not functioning correctly.

We ended up creating an ad campaign that touted our guarantee. It was not aimed at sales departments. The salesperson couldn't have cared less about service costs. He had made his commission and was off to the next opportunity. Instead, we targeted the security company's owner and finance team: "BCDVideo understands your bottom line." The owner got the message loud and clear. Those truck rolls dinged his bottom line every time.

We considered ourselves to be an "equal opportunity builder." Every system was built with the same attention to quality, regardless of scope or size. Our customers ranged from giant nationals, such as Siemens, Johnson Controls, and Convergint, to mom-and-pop shops buying our four-camera solutions. We knew how important that four-camera system at the retail store was to that store owner, so we approached it with the same care that we brought to the server recording hundreds of cameras at the Pentagon.

In 2013, having established our brand in North America, we thought other parts of the world needed to become aware of BCD as well. Late that year, we signed a distribution agreement with Mayflex, a company based in Birmingham, England. Their focus was on data infrastructure, networking solutions, and Internet Protocol (IP) camera security for businesses. IP cameras had been introduced by Axis Communications 15 years prior, providing digital video surveillance by sending and receiving footage over the Internet or local area network (LAN).

We thought our shared "IT/IP" business mentality with Mayflex would create synergies for both our businesses. Most importantly, as they were also a distributor of Milestone Software, we expected increased opportunities to attach our recording appliances to their software quotes. After all, the customer needed to load the software on something!

After roughly six months, we realized that capturing the attention of distributors was a problem not limited to North America. Like Anixter, Mayflex was reluctant to push our products, at least initially. But after numerous product positioning training sessions in a time zone six hours ahead of us, we began to have some success. Finally, Mayflex began to advertise and promote our brand, which increased our name recognition in the UK marketplace.

Around that same time, I got a phone call out of the blue from an English gentleman. Roughly two minutes into the call, I replied with, "What did you say?" His accent was like the thickest English Stinking Bishop cheese, and I found it incomprehensible. It reminded me of watching *Braveheart*, except a) they were Scottish, and b) I could always use the rewind button.

He started over, speaking somewhat more slowly and a bit more clearly. His name was Gary Sykes, and he was an independent manufacturer's representative living about an hour or so north of London. That explained the accent. The further north of London one went, the thicker the cheese. (I learned that firsthand months later, when Gary and I visited Manchester for a security event at Old Trafford.)

He had been at a company called Pivot 3, which was known as a high-end IT-centric company focused on software-defined infrastructure, also known as hyper-converged infrastructure.

Although at the time we did not support this technology, Gary's high-end IT background certainly gained my attention, along with his knowledge of the video surveillance space. We struck a deal, and Gary spent over a decade as a salesperson with us. During that time, I still had an issue with understanding him, so for the last few years, everything was done either on a Teams or Zoom call. I figured if I could at least read his lips, it would give me more of a fighting chance!

Gary did great work with us, bringing BCD into three of the largest UK distributors—Mayflex, ADI, and, yes, Anixter UK. He also arranged for on-site training sessions at all these distributors, which I was more than happy to attend in person.

Every year, Joanne and I would take a trip to London, usually in August around her birthday. Gary and I held court at the bistro in Flemings Hotel in Mayfair, where Joanne and I stayed. He and I would meet with five or six customers, one at a time, starting at 10 a.m. and running through 5 p.m., while Joanne was reveling in all things London. BCD also attended the annual security event at the NEC in Birmingham. Gary was our tour guide; he knew everyone on the show floor. Those visits brought us great exposure.

One year, my son Max was spending the third trimester of his junior year at Lawrence University's South Kensington campus. He took the train up to Birmingham and walked the NEC show floor with me. It was so much fun taking him through the event, introducing him to my new UK contacts, and watching him react to all the bells and whistles. Out of the corner of my eye, I could see the pride on his face.

Back in the US, I reached out to our old friends at Ingram. Anixter was never interested in pitching our storage solutions to their camera customers, but that did not mean it was a bad idea. I got in touch with Tom Burns—he of the famous 2009 quote about Anixter, calling them an "outstanding competitor." I proposed that we develop a series of video storage solutions exclusively for them to offer their customers whenever they were quoting cameras. After all, Ingram's entry into the security market brought us millions of dollars in Anixter sales. I figured this was the least we could do to even things out!

We came up with their own brand, Video Storage Solutions, and signed them to a distribution agreement. In a role reversal, we were now their distributor for video storage products, as they were our distributor for all IT products.

As 2013 was ending, we were buzzing. *Computer Reseller News* again named us on their Solution Provider 500 list. For the first time, we were included in *Inc. Magazine*'s List of America's 5000 Fastest-Growing Private Companies. Security integrators continued to reach out to us with their project opportunities. Our salespeople were inundated with quote requests.

While still committed to maintaining the quick turnaround times that had made our reputation, we were wary of rushing the salespeople, which would create the potential for mistakes. A company that guarantees its solutions must guard against preventable errors. We needed a solution.

Thanks to our technology lead, Eugene, we came up with team email boxes that were easily set up in Microsoft Outlook. To expedite replies, several select sales reps monitored customers' emails to the team boxes, deciding internally which could respond most rapidly. This prevented a single sales rep from being slammed with quote requests, while making sure no customers ever felt they had fallen into the black hole of email. There is no customer "black hole of email" fan club that I am aware of.

The approach worked just as planned. Our response turnaround times were even faster than before, with no degradation in the quote quality. Soon, we were offering customers like Siemens, SimplexGrinnell, and Johnson Controls their own team boxes as well. These dedicated team boxes provided a super-easy path for customers to reach us and were very well-received. It made them feel important and special within BCD and gave them an even greater sense of our focus on immediacy.

I could only imagine how much easier life would have been back in the 1980s if we could have had this dedicated email box tool for the State Farm account and my 32 assigned CSRs. But, of course, email was not widely used until the 1990s.

CHAPTER 38
MAXIMIZING THE OPPORTUNITY

———

March 2014

When 2014 arrived, we gave the usual greeting to what we thought would be another year of usual growth. We did not expect that, by summer, we would sign a deal that would transform our business.

We were optimistic about 2014. The aftereffects of the Great Recession had almost totally disappeared. Companies were hiring, and inflation was falling. We were doing a lot of business with Milestone resellers. But we noticed we were getting more and more requests for systems built around both Omnicast and Security Center software, both the property of Genetec, a company based in Montreal.

Genetec was considered *the* enterprise video software. It was the standard used by US government facilities worldwide and was widely used by foreign governments, casinos, arenas, and airports. We had been building Genetec-ready servers since late 2011, but most of our focus had been on Milestone, the first security vendor we partnered with back in 2009.

Over the first six months of 2014, however, Genetec's security integrators had installed our servers in the AT&T Center, home of the San Antonio Spurs; MetLife Stadium in New Jersey; the Rolls Royce factory in Goodwood, England; Churchill Downs in

Louisville; and the Staples Center/LA Live in Los Angeles. There seemed to be chatter within the security industry that BCDVideo built the best servers to use with Genetec software. Integrators from all over the world were pinging us with quote requests. And the places they were landing were all eye candy to me!

After the first quarter, our Genetec-based video servers were running neck-and-neck with Milestone XProtect-based solutions. The eye-opener was that even though we sold virtually the same number of pre-loaded Genetec and Milestone systems— roughly a hundred systems of each—the revenue delivered on the Genetec systems was triple that of the Milestone units. This was mostly because the Genetec systems used hard drives to generate throughput, so they needed more hard drives in each system. Most other software companies gained throughput with faster processors.

This development was even more intriguing because customers bought storage solutions from us, even though Genetec had its own storage devices (which they called appliances.) They were good ones, just somewhat limited. Their offering at the time, the SV-32, could only support up to 32 cameras, which explains why so much business was coming to our door. The SV-32 was just not big enough. Many integrators using Genetec software were working on projects with fifty or one-hundred cameras—in some cases, hundreds of cameras. Some integrators tried to push off-the-shelf Dell or HP servers. But while those servers had enough juice to manage the software, they couldn't ingest all the camera streams involved in big systems.

Our servers could handle any load. Over the years, we took the initiative to develop large servers, and Eugene invested time in learning the intricacies of both Genetec and Milestone software. This allowed us to create individualized catalogs offering a full range of storage solutions, from a four-camera system suitable for mom-and-pop shops to a system that could handle up to 1,000 cameras at a time, more than double any other server builder.

The catalog listed each system's maximum internal storage as the maximum number of high-resolution cameras it could support. All guaranteed. Both Genetec's and Milestone's customers ate it up. Especially Genetec's, as those systems needed much more throughput than the typical Milestone build.

As the volume of business increased, we continued to work on delivering even more throughput. Eugene continued to upgrade our Genetec server technology—splitting the load, eliminating superfluous functions and updating the operating system registry—all of which helped the data streams run even more smoothly. Eugene was far and away the Most Important Person (MIP) in the company and I made it a point to tell him so. He was the one kicking the living crap out of our wannabe competitors. Every time they got a little closer to system performance, he would widen the gap, again and again. I made sure he knew that, often, and especially at every year-end review that HE was the company MIP.

Our most popular unit was from our Supernova series, a single server with 224TB of available storage within the unit. Capable of supporting up to 1,200 cameras, this had become a de facto standard in hotels and casinos, supporting Genetec's Security Center enterprise software. This certainly caught the attention of Genetec's resellers. By the end of that first quarter, we were getting slammed with project quote requests needing this particular unit from Genetec integrators from all over the world. We thrived in that global environment!

Even though we were bombarded with these project requests, we never lost sight of the need for speedy customer service. We added Genetec to our list of team email boxes, and we made sure it was monitored by salespeople well-versed in the nuances of Genetec-ready video servers. We also added Eugene to the team box. He had taken it upon himself to do a deep dive into Genetec software, and he was personally embedded into all our Genetec build requests. By including Eugene, we cut out the middleman. The salesperson did not have to reach out to him; Eugène would see the request and proactively send an email to the team members detailing the best system for that project.

Having Eugene on the Genetec team box provided salespeople with an extra level of expertise that helped ensure that their quotes were both accurate and technically proficient. In some cases, he would realize that what the customer requested would not work. Catching that upfront was a major asset.

> **The key to our company's success has always been "quote integrity." If an inaccurate project quote leaves the salesperson's desk, the sale is doomed from the start, and the fix is never simple. Undoing mistakes results in a loss every time. At BCD, our reverse twist on that age-old mantra was "Garbage Out, Garbage Back In."**

This was a beautiful time for our business, both electric and exciting. Genetec had the most buzz in security software, and we were the company with the most buzz in building servers for Genetec. When the numbers for the first half of 2014 came in, they showed that we had sold $4 million of Genetec-based servers, more than doubling the amount we sold during the second half of 2013.

As all this was happening, my son Max was just a month away from graduation from Lawrence University in Appleton, Wisconsin. Many graduating seniors have angst about life after college, and Max was no exception. I came up with an idea, but I had to get it through Joanne first. Call it a slight case of mother-hen syndrome: She was very protective of her flock. (I am happy to be part of that flock since she is incredibly protective of me.)

From childhood, Max had a gift. Everyone loved him. His friends' parents wanted him as their son, or they wanted to marry him off one day to their daughters. I can safely state that he did not get that gift from me. (At most, 2% of it came from me, with the balance coming from my wife's gene pool.)

Max was extremely bright, but his brain worked a bit differently. As opposed to learning from A to B to C, Max's brain learned from

A to C to B. With written assignments, Max had to focus with full attention to grasp what was being asked. Yet on the baseball diamond or basketball court, he knew the play before the ball even came to him.

To help him succeed in the classroom, he met twice a week after school with Mara Lane, a comprehensive speech and language pathologist, at her home in Deerfield, near where we lived. Mrs. Lane guided Max into "learning how to learn." To this day, Joanne and I credit Mrs. Lane, along with Max's incredible work ethic, with Max being accepted into Lawrence, where he was a four-year member of the basketball team. But I think most of the credit goes to Joanne, as she was the one driving our son back and forth and following up with Max on any assignments Mrs. Lane gave him.

I knew how bright Max was, and how hard he worked. He also has superb listening skills. He listens with compassion and sincerity, asking relevant follow-up questions along the way. So why shouldn't he come to work with me?

That became my "soft" argument to Joanne. "I can teach anyone the IT or security marketplace, train them on our products, tell them where we fit and where we do not. But I cannot teach them how to make the customer love them. Max has that gift. Why should someone else capitalize on it?"

Sure, I'm a closer. But convincing your lioness that her cub will not fail in something he had never done before was far from easy. She never doubted his ability; she just did not want him to be hurt.

Our daughter Lizzie had already worked for us part-time over a few summers, helping in human resources and accounting. But Max became our first full-time family employee (other than me), a month after his graduation. I took him on as a global business development manager, and he has opened doors ever since, and, yes, made customers all over the world love him first, and BCD second. I was more than okay with that. Love apparently *is* universal.

CHAPTER 39

HISTORIC TIMES

April 2014

April in our industry always meant one thing: the ISC West security show in Las Vegas. In 2014, we were more excited than usual. The show was going to be our coming-out party, as we were peaking at the perfect time. I was eager to gauge the reception we would receive when we walked on that show floor. Based on the volume of opportunities being presented to us, we knew the security integrators trusted us, regardless of which video surveillance software manufacturer they supported—Axis, Exacq, IPVision, Genetec, Milestone, Verint, or whomever.

We planned to meet with all those software companies, hoping we could position BCDVideo as their go-to server builder. We expected to spend most of our time at the Genetec and Milestone booths, mingling with their salespeople and, most importantly, exchanging business cards with their customers. Especially intriguing was that a month earlier, both Genetec and Milestone had requested to meet with us during the show.

Their intentions weren't clear. Indeed, maybe they had none; so many, many meetings during conventions are held only to attach a face to a name or a voice on the other end of the phone. But if something was cooking, my hunch was that there was more of an opportunity with Milestone. They had popular software, but the server they offered was inadequate. That left their customers shopping around for whatever they could find on the cheap. Regardless of where the customer bought the hardware, their first call went to the software vendor, wasting everyone's time and money.

Genetec needed a better server, too, but we had already built them for so many Genetec customers. By cutting a deal with Genetec, we would take all that existing direct business and move it through Genetec. Not much gain there, other than better financing. Becoming Milestone's system builder seemed the more advantageous move for us. I wanted to have my cake and eat it, too; I wanted to build for Milestone and remain the Genetec integrators' choice for their systems.

So that was our game plan as we went to the convention: have the best of both worlds. Additionally, we wanted to expand our hardware range with as many other software companies as possible.

The show was held in the Sands Hotel, which was attached to the Palazzo at the Venetian Resort. Companies rented booths of various sizes and locations within the venue. The larger the booth and the closer to the center of the show floor, the higher the cost. All the major camera and software vendors were in the largest booths in the center. Those booths had meeting rooms, and a few had stairs leading up to more meeting rooms as well. Rather than invest hundreds of thousands of dollars in floor space, we just walked the floor for free.

Seagate Technology, the hard drive company, had a large, prominently located booth. It was so very cool when I walked up that external stairway to meet Clayton Bailey, our Seagate sales rep, and Danny Lim, who ran Seagate's play into the surveillance market. Everyone at the show saw me walking up those stairs, either thinking "Who *is* that guy?" or, for those who knew us, "Wow, BCD must be a huge Seagate customer!" Which we were. After the meeting, we walked down the stairs very slowly, just to make sure everyone saw us leaving the meeting with Seagate. I had to resist waving to the crowd.

The next meeting was with Milestone. As we made our way to their booth, I realized that everybody in the security industry seemed to be there. I recognized so many names by glancing at their badges as they were walking by. I told each person that I would catch up with them on the show floor after the meeting.

As I scurried over to see Milestone, I reminded myself to let them talk first, to hear what was on their minds. Unlike most salespeople, I believed that listening was more important than talking. It's a great way to learn, and an even better way to identify their pain points. In this case, I needed to learn Milestone's intent here, as I had no idea what they were even looking for.

I met with what we considered Milestone's brain trust— John Blem (company co-founder in 1998), Eric Fullerton (chief marketing and sales officer), and Tim Palmquist (VP of the Americas). Certainly, these were three people with the capability and authority to make decisions. At least, one would think so.

Tim did most of the talking. He walked through their global distributor model. (They referred to their resellers as distributors.) There were roughly 190 of these resellers/distributors globally, of all shapes and sizes. Milestone was looking for a new system builder. Many of their existing system builders were having trouble shipping anything outside of the European Union because they couldn't figure out the necessary export paperwork. Systems got stuck in customs for weeks at a time, and customers were very unhappy. And when they felt unhappy, they called the head office in Copenhagen, not the system builder.

Their need for what we brought to the table seemed obvious. Obvious to us, anyway. BCD had systems of all shapes and sizes that could support their XProtect software. We also had global logistics in place, so we would not have to learn as we went. Moreover, our customs and export documents were in order. We never had trouble with customs internationally.

I felt it was a strong one-hour meeting. We were with their brain trust. There was no, "Let us check with the boss" moment.

They left it with, "You certainly gave us a lot to chew on here. Let us walk through this and get back to you."

The next day we met with members of the Genetec Product Appliance team, led by Francis Lachance, their appliance manager. In Genetec lingo, an appliance was a non-software product. We had a good conversation with this group, lasting forty-five minutes, where we name-dropped the marquee locations where BCDVideo servers were recording via Genetec's software. I am pretty sure they did not need me to tell them all those places; they already knew from their salespeople who had lost the hardware to us.

They were either good poker players or not impressed. Their response was not quite, "Do not call us, we'll call you," but we certainly did not have a sense that they were even interested. After I left their meeting room, I remember feeling like they were just picking my brain for information they could pass on to whoever was doing their system-building.

Frankly, we had expected more, but we did not dwell on it. We were still salivating over Milestone. That meeting was electric, with both parties exchanging information freely. The Genetec meeting was bland.

ISC West generally runs from Tuesday through Friday. Three days of meetings and being "on" non-stop was enough for me, so on Friday, I was on the 7 a.m. flight back to Chicago. I boarded that flight without an answer from either company, but I was determined to be patient.

A few Tuesdays later, I received a call from Francis Lachance, the Genetec product appliance manager we had met in Vegas, requesting a meeting. Two weeks later, three Genetec executives came to visit us at our offices: Francis, Marketing Manager Andrew Elvish, and Logistics Manager Francine Le. (A decade later, I'm still waiting to hear a decision from Milestone.)

Andrew's presence led me to assume they were looking for a private-label opportunity. Unless branding was involved, why bring the marketing manager? I couldn't have been more wrong.

Andrew made short work of the conversation. "BCDVideo is the brand we keep hearing about from our security integrator customers," he said. "We want to sell the BCDVideo brand."

I sure never saw that coming! I began experiencing an internal tsunami of bursting pride and this-is-too-good-to-be-true elation. Visions of sugarplums danced in my head. We were currently selling approximately ten million dollars a year in Genetec-compatible servers. This proposed co-selling arrangement would likely triple that. I was finding it hard to keep my emotions inside and the poker face on the outside. For years we had practically pleaded with Anixter to push our servers, all for naught. Now Genetec, almost nonchalantly, was offering to take on that role, no pleading necessary.

We spent the next hour discussing how our salespeople would operate, how orders would be placed, and other nitty-gritty details that may be boring to hear but are crucial to this kind of arrangement. All the while, my head was spinning. We certainly did not need to re-invent ourselves. Everything Genetec wanted us to do were things we had already been doing. I couldn't believe our good fortune.

We decided to take a break for lunch. At the restaurant, Francis asked me, "If we do this deal with BCD, will you offer this hardware co-selling to any other software company?"

Instantaneously, I replied, "If we do this deal with Genetec, we will not need anybody else!" Let's face it, we were cutting a hardware deal with the most powerful software company in the security industry.

That answer seemed to seal the deal. "Here's to Genetec and BCD!" we said and raised our glasses.

After they all left, I sat in my office with the door closed, which was unusual for me. I was absorbing all that had happened in the month since those meetings at ISC West. While I had no idea where this was going to lead, I knew that, with this co-selling arrangement, BCD and our team had accomplished something that had never been done before. We were indeed pioneers!

As awesome as the "Bank of Anixter" had been in taking our potential credit risks with new and unknown security integrators, the Bank of Genetec would be even greater. So, this was a win for us on many counts. All we were waiting for at that point was the contract.

On July 8, 2014, I was in Montreal signing the distribution agreement with Alain Cote, Genetec's legal counsel, and the number two man in the company. Alain had known the founder Pierre Racz since kindergarten. I can certainly relate to lifetime friendships.

As we were signing the agreements, Genetec team members in the room took pictures. Before we finished signing the multiple copies, those pictures were circling the globe. We received copies of that same photo with congratulatory messages from London, Paris, Sydney, Mexico City, and all the way back to Montreal. It was one of the most memorable events in my business life, and that is saying something.

The next day, the agreement was announced to the world via a global joint press release. The security press ate it up. I was soon flooded with calls from customers and vendors congratulating me on this historic partnership.

And they were right. It was a historic partnership. I was always that guy pushing limits, especially for myself. Closing this deal escalated BCDVideo into another stratosphere. Of all the server builders in the marketplace, the biggest brand name in the industry chose both our brand and our mutual go-to-market plan. It truly gave me the greatest sense of accomplishment I ever felt over the lifespan of my business career.

Everything and every decision, good and bad, that I had made over those past twenty-six years had brought us to that table in Canada with the behemoth of the security industry. And all because some guy named Ray messed up our GE Security server at the Illinois Tollway.

Extreme personal satisfaction is rare air. I was vaping it!

CHAPTER 40
EXPANDING OUR REACH

—————

July 2014

With me, you are always either "in," or you are "out." I have always been a 100% person. I never did 50%, 87%, or even 93% very well. It's the same with my company.

As soon as the worldwide press announcement was released, we stopped all direct sales to the security integrators on Genetec-based projects; everything had to go through Genetec, and we would lead the charge. It was the professional thing to do.

We formed a four-person sales desk of customer sales representatives focused on quoting Genetec products. All incoming Genetec sales projects were exclusively quoted through this sales desk. In order not to penalize the territory sales reps who had Genetec customers in their regions, we made a split on the commission, with half going to the Genetec team, and the other half hitting the appropriate region. Everybody wins.

Timing is everything. Thanks to our momentum, we were able to establish a new senior credit line through MB Financial Bank. The deal was important enough that the bank published a press release announcing it. This began a decade-long relationship with Rob Hallberg, MB Bank's lead relationship manager on our account, who would play a vital role in my company's future.

We all had Genetec on the brain. It was a passionate love

affair, and globally mutual. We worked on projects with Genetec sales reps all over the world. BCD's efforts to utilize Genetec's part numbers to co-sell hardware had been working flawlessly. Genetec's purchase revenues were tracking at a $10 million run rate for their first 12 months.

But unless you're married, love affairs are fleeting. And we were not married to Genetec. It was not like they offered to buy us or anything like that. It was nothing more than a business relationship—a strong one at the start. But I was aware that our blindly loyal, 100% approach to our customers had never been completely reciprocal, and I did not want to get burned again. As great as the Genetec deal was, I knew we needed to continue to find new customers and new paths to the market. So, I took the opportunity to get out of the office more and visit customers.

I always loved being in front of customers. I traveled around the United States, making it a point to visit our Milestone resellers and stress that we wanted to continue providing them with the hardware they needed for their projects.

I also went to Copenhagen to meet with Milestone directly. I certainly did not go there to gloat. Instead, I was there to reassure them that it was business as usual with all their customers. We were not on a mission to convert their customers over to Genetec. On the contrary, I saw it as an opportunity to expand our base. Man does not live on Genetec alone.

For several months, I had been speaking with Christian Bohn, Milestone's VP of marketing and product management. It was great to meet him in person, and I certainly was not treated as a leper in their offices. After all, we shared a common goal: happy Milestone customers. Milestone really could not have cared less that we were Genetec's server builder. They were happy that their customers were getting BCD's quality engines to run their projects. And they trusted me enough to know BCD would never flip a Milestone opportunity over to Genetec.

The face-to-face meetings were time well spent, as the phrase "business is business" is universal. To this day, BCDVideo remains the Milestone resellers' choice for project hardware. Even though Milestone markets their own in-house digital video recorder (DVR), the Husky, we maintain a healthy mutual relationship.

We came away from that Denmark visit with a trove of amber cufflinks and pins for Joanne, me, and my employees back home, as well as an enthusiasm for the cuisine. Joanne and I could not get enough of the open-faced pumpernickel sandwiches for lunch and the herring appetizers at dinner.

After Milestone, we took the 45-minute train ride across the strait to Lund, Sweden, headquarters of Axis Communications—the largest video camera company in the world. I met with their OEM manager to talk about the possibility of BCDVideo building recording appliances for Axis Communications. Nothing much came of my one-hour meeting, but Joanne had a wonderful time walking around Lund University. She loves older architecture, and this 350-year-old campus remains among her favorites.

From there, it was off to London, Joanne's favorite city in the world and one of my favorites as well. As Gary Sykes and I took the Underground to make our way to customer meetings throughout the city, Joanne was busy exploring Buckingham Palace, Hyde Park, Windsor Castle, the Tower of London, and other sights. During those two days with Gary, we met with more than 15 customers. Half were already happy sellers of BCDVideo products, while the others were still on the fence. Gary had done a nice job of setting us up, and I was there to push them over the edge. Today, all but two of those companies are customers of BCDVideo.

Joanne saved her visit to Covent Garden for Saturday, so she could spend it with me. After wandering through the open market, finding things to take or ship home, we popped into the White Lion pub next to the Tube station for our fish 'n' chips lunch on the way out. Joanne is convinced she had spent a previous life in England, and I tend to believe her!

Back home, Eugene was busy working with Peter Moeller, Milestone Systems' pre-sales engineer. Peter led Milestone's system-testing certification process, and Eugene was performance-testing our Milestone-based servers. The Milestone Solution Certification verifies that a company's products are interoperable and optimized for performance with their XProtect Video Management Software. After our initial testing was completed, Christian Bohn, Milestone's marketing VP, told an on-line security publication: "The BCDVideo storage solution to date is among the best that Milestone had tested with the given parameters."

Our Milestone Solutions certification helped us send a clear message to the market that we were not just a Genetec shop. They were just a very large—*extremely* large—customer.

This open market philosophy would serve us well. In a very short time, we would become the "unofficial" system tester to the security software market. We began doing testing for numerous Israeli technology companies, and we made the eight-hour time difference work for us. These long-distance testing events began with determining the baseline, the customer's minimum specifications to run their software. We would set up a system on the bench with internet connectivity.

Once we made sure the system met those minimum specifications, Eugene would begin "tinkering"—adding more memory to gauge if the increase in RAM would alter the performance. Then he would try hard drives of different sizes or alternate technologies. He would leave password-protected notes detailing the system performance increases (or perhaps decreases) with each change made.

At 9 a.m. their time, 1 a.m. our time, the Israeli company would remote into the system and run their own tests. When finished, they would leave their comments and suggestions on that same note tab. Many of those notes were testing suggestions, such as seeing how the system would perform with double the memory or switching to more expensive solid state hard drives.

This would generally go back and forth for two weeks. Consider it server ping pong. This approach was so much more efficient and so much less expensive than shipping the unit back and forth through customs on both sides. Why make FedEx any richer?

We also invested time in maintaining our relationship with Hewlett-Packard. We were one of the few security system builders that remained on the HP platform; everyone else had bolted over to Dell. In May, HP invited me to become a member of the HP OEM Council and attend its weekend meeting in San Jose. At the meeting, there were seven other HP OEM customers and quite a few HP senior executives. I was the only HP OEM customer there who was in the IT/Security market. The others were using HP products in communications, manufacturing, and construction. The meeting widened my view on OEM and reinforced the importance of OEM customers to Hewlett-Packard. It was a great learning experience.

Just four months later, Hewlett-Packard split into two companies—HP Inc. as the PC and notebook company, and Hewlett-Packard Enterprise (HPE) as the server company. Now we needed to set up two new vendor accounts in our system. Luckily, our credit lines stayed intact; however, it was initially challenging to try to figure out which HP company to contact for what.

Dean Ruggles, who had been our HP sales rep for years, was now our HPE sales rep. This was good for us both, as we were building primarily off their servers. Dan Dankowski, whom I had known for years at HP, was now covering us on the PC side. For us, most of that business was in HP's workstations, many of which we used as desktop servers for locations without a rack infrastructure, primarily corporate branch locations.

While all this was going on, Eugene was finalizing a two-factor authentication program (2FA), called SmartControl, for our servers. SmartControl added another level of protection to our systems. To gain access to the server, a user had to supply not just a username and password, but a unique six-digit code that had been sent to the user. SmartControl was awarded with security industry publication *Security Sales & Integration's* 2015 Stellar Service Gold Award Winner.

SmartControl did more than secure access to the server; it was a management tool. Through a secure portal, the program delivered advanced system analytics and provided incident notification regarding power usage, CPU usage, memory usage, and hard-drive utilization, all to the person responsible for managing that device.

This BCD-created software also included a disaster recovery program and a proactive support solution. On any Internet-connected BCD server, support tickets were sent directly to BCD's support teams. Technology managers could now manage their servers from anywhere in the world.

While all this activity was going on, we went in search of a new procurement manager. Soon after posting an ad, however, I realized I knew just the right person, and this time, I would not need to sell his mom on it. Our eldest, Alexander, had graduated from the University of Wisconsin three years earlier. His first job after UW was at STATS, Inc., known for feeding instantaneous data to ESPN. For a sports-loving double-major in economics and statistics, this appeared to be a dream job. But as much as he loved the work, he hated the "meat market" aspect of it, and the company was constantly comparing his rapid statistics percentages against his colleagues.

Within five or six months, the buzz of working at STATS, Inc. had become the hassle of working at STATS, Inc. Alexander moved to W.W. Grainger, Inc., the Lake Forest, Illinois-based Fortune 500 industrial distributor, as their global sourcing forecast analyst. Soon he was promoted to global sourcing planning analysis, with responsibility for their international partners in Mexico and Asia, primarily China.

Like a lot of people, Alexander developed a severe case of Fortune 500-itis. His first year at the Fortune 500 company was wonderful and new. His second year? "Fortune 500 sucks." So, I reached out to him and told him about the job we had just posted.

"Why not you?" I asked. Although he would need to interview for the position with the operations manager, let's face it: The job was his if he wanted it. Who were we kidding?

A decade later, he is now our vice president of global supply chain operations. He manages the company's most important vendors, as well as our entire supply chain, warehouse operations, and accounting. Most importantly, Alexander is one of the most respected people at the company, and this respect extends to all our vendors.

BCDVideo finished 2015 with $35 million in revenue, half of which came through Genetec. That is impressive, but perhaps not as impressive as it seems. Most of those Genetec purchases were for BCD customers who had been buying our Genetec-ready servers for years. At that point, Genetec was merely acting as our credit department. We were just trading dollars. Most of the rest came directly from the national integrators, primarily Siemens and SimplexGrinnell.

Nevertheless, we were in a healthy place. Our North American video surveillance engine had a constant stream, and we were walking into 2016 with a global buzz. Double-digit growth was within our reach.

CHAPTER 41

ROUGH WATERS, CALM SEAS

January 2016

I spent my New Year's weekend break contemplating, well, everything—how we got here, what was working great, what needed more attention, whether we had enough team members, whether we had the right team members, and how I could get sales to sync better with the rest of the company.

On a more personal note, I spent time thinking about how proud my dad would have been of his "unemployable son," as he said laughingly. His opinion always meant more to me than the numbers. I had succeeded in building a company that he would have built. We had employee pride, diversity, and a general sense of camaraderie and teamwork.

If you had asked me then what my objectives were for the company, I'm not sure I could have given a definitive answer. I knew I wanted to complete our transformation into a security company, but that goal was nearly achieved. All our top 10 customers were video surveillance/physical security focused. They brought in a combined total of $22.4 million in revenue.

> **Everything I had accomplished (and failed in) was based on my gut feeling. I generally knew what would work, and I was never afraid to quickly yank something that did not.**

It would have been nice to have had a five-year plan that was full of charts, graphs, and projections, but I was never that kind of businessman. (Perhaps during that one year at Illinois State University, I would have been better served by taking Business Law, instead of scoffing at students lugging thick textbooks across the quad.)

I knew I wanted to keep growing the company, and that we were in a prime spot. It was obvious that everywhere in the world, the security industry was expanding. Banks and insurance companies wanted it, people wanted it, law enforcement needed it, and technology was making it possible for everyone to have it. I knew we had what people needed. Now, I wanted to extend our reach. We were taking over North America. Why not the rest of the world?

We had great products, a great formula, a great guarantee, a great reputation, and even greater relationships. Our systems were now recording surveillance at the most critical infrastructures in the world, as well as some of the coolest places on Earth. I wanted to keep the ball rolling, to keep growing the company, to keep solving people's problems. So, we continued to go after the bigger fish in the security sea.

We signed a vendor contract with Siemens Building Technologies, the global billion-dollar physical security company. Very early on, we jointly won the deal at the Chicago Housing Authority (CHA), one of the largest public housing organizations in the United States, with 187,000 tenants.

CHA was one of BCD's first "gut jobs." A gut job is a project your company loses to another vendor but regains the deal a few months later when the end customer realizes the other vendor is not meeting performance expectations. We helped CHA determine that their integrator purchased and installed $1 million of counterfeit Cisco network hardware in their facility. Those had to be removed and replaced with our legitimate Cisco switches. BCD security customers went on to do installations at several housing authorities around the United States, most notably the

New York City Housing Authority (NYCHA), the largest in the country.

Housing authority rollouts generally take more time than any other market. Roll-outs involve installing the same systems in multiple locations. The systems are delivered and installed on a timetable. Phasing in the installation is necessary because delivering hundreds of systems to a single location at one time is not going to win you many friends at the site.

Housing authority sites pose unique problems, since many locations are not up to code, are infested with insects, and are plagued with gang activity. Installations at these sites could never be one-person jobs. A second person, legally armed, would always accompany the installer. No work could be performed until the unit was wired to code and cleaned. So, a planned installation that normally would take only one day could take up to ten days to complete.

Our work with Siemens also marked our first venture into private labeling. We used HPE servers but affixed the Siemens logo on the system bezel. This provided Siemens with brand-name recognition and protected them against competing integrators, who could not tell exactly what was inside the server. (We now brand for more than fifty large security integrators globally.) Siemens bought $1.2 million from BCD in 2016, their first calendar year, and Stanley Security added just short of a million dollars as well. We were on a roll.

We signed direct contracts with two significant customers, Johnson Controls and General Dynamics, a major government contractor.

Through Johnson Controls, BCDVideo servers are recording almost everything that happens in Milwaukee, from Milwaukee Mitchell International Airport to Miller Park (now American Family Field) to the facilities in the domain of the Milwaukee County Sheriff's Department.

General Dynamics Information Technology (GDIT) was one of Anixter's largest customers. Patrick Larkin, GDIT's lead buyer whom I worked with through Anixter, reached out to me directly to quote on the items in their security catalog. It was like shooting fish in a barrel. Those part numbers were the same as we had quoted to Anixter, so we just gave GDIT the same price. Fair is fair, right? He never brought up the price being the same; Patrick was sold on my availability, the service, and order turnaround.

We finished the year by signing our first non-U.S. OEM partner, Agent Vi in Tel Aviv. We were building micro-PCs about the size of a shoebox for them to access cloud connectivity for their worldwide customers. You certainly need to sell a lot of $365 mini servers to make a profit (which we never did.)

It was an exciting time. Everything seemed to be clicking. My goal at the beginning of the year had been to broaden our reach. Here it was only March, and we had already signed deals with two ginormous security companies, plus new deals with a company in the UK and another in Tel Aviv. By the end of the year, security integrators had crisscrossed the world to install BCD's video servers in Brazil, Saudi Arabia, Japan, Australia, and another 20 countries in between.

We had tremendous momentum and were cranking out more than 30 security server project quotes a day. The company was electric, and our employees could feel it. Everyone was in the office a little early every day, as if they could not wait to start the day.

That was the kind of company I dreamed of creating; a company just like me. Now we had to maintain that buzz.

CHAPTER 42

ACTING THE PART

———

January 2017

As I did almost every year, I used the holiday downtime to revisit BCD's lot in life. We left 2016 with $46.5 million in revenues, our biggest year ever, with 25% growth over last year! Still, I felt a little uneasy. Just because we'd had a great year, which did not mean we could not have done things better. We likely left money on the table, which you should never do without a good reason.

Our product margins were good, but I wanted to raise them somewhat—not to gouge our customers, but to establish fair market value. I had confidence in our brand, and in the trust that our customers had in our brand. Our competitors liked to say, "We are just like BCD." No, they weren't. They offered servers; we offered solutions.

Our competitors often said that one server is the same as another. But that is not true, even with the same product from the same company, because one situation is different from another. Our competitors were just slinging boxes like they were flipping burgers at a fast-food joint (speaking of which, we won the McDonald's project!) Our systems, on the other hand, were like meals made by a private chef who had come to your home to prepare a customized menu.

We were the *only* server builder in the industry who customized the server to meet the needs of the project, and the customers who understood the value of that did not try to nickel-and-dime the cost. It reminded me of a TV commercial from Sym's clothing store that ran over and over in the 1970s. It carried the tagline, "An educated consumer is our best customer."

Yes, our systems cost more, but they cost less over the three to 10 years that the server was expected to work. All those truck rolls to the site to fix yet another server issue come out of the security integrator's pocket, not the end customer. We had to make the integrators realize that, over the life of the system, we were the lowest-cost solution on the market.

The challenge was to educate the consumer. But that had to be done through the security integrator, and that meant persuading our salespeople to do the training.

Salespeople are not by nature teachers. Moreover, salespeople tend to be susceptible to price traps. They get paid by commission, and they're not stupid. They would rather earn a 10% commission on a $100 sale that goes through than earn no commission on a $2,000 sale that never happens.

I told our salespeople that if a customer calls and asks us to beat a price on a piece of equipment, do not be a lazy shit and just beat the price; use the opportunity to educate the customer. No one else in the industry offered customized solutions. And no one else in the industry had the brains or the balls to guarantee their calculations and the solution.

We needed to train our people to stop focusing on what they were selling and start focusing on why. To begin with, we prepared customized data sheets for every product. They detailed all the specifications, from which Intel processors were installed to how many cameras the system could support. These data sheets were not meant to replace the salesperson's knowledge or effort; they were there to help the salesperson present our offering, or submittal, to their customer.

A submittal is an information sheet that the security integrator provides to the end customers as written proof that what is being offered matches, at the very least, their minimum bid requirements. It's a proof of concept that the security integrator is delivering what is expected by the eventual buyer.

However, it would not be enough to tell the customer what size and type of hard drives were being used. Our salespeople had to be able to explain the reason why they were being incorporated into the solution, to position themselves as trusted advisors.

That meant we had to change our salespeople's behaviors. There were many times when a customer came to us and asked a salesman for a quote based on their specifications, and all the salesman did was quote a price on whatever best matched their request. I was tempted to change his title to "Lazy Fuck." That kind of simple-minded response offered zero added value. It was department store sales clerk behavior, which needed to be corrected immediately.

I developed a new approach for our salespeople. Under the new system, our salespeople would not give a quote without a little homework. Instead, they would ask a set of basic questions: "What software are you using?" "What model and how many cameras are you capturing?" "How long do you need to retain the footage?" It was now mandatory to gather this data before preparing a quote.

We expected that this approach would not always go over well with the customers, but we felt we were doing them a favor. If we came back with a different solution than the one they had asked us about, we explained why our solution would work better. And we made it clear that we would guarantee our calculations.

If the customer balked and still wanted what he requested, we would kindly tell them we were unwilling to quote it, as we did not feel it would work correctly, and we did not want the company liability. I knew this was radical, but to me, it saved the company tens of thousands of dollars in open, used products coming back through our doors.

On the positive side, we were sending a message that we ensured the customer would get the proper solution for his project, not the cheapest piece of crap that barely met the spec. And we were, and still are, the only company standing behind our offering.

To help educate customers, I had our marketing department create cost-of-ownership trade magazine ads, as well as slides for our sales team to use in their PowerPoint presentations.

To reward the sales team's compliance, I decided to implement a new sales compensation plan. I believed we had a superior product, and I expected superior, trained salespeople to present it and to be rewarded highly for doing so. The higher the profit margin on the deal, the greater the percentage for the reward.

I did not need to be a mind reader to know that this proposal would be met with skepticism, if not downright hostility by the sales team. I do not think I would have been happy if I had been asked to turn down sure commissions on sure sales.

For this to work, the salespeople had to buy into it. So, I presented it with a little tough love. I told them we were paying them to be salespeople, not salesclerks. We did not need them to take orders; we needed them to guide the customer to the proper solution. That is how you gain respect from your customer. He may be able to get a price from anybody, but he gets the truth from you. I added that, if they followed my lead, their commissions should double. They just needed to trust me.

The new compensation plan was based on our expected 20% minimum profit on our video servers. Pricing on the PCs, monitors, and other commodities would be subject to whatever the market would bear. But we controlled our video server pricing, not the customer or the competition. When it came to these servers, there was no "me too" in the industry, just a lot of pretenders. ("Just like BCD," my ass.)

We scaled the compensation plan rewards based on both the margin percentage and the total profit amount. This rewarded good selling and stopped the company from overpaying on lower-margin deals. Those salespeople willing to do the work to become trusted advisors had the opportunity to make six-figure commissions by the end of the year. And we would be thrilled to pay them.

Happily, four of the seven sales team members embraced the challenge. Greed really IS good! Those four had their titles changed to Advanced Systems Specialists, with double the commission plan. They split the previous year's top 32 customers among them and would receive additional opportunities as they came into the company.

The other three sales reps were still in a good place within the company. I appreciated that they were honest about their fears of taking over the bigger roles. There was still a need for what they brought to the table, especially for all those under-20 camera opportunities. And I left the door open for them to go to the next level should they choose.

January was sure off to a great start.

CHAPTER 43
GO BIG OR GO HOME

April 2017

In April, Hewlett-Packard announced a new server specifically engineered for large storage applications. It was an amazing machine; it combined on a single server the capacity of sixty hard drives, with the power of built-in, high-speed Intel processors.

It was the largest internal storage server on the market, and it was physically enormous, taking up five rack spaces. Generally, rack servers came as either 1U or 2U in height, the "U" being server terminology for "Unit," as in how many spaces within the rack it takes up.

Server racks range in size from 4U, regarded as a desktop rack, to wheeled 42U racks capable of supporting 3,000 pounds of metal devices. HP's new server was a 5U chassis. Because other components take up room as well, a 42U rack generally has only 30U of space available for servers. A single 5U server would take up 17% of the available rack space. However, bigger projects generally required a 2U rack-mounted server attached to a 4U storage bay that was also inside the rack—6U altogether. Although the 5U server was larger, it was a more efficient use of space. Even 1U of saved rack space was valuable to the customer.

Eugene and I were out of our minds with excitement, thinking about all the ways we could use this server within the vast vertical markets we served. But just because the system could support 360TB of built-in storage, we couldn't assume the software could support it. No one had ever seen such a beast before, and we had to be sure. Within days, we had a demo model on Eugene's tech bench for testing. As it turned out, our two top server-installed video software products, Milestone XProtect, and Genetec Security Center, supported the system famously.

We were beside ourselves. As usual, I was itching to announce that we were offering this product to our customers. But this was no ordinary product, to be listed in this BCD catalog with an ordinary BCD part number. This thing needed a name! But what to call this behemoth?

We bounced it between ourselves and then expanded the name search to the sales team. We wanted to make them part of the process since participation in the product generally made them more willing to sell it.

Someone suggested Big Boy. That name was accurate, but I was unsure it would resonate. Big Boy made me think of the Big Boy casual dining restaurant chain (which a quick search found to be a trademarked name.)

I thought of Big MF, but feared the repercussions should someone "break the code." It would have been a statement, though!

Then I thought of Big Bertha, the Callaway-branded golf driver that had been on the market for over a decade. I bounced the name off Eugene. He loved it. After a quick search showing no copyright issues, we sent the product information and capabilities, along with the Big Bertha product name, over to marketing. Before long, the item was in our catalog.

Timing is everything. Within days of announcing the availability of Big Bertha, we heard from one of our larger Milestone security integrators. Jeff Wooten, CEO of Cincinnati-based Datalink, had an immediate need for two massive storage systems at the Cincinnati/Northern Kentucky Airport. The airport had two terminals, and he wanted to put a large server in each. One hitch: Jeff wanted to run a demo, and all we had on hand was the HP demo system on Eugene's bench. Even though HP would hold us responsible for that unit, it was an easy decision to send it to Jeff. He had a live deal going down. I would deal with HP later if needed. It sure beat waiting two weeks to get their approval.

The system ran flawlessly, and Datalink ordered the two fully loaded systems, each with 360TB of storage built in. We let him keep running the demo system until the actual units were delivered. They have been running ever since.

In May, I signed off on BCD's future home. By September, we exchanged a 14,500-square-foot facility, with 800 square feet dedicated to the configuration center, for a 51,000-square-foot complex with more than 15,000 square feet of server configuration space.

Our new HQ was in Buffalo Grove, just two towns over from our Northbrook offices, so the move did not cost us any employees. We took them on tours in shifts to show them the progress being made during remodeling. It was a big step up for us, and the employees were excited.

In the fall, we began hearing talk on the street that CDW was losing IT market share to Amazon. That made sense. CDW had become a billion-dollar company selling IT peripheral parts; now those items were all available from Amazon, the home of quick, easy, price-competitive transactions. Amazon was disrupting commerce at every level, and now CDW was affected. I thought we might have something to offer CDW.

My CDW plan was interrupted by hip replacement surgery, followed by weeks of rehab. But once I was back on my feet, I set up a meeting at CDW. I started by telling them that, decades earlier, I was working at Elek-Tek, selling hundreds of Toshiba notebooks to a company named MPK Consulting. That stood for Michael P. Krasney, now the CDW founder and CEO. The tale gave a kind of "street cred" to the rest of my pitch.

I then flattered them by acknowledging the obvious: They were hugely successful, and they did not get that way by chance. They knew what they were doing. But right now, they had a problem with Amazon. I thought we could help them, and at the same time help ourselves.

"I think it's possible that every K-12, college, and government entity has an account with CDW or CDW-G, and at least half of corporate America does as well. You already have the customers; you just need to sell them more. But not more parts. You need to go wider. You need to sell solutions."

Explaining the obvious, I said, "If you sell parts, customers can compare prices among dealers. They can even get competitors to drop their prices to beat you, which is how sales margins get devalued."

The answer was to turn CDW into a one-stop shop, offering bundled solutions. CDW was already selling Axis Communications cameras and Milestone Systems software. All they needed were the servers that allowed everything to work together. "We're offering you the missing piece of that puzzle," I said.

Drawing back on the systems we developed at Anixter years earlier, we had come up with a line of "camera-ready video storage solutions," based on Milestone Systems software and optimized for 10, 20, 30, 40, or 50 cameras. Under this plan, any time a CDW salesperson entered a customer quote that included cameras, the appropriate storage system would be automatically added as an optional item. If, for example, the quote included 22 cameras, the CDW system could include the optional 30-camera solution. That would meet their current need and enable the addition of eight more cameras in the future.

This was hardly unknown territory for CDW. The company was an early pioneer in utilizing technology to offer related products on their quotes to customers. Whatever was being quoted, the CDW system would also add a small section on the quote titled, "Customers Who Ordered This Generally Order This as Well."

CDW would win whether the customer bought the optional server or not. Either way, customers would start to grasp that CDW now sold video servers, too. This automated suggestion took the human factor out of the equation. With Anixter, we had hoped and prayed, usually in vain, that the sales rep would think of adding the server. Here, the suggestion would just pop up. CDW's technology would do the salespeople's thinking for them.

The fact was the customer was already volunteering all the necessary information by asking for a quote on video software and a particular number and type of cameras. Nothing else was needed. Of course, salespeople could still engage the customer and ask what they were considering for capturing the video footage, but the beauty of the idea was that they did not have to do that. Comfort zones were never challenged.

It was impossible not to pick up the vibe of excitement in the room, and it made for a great conversation with Joanne as I was heading back to the office. She always wanted me to be happy, and I always wanted to share that happiness with her.

CDW was soon featuring our "related products" offerings on their quoting system. While the success of that program did not yield the rampant growth we had envisioned, we have enjoyed a healthy relationship with CDW ever since. They have since done several three-year security rollouts in counties within Florida.

I certainly had come full circle since selling Michael Krasney at MPK Consulting almost four decades before! Once again, everything happens for a reason. There are no coincidences.

By the end of the year, *Computer Reseller News* included us among their "Solution Provider 500" for the third time. But I was happiest when *Inc. Magazine* named BCD as one of their "Best Places to Work." That honor is based on a confidential employee survey that asks about management's credibility, overall job satisfaction, and camaraderie, as well as questions about pay and benefit programs, hiring practices, internal communication, training, and recognition programs. Our application for this latest honor had been orchestrated by our newest team member, Sue Komarchuk, our human resources director. Sue brought an unprecedented level of professionalism into BCD, where we needed it the most.

CHAPTER 44
AN EVOLUTION REVOLUTION

———

November 2017

Computer products evolve as technology advances. Whenever Intel announced new, faster chipsets, Seagate or Western Digital would announce new, faster hard drives. Whenever Microsoft released updated versions of their Windows software, HP and all the other server manufacturers would roll out new generations of their existing lines.

These manufacturers were not making slight tweaks. A lot was involved. For one thing, they needed to test the new products with their existing products to make sure they were compatible. Frequently they weren't, and the manufacturers would have to revise the existing products to perform optimally when operating with these faster or more powerful internal playmates.

Once the process was completed, these revised products would often be announced as a new and improved generation of that manufacturer's product line. But "improved" is like "beauty." It's totally in the eye of the beholder.

Two days before Thanksgiving in 2017, Dean Ruggles, our HP account manager, came out to present Hewlett-Packard's latest server platform transformation from the 9th to the 10th generation. While going through the various models, we noticed there was no planned continuation of the ProLiant DL160 and ProLiant DL180 servers from Gen9 to Gen10. These 1U and 2U rack space solutions were HP's entry-level rack server models, at an entry-level price. (Well, entry level for HP, anyway.) This out-of-left field news was a major jolt to our systems. Those servers were our go-to-built models. They represented over half of our video server builds.

While those home-run 500-plus camera projects were exciting, most video surveillance projects require 50 cameras or less. For those entry-level projects, all a customer needs is an entry-level base unit. They certainly do not need a datacenter-quality server to run surveillance systems in motels, secondary schools, churches and temples, car rental agencies, and village police departments.

HP's DL160 and DL180 servers were our best choice for such jobs. If they were unavailable, we would have to move customers up to the ProLiant DL380, which was our server of choice on all enterprise-size projects, such as Madison Square Garden all those years ago. This was an exceptional server for IT applications, and I sold thousands of them throughout my career, many of them to HP's customers on behalf of HP. But I sold almost three times as many of those entry-level servers.

Substituting the DL380 would have killed us. For BCD, the $4,000 price delta between the DL380 and the DL180 would have been the equivalent of a torpedo in the engine room. I'm a pretty good salesperson, but not that good, especially in a price-conscious marketplace. There just was not enough yarn for us to weave that story.

As my mind was already scrambling for what could replace it, I challenged Dean about why the DL160 and DL180 entry-level servers were not on the Gen10 platform, reminding him of the large share of our product line they represented.

He told me the CEO, Antonio Neri, decided to drop them on the generational change as "he was tired of the HP server team dumping low-margin entry-level servers to their large customers' (Apple, Facebook, and others) data centers in China."

That had to have been one of the most idiotic reasons for drastically changing something that would adversely affect tens of thousands of customers that I had ever heard of in my business life. And it still is.

But what bothered me the most was not Antonio's short-sighted logic. We were making 30% margins on the BCD versions, while HP's cowardly, selfish SOB of a salesperson was dumping servers at a 5% margin. He was, at best, making a $200 commission per server, 40% below the HP norm. This salesperson's weakness led HP's CEO to drop the entire low-end server line. All for a measly $200 commission per server.

Using what I refer to as "servernomics," the server is just the front end of the expense. Whether it is a $4,000 server or an $8,000 server, the real cost is in the server's deployment. There is always an additional cost associated with sliding a server into a rack. It's known as "people, pipe, and power". The "people" are the IT technician teams managing the server. The time they devote to deployment represents a slice of their annual salary. It's a sunk cost, but it's still a cost linked to that server.

The pipe consists of the connection to the wide-area network. In some cases, the network switch may be at full capacity, so a new switch is needed. That is another cost. And, if there is no available rack space, another rack must be ordered, along with all those pieces and parts needed to make it functional. More costs.

Then there is the power, managed through the Power Distribution Unit (PDU). The PDU is always ordered when the rack is purchased, as the rack cannot function without power, and the server must connect via the PDU. It is not as simple as plugging it into a wall outlet unless the plan is to blow out the power for the entire building.

Regardless of whether we're talking about a $2,000 server, a $4,000 server, or a $20,000 server, the "people, pipe, and power" equation applies to all of them—roughly 18% of the server price. The true cost for the customer buying the $4,000 server was actually $4,720.

It would be easy to say that Antonio "cut off his nose to spite his face," but in this case, it may have been a more southern appendage.

Why cut the entire line from the worldwide customer market because of the dump-and-dash actions of their China server team?

Maybe what pissed me off the most was that he never even did his homework. Just change the compensation plan and make it margin-based. If HP would not pay commission on anything under five points, 10 points, or even 15 points, the problem was solved.

That was pretty much the gist of what I said to Dean. I admired his having the balls to present it, knowing that we were going to have a major issue with it. HP's decision did more than threaten my pocketbook—it hurt me personally. I was a loyalist. I never cheated on them. I was faithful to a fault. We were hit on continually by other vendors, like the high school girl with a reputation, and they were always rebuffed.

I was a member of the HP OEM Committee, helping them chart their future course for OEMs in all vertical markets. BCD literally sold its soul to HP, forsaking all others. I always seemed to have this sense of loyalty that was lacking in others. But I would never have traded that away. Why stoop to their level when, at the end of the day, you need to be able to look at yourself in the mirror without blinking?

I had lost count of the number of times over the years that I could have moved to Dell. It would have been easy, even logical, to add a small segment of their line to broaden our spending power. But I was a never-Dell HP purist, proud of being important within HP's ecosystem. Was HP perfect? Hell, no. But neither are my kids. Neither am I, for that matter.

Only yesterday (okay, thirteen years ago), HP's Ron Pope was my hero, saving BCD's financial ass less than a month after our accountant told us we needed to drastically reduce our SGA. Like the Lone Ranger, Ron Pope rode into my life (with my decades-long relationship with GE and GE Capital serving as his faithful horse, Silver. Hi-ho, Silver!)

I had to face the fact that we did not have a relationship with HP; we only did business with HP. The only HP relationship we truly had was the one with Ron Pope. Ron was the man. And I was his. And Dean Ruggles as well, as he was only the messenger. But in the end, HP couldn't give a shit about BCD. We weren't even on their radar; otherwise they would have asked our opinion before making the decision.

Jeff's misguided passion got him dinged yet again. However, this was not my first rodeo. My whole career has been about adapting to change—jobs, managers, and titles, with no title better than BCD CEO. I always landed on my feet in a better situation. This would be no different.

As Dean continued going through the HP roadmap, I was barely listening. HP was already "dead to me," to quote Tony Soprano. My brain was already in overdrive, scanning which vendor would be the next lotto winner, hand-picked as the base for our world-class solutions.

I knew we would land on our feet. As we had been doing for the last 30 years, and always for the better. We had the advantage. We could build our systems on whatever we chose to build them, while controlling our destiny.

They were fucking with the wrong company and the wrong man.

CHAPTER 45
NEVER SAY NEVER

———

December 2017

For over a decade, my company had earned an IT-savvy reputation for building solutions on an HP platform. Now there was a gap in a major part of our product line. We were at a turning point. But which way would we turn?

We thought through our options; there weren't many. We considered, though not too seriously, filling that hole with a white box brand like Supermicro. A white box computer is nothing more than a box of parts. While it could have the same parts our HP servers had—hard drives, memory modules, Intel processors, fans—those parts would not have been configured nor tested to work together. I felt we would be jeopardizing our well-earned reputation as a quality system builder by bringing in Supermicro.

It did not take long to realize that Dell Technologies was the only logical choice. They had a product line that matched HP, server for server. Of course they did. They were archrivals! Recognizing that was the easy part; the hard part was going to be me.

I always had a chip on my shoulder about Dell. This went as far back as my Tek-Aids years. I was aware of Michael Dell back in his senior year at UT-Austin, when he founded his company in his dorm room and revolutionized the build-to-order model. I admired him for that. It was the aftermath that became my issue. He single-handedly turned the phrase "Inventory is King," or as I liked to say it, "Inventory is Truth," into "Inventory is a Liability." Perhaps if I had still been in Austin, he and I could have met for a beer and a bite at Fonda San Miguel or even Sixth Street. But by that time, we were thousands of miles apart, and he was singlehandedly fucking up one of my key strengths—namely, having ready-to-build inventory on hand.

At the time, I thought Dell's innovation was nothing more than change for the sake of change. I believed manufacturers took it too much to heart. Almost everyone seemed to jump on that bandwagon, but I did not join them. Sure, we had to change. We shifted to keeping two weeks of inventory, rather than six weeks. It made us nimbler, still turning around customer orders in days.

It also made us smarter. We began getting away from reading specifications off a data sheet. Honestly, everyone's sheet said the same things—CPUs, memory, hard drives. Instead, we started explaining to customers the benefits of our solution: the performance guarantee, and the number of cameras they could run off our server, which was more than anybody else.

Dell sure was not offering that. Because they couldn't. THAT was our one-up on them. We purpose-built solutions for specific security projects.

My opinion was that Dell sent servers to customers with no idea of their usage. They just gave the customer what they asked for, even when the customer did not know what they really needed.

I would not have been surprised to learn that several of the proposals we put out to customers were sent to Dell for a price match. I couldn't begrudge a customer doing a little comparison shopping. However, it should have been the reverse. They should have been asking Dell how many cameras they could support, and what were their frame resolutions, expected motion, and days of retention.

We encountered many customers who wanted to purchase our

solution, only at the Dell price. (I never heard of a customer who asked Dell to match our performance guarantee.)

When a customer forwarded one of our purpose-built quotes to Dell for price checks and told us he "found what we quoted cheaper at Dell," we acted. We locked them out of their discount and would only quote them MSRP. Nor did we offer any camera calculations. It was my newly created FIFU program—Fuck It and Fuck U. "You want to buy our project specifications from Dell? Not today, pal."

These customers would usually escalate up to me. I would call and ask each of them the same questions: "When you called Dell for the quote, did you give them the camera counts, days of retention, failover, or any of that?"

"No," they typically answered, "Dell doesn't offer that."

"So, you took our work, which is noted as confidential on your proposal, and shared it with them? Why should we ever trust you again?"

The customer would dance a little on the phone, mumbling under their breath. Most of them had the decency to be embarrassed, and we would soon reach a moment of uncomfortable silence. I let that fester for a moment. Then I would ask if we could trust him not to do this anymore. I reminded him that we documented every project quote, and tracked wins and losses. On the losses, which gladly were few and far between, we had methods to find what ultimately was ordered, generally from the end customer.

I had spent my entire IT career selling customized solutions that were HP-based systems, and selling against Dell. We frequently competed head-to-head. When we prevailed, one win would count as two for me—we got the order, and I slayed the mighty Goliath, aka Dell.

But you cannot deny success, and Dell was certainly successful. Eight years after the company was founded, Dell entered the Fortune 500 and never left. The computer trade rags were smoking from Dell's hookah. According to them, Michael could do nothing wrong.

That is what made this turning point such a crisis. We weren't just trying to fill a hole in our product line, I had built an identity as Dell's most ardent critic. What should I do? Should I continue to feed my reputation as the leader of the anti-Dell rebels? Or should I solve my company's need for all enterprise-quality systems?

On the other hand, if I were to swallow HP's insulting disregard for my company's business this time, who's to say they would not pull this shit again the next time Antonio got a bug up his ass?

We made the obvious choice. We would dump HP for Dell and transition the entire HP portfolio to Dell along the way. It would be a massive undertaking, but a "fuck them" mentality is a wonderful motivator. My whole team knew that I felt HP disrespected me personally. More importantly, they had disrespected the company—all of us. Along with the insult, HP gave us a common cause.

Although I was quite ready to leap to Dell, I was smart enough to make sure we did some looking first. Acting under the radar, we began cross-tweaking our HP builds into Dell builds, using the same specifications. We weren't in any rush; the holidays were weeks away, and nobody would be shipping us anything until the New Year. On the down-low, we placed a $25,000 mini-order for three different Dell servers, which allowed Eugene and his team to begin investigating their server architecture. They double- and triple-checked the servers against the comparable HP models. We could see from the product descriptions that the specs matched, but for Eugene, this was just the baseline. To get a true test of maximum performance, we needed to get some machines on our benches. He liked what he saw.

Although we were trying to act in "stealth bomber" mode, word of our interest got out. Maybe someone in Dell's sales or accounting departments took note of our new customer application. Maybe somebody saw our modest order, looked us up on the internet, realized we were heavy in the security market, and sent the internal lead to their colleagues in the video security division. But more than likely, someone reached out to one of Dell's de facto video security leaders, Ken Mills or Kristin DeLeeuw Pavlovich, and spilled the beans.

Whether it was through their initiative or ours, the week before Christmas, Ken and Kristin came out to our offices to meet with our video security team managers. As it happened, Joanne and I were out of the country at a Genetec customer event in Cancun at the time. As the story goes, when Ken realized I was not going to be at the meeting, he asked, "Does Jeff even know we are here?" After the visit, I was briefed on the meeting and told that it went well. "It's probably good you weren't here," I was told. "At one point, Ken said he always heard that you thought there's a reason Dell rhymes with hell."

It seems my "Dell is the Antichrist" reputation was well-known within Dell. That made me somewhat proud! It was my "Steve Martin in *The Jerk* finding his name in the phone book" moment. I was somebody! I was in their phone book! This was 180 degrees from how I was feeling within Hewlett-Packard.

Ken and Kristin returned soon, and this time I was in the office. We hammered out a framework, enough to get Dell's legal team working on a contract. By January 1, we were locked and loaded.

Then the moment happened. I was at home on a January Saturday afternoon, working on my notebook with the noise of some college football game on the TV in the background. Randomly, I received an email with the subject line, "Welcome to the team!" I looked at the sender. It was michael@dell.com. Yes, apparently that guy. I motioned Joanne over to look. She thought it looked real as well.

That was a historical moment for me. During my career, I sold roughly a quarter-billion dollars of HP products. Starting with Carley Fiorina, I had made money for five different Hewlett-Packard CEOs. Never did I receive a "thank you" card, a holiday card, a birthday card, or even a "How ya doin'?" email. Other than Dean, I never heard a peep from anyone at HP expressing the hope that we would stick around.

So, my company had yet to spend a nickel at Dell, and this industry icon was already welcoming me to his team. Any doubts I may have had were gone at that point. I felt great about our decision, and my brain started to go into overdrive on how to make a positive impact on Mr. Dell's company.

CHAPTER 46
EXPANDING OUR REACH

———

March 2018

Early in our history with Dell, even before we received our first stocking order, my son Max, our Global Sales Director, got us in front of a deal in the Middle East. Max had now been with us for four years and had broadened his reach with global contacts and customers. Through his relationship with Peter Lintzeris, who is video software manufacturer Milestone's country manager in Canada, Max was sideways introduced to the Milestone team in the Middle East. Our work with Milestone had blossomed into a rewarding relationship since BCD was named Milestone's 2012 Technology Partner of the Year.

Through his connections, Max learned that Milestone had contracted to install an enormous network project for the city of Ras Al-Khaimah, approximately 120 kilometers north of Dubai in the United Arab Emirates.

This was a citywide video network project, where the surveillance covered all government buildings in the city, including police stations, City Hall, hospitals, emergency services, and everything in between. The sheer size of the project required fifty-two high-performance servers, all built to specification.

The contract required an on-site Field Assurance Test (FAT), a process that ensures the products the customer is buying reach designated standards of performance. These tests eliminate finding out the hard way—on site—that the expensive hardware you just bought and installed does not work. Dominic and Steven, the project consultants, were required to monitor the servers in person as they underwent these tests and to verify that the servers passed. But Dominic and Steven had a problem. They couldn't find anyone to run the tests, and now their reputation was on the line.

At first, Dominic and Steven reached out to Dell, which had built the servers. They asked if Dell could conduct the test at their facility in Round Rock, Texas. Dell said they could conduct the tests, but that Dominic and Steven couldn't attend, since only Dell employees with appropriate clearances could enter the server-building facility. That made sense to me; a company like Dell has a lot of trade secrets to protect.

Dominic and Steven then reached out to us through Max. We were eager to prove ourselves, especially after Dell turned them down. Did I mention we were in the hero business?

We gladly seized the opportunity, although the logistics were daunting. We would have to rent space in Dubai, hook up power, transport the servers and our team to the UAE, and hope that everything worked. Dominic and Steven then stepped up and made everything easier. Instead of us going to the UAE, they agreed to come to our new location in Buffalo Grove to observe the test.

Never underestimate what a promise of deep-dish Chicago pizza for lunch can accomplish.

Now all we needed was the inventory. We were still waiting for Dell to begin filling our initial order. By pure chance, however, the same high-end, maximum-performing servers we needed for the testing were already on our initial PO. John at Dell agreed to peel them off the order and have them expedited to us within a couple of days.

Once the servers arrived, we immediately put them on the bench in our Innovation Center. The first 38 systems were hooked up and ran smoothly. As we got to the 39th system on the bench, however, we noticed random power surges breaking out. The lights throughout our office blinked. The coffee maker in the break room went off and on.

Think of a power surge as a kind of hiccup along the course of the electrical current running through a building. You've probably had them in your home. When power surges break into *Real Housewives* or *Monday Night Football* for an instant, they are not a big deal. But they were a very big deal to us. This was not a hiccup; it was acid reflux. If a surge happened during a test, the servers would fail. That would be a huge embarrassment to Dominic and Steven, and it would be humiliating for us.

This had never happened to us before. On any given day, our benches were full of systems, and we never suffered any surges. Even when we had half the benches in the room stacked four-high with 160 Genetec surveillance appliances destined for Starbucks, we never had power surges. But quickly we realized that on most of those occasions, the systems were workstation-based, which drew one-fifth of the power of the typical server.

And we were running only thirty-nine of the fifty-two systems. Crisis, what crisis? We would have to pull a rabbit out of a hat, and fast.

Eugene quickly realized we were overloading the circuits in the part of the building where we were doing the tests. The solution, he calculated, was to spread the current throughout the building.

Thankfully, we had that hat, and the rabbit that went in it. Our 51,000-square-foot facility included an open room with a cement floor, a twenty-foot ceiling, and a brick wall painted white on the upper half and dark, royal blue below. It was 15,000 square feet of unused space that we called the "blue warehouse." We had never really found a use for it. Now we had one. By conducting part of the testing there, we could redistribute the power throughout the facility and avoid surges. In theory, anyway.

What we did not have was a lot of time. In four days, Dominic and Steven would board a plane in Dubai and fly for fifteen hours to see us perform our first-ever Factory Assurance Testing.

Fortunately, no one scrambles like BCD! Then again, we've had so much practice at it.

The first thing we did was go to Home Depot and buy seven unfinished oak doors, solid rectangles without any openings cut for doorknobs. BCD's tech benches have always been these doors, mounted on metal legs. We found them far preferable to the fancy linoleum benches that quickly get all scratched up when 80-pound metal chassis servers slide on and off them. As soon as the doors arrived, we stained them, then left them to dry overnight.

Then we got in touch with Ingram Micro and ordered 28 computer monitors, keyboard/mouse combos, and power filters, four for each of the seven stations. We were planning on four systems on each bench for better power load balancing.

Our new Innovation Center came together just in time for Dominic and Steven's arrival. I was absent; I had torn the meniscus in my knee and was sidelined. But Max played host, and Eugene ran the show. As we all expected, the Field Assurance Testing went flawlessly. There were no power issues whatsoever, not even a hiccup. The performance of those 52 servers was off the charts.

Dominic and Steven must have had confidence in our capabilities; they had brought the FAT certification with them and gladly signed it on the spot. We made a copy, which Eugene had framed and hung in the Innovation Center, now our main tech center in the building. Yes, because of that high-end testing, BCD now had two build centers within its facility.

Once we passed that first significant test, we never looked back. We impressed Dell; they liked the way we stepped up. We certainly impressed Milestone, whose bacon we saved on the highly visible Ras Al-Khaimah project. We probably even impressed our customer Genetec, Milestone's main competitor, who had been salivating at the thought of swooping in and replacing Milestone if they floundered. Milestone did not fail, with our assistance. Have I mentioned we are in the hero business?

In the meantime, we received another special delivery: our first shipment of Dell-logoed polo-type shirts from our apparel vendor.

I spread them around the office and sent one to each of the Dell people we had met over those first few months. From the selfie texts I received showing recipients wearing the shirts, they were an instant hit.

I took a chance and sent an XL shirt to CEO Michael Dell at the company's Round Rock headquarters. I added a note inside the shirt, stating *"As you welcomed me to the team, I figured you needed a uniform."*

CHAPTER 47
PREPARE FOR THE UNEXPECTED

———

April 2018

We had been using up our HP stock for months, looking forward to the day we would turn the page and start dealing with Dell. We counted down the hours. With the delivery day in sight, we began tracking the inbound semi-truck, following it from Dell's dock in Round Rock, to Dell's local branch, and finally down the highway to Buffalo Grove.

One of the things I liked about our new space was that my office gave me a view of the road. I loved seeing trucks, from FedEx vans to large 53-footers, arriving and leaving our lot all day long. When I watched them, I thought to myself, "That is commerce!" On the day the truck arrived, I thought I would shout those words out loud.

And there it was! I shouted loud enough to be heard throughout the front office, maybe even the warehouse, too.

That day I wore jeans, because I knew I would be spending time on the loading dock. When I saw the truck carrying Dell's load enter our parking lot and pass by my window, I grabbed my work gloves and headed for the dock. I do not know if my feet touched the ground.

When I arrived, the warehouse crew had the back of the trailer open. I could see the wall of servers, stacked on their pallets and beautifully shrink-wrapped. I grabbed a pallet jack and began helping the team move the cargo off the truck and into the spotless warehouse space we had prepared for their arrival. Fifteen pallets later, we went back onto the trailer to start pulling out the hard drives.

I was expecting to see clean, sturdy cartons stacked on a pallet, ready for an easy exit from the trailer. Instead, I was struck with a vision that resembled the scene from *Used Cars*, when Luke saw the crappy cars that Rudy Russo planned to sell to the school district at full price, if only to get the auto shop expertise. I was shocked.

There were no pallets. No uniform boxes. No standardized packing. Instead, there were a bunch of loose boxes of every shape, size, and condition semi-stacked in the trailer. You couldn't use a pallet jack to lift this mishmash; instead, we had to use two-wheeled hand carts and go back and forth. Many of the boxes were in such poor condition that they had to be hand-carried and immediately inspected for damage. Surprisingly, the drives were all okay. Still, what should have taken 15 minutes took two hours.

This was a far cry from the "Welcome to Dell" moment I had dreamed of. Nothing like this ever happened on HP's watch.

"There's a screw-up somewhere," I said to the crew, thinking I was pointing out the obvious. My expectation was that we would quickly get to the bottom of this mess and that we would soon be shipping them back. "For now, let's get them off the truck and leave them by the dock." I then headed back to my office to call John at Dell. On this trip, my feet definitely touched the ground. In fact, they kind of stomped.

John and I shared a "WTF moment." I told him I had never heard of products being shipped this way. "Me neither," he said, pretty convincingly. "Let me look into it." He called back minutes later. "You ordered the drives a la carte, instead of having them installed into the servers."

"No kidding," I responded. "That is how we've always done it!"

But that was not the way Dell had ever done it. Apparently in our haste to get the order in, we neglected to do our homework. Dell orders had to be coded in a certain way, and we did not do that. We were excited to get started, and I was likely in "ready, fire, aim" mode. Granted, that responsibility generally falls on me. But surely Dell would have recognized how out of the ordinary our order was; it would have been nice if they had given us a heads-up when they began processing the order.

While the guys were moving the drives off the truck, they noticed something about the hard drives that was even more alarming than the haphazard packing. There were no serial numbers we could import into our system. All the packing list showed was 4,000 hard drives, broken down by how many of each type.

"Can you send me the serial numbers?" I asked John.

"No," he replied. "We do not maintain hard drive serial numbers. The server is the warrantied product, and the drives are inside the warrantied server." Now steam was coming out of my ears, but I began to see what had gone wrong. HP drives could be used with many brands of servers, so each needed its own serial number. But Dell drives could be used only in Dell systems, so the serial number of each drive was affixed to the server it had been loaded into. Granted, my fault for assuming like-for-like. But why would you not?

Still, I was angry, and John, unfortunately for him, caught the brunt. "This is the most fucked-up thing I can remember ever happening to my company in 20 years. Helluva way to make a first impression. Lesson learned. It will never happen again."

That ended the call. I knew what was ahead of us. We were facing a bear of a job, sorting the drives and labeling them with their serial numbers.

I went out back to meet with the warehouse team and repeated the conversation verbatim. Wanting to lead by example and not just dump it on them, I said, "Let's get started." I grabbed a skid, pallet-jacked it to the dock area, threw six or so of these mix-and-match boxes on it, and said, "Who's with me?" They all were. I took the jack to an open bench and started counting and documenting drives. They all did the same.

Unfortunately, my day job did not allow me to keep sorting drives for long. But the four hours I put in went a long way to maintain morale. It ended up taking us several weeks to identify, label, and stock all the hard drives. I did contribute with daily donut and coffee cake deliveries, which Joanne augmented by baking her fan-favorite brownie cookies!

Once the Dell pieces and parts labeling and sorting were behind us, we could see what had gone wrong. We had assumed that the "HP way" was the universal way of shipping hard drives. Not so. Shame on us, not Dell. And the onus to adapt was on us, not Dell. We needed to convert to the Dell way, not make them deal with us the HP way. As it would turn out, doing it the Dell way would be a financial benefit to BCD. Everything happens for a reason.

We began placing orders through Dell's online ordering system. Very quickly, we noticed that as we added components, the server chassis price automatically adjusted downward. The more we messed around with the system, the further the price dropped. We added hard drives, and the server chassis price went lower. We added processors, and the chassis price went even lower. At that point, we would have added a sunroof if they offered it. Sometimes the savings reached as high as 20%. For example, if we separately ordered a server and a group of drives and other parts, we would have expected to pay $29,250. But when we ordered the server already loaded with those parts, we would pay $25,000. It was crazy.

On all future orders, we ordered servers with each system already fully populated with the hard drives we wanted in each server bay. When the order arrived, our warehouse staff removed the top case, popped out each hot-pluggable hard drive, and then labeled it with our part number. Then, based on what the customer needed, we would reload the server with the appropriate drives.

Rarely did a Dell server hit our dock with an open drive bay or an open motherboard slot. Usually, when we bought a server from

Dell, it was as fully stuffed as one of John Madden's turduckens. Now when BCD was buying a server from Dell, we weren't ordering a $4,000 chassis. We were ordering a $25,000 solution, fully loaded with hard drives, NVIDIA GPUs, and every other option we could fit inside that chassis that we could pull out and put into stock.

Consider that we were ordering 50 to 100 of these $25,000 systems from Dell at a time. Our orders went right to the top of the line. While the world was waiting up to two months for their Dell servers, BCD was waiting a mere two weeks.

BCD finished its first fiscal year with Dell (February 2018 through January 2019) as its top OEM customer in the surveillance arena, ending Motorola-owned Avigilon Systems' five-year run in that position. We ranked fourth in the Americas for all OEM customers, and number eight in the world!

And if that was not enough momentum, I received an email from Michael Dell, *thanking me for the uniform.* Perhaps I sometimes put too much emphasis on such things, but this told me a lot about the man. He did not brainlessly thank me for the polo shirt; he thanked me for the uniform. He read the note! I was pretty jacked.

Joanne and I were invited to the Dell Match Play golf event at Austin Country Club a few months later, "inside the ropes." Of course, we were wearing our BCDVideo polo shirts. We walked the course over 18 holes with Jon Rahm and Sergio Garcia. It was certainly a once-in-a-lifetime experience.

As for the golf match, it was fortunate that pro golfers take a long time on the greens reading their putts. This gave me a chance to catch up after lagging during the walk from the tee box to the green. (I was less than a year away from replacement knee surgery.) I got a couple of looks, not necessarily sneers, from the two golfers. It's understandable, as they were playing for money, but I do not think I distracted them that much. I did not intend to, anyway.

After that match play round, Joanne and I were able to make our way over to the Dell suite, parallel to the 14th fairway, where we enjoyed the incredible food and views. Every match had two golfers walking past us. Phil, Rory, Scottie, Jordan, all of them. We had a great chance to meet the extended Dell executive family, and yes, Michael as well. When I was formally introduced to him and we were shaking hands, he said, "I know you. You're the shirt guy!"

Thus, my claim to fame. I made an impression on one of the world's most famous people, all over a $20 shirt. I still beam today knowing that Michael Dell read my note; the shirt is secondary.

CHAPTER 48

PLAYING THE GAME

December 2018

We had a great first year with Dell. In fact, through our first five years with Dell, we were a $275 million customer. I was supercharged with enthusiasm; we had opened the door to a new line, a new partner, a new day, and my excitement about building off our popular new partner's line spread through our entire organization.

But not everyone outside our company saw it quite the same way. Over the first two years with Dell, our revenues grew consistently at the same 19% year-over-year rate we'd had for the three years prior, but our win ratio on quotes dropped 12%. That told me that we were still losing sales to customers who preferred to buy from Dell directly.

Eventually, it dawned on me that we were trying to pull off a tricky combination shot. On the one hand, we were proud of our affiliation with Dell. At the same time, we had to separate ourselves from Dell, to focus on the value we added. One day on a sales call, a customer shrugged at my pitch. "It's just a Dell," he said.

"No," I quickly replied. "It used to be a Dell. BCD is Dell for Video. We take the best IT servers in the world and customize them to do a better job capturing video surveillance. Dell for Video servers can manage two or three times more cameras than the original Dell server ever could."

I saved the trump card for last. "Plus, we guarantee the servers, for the project and for Dell."

That seemed to stick, so "BCD is Dell for video" became our five-word answer to "Why BCD?" Over the next 90 days, our quote-to-order ratios jumped up to 23.6%, returning us to the norm of our HP years.

As important as it was to define this line of differentiation, I did not want to waste our momentum. I saw this alignment with Dell as yet another chance to expand our reach.

Although our success rate with distribution had been disappointing so far, we were now a totally different company, and years had passed since our last effort. There were many security integrators across the world, and I was certain that a lot of them would find value in our approach.

Our best opportunities seemed to lie in META, as the territory encompassing the Middle East, Turkey, and Africa was then called. We had done many projects with Genetec in that area, primarily in Saudi Arabia, Qatar, and the United Arab Emirates.

Our experience showed that projects there generally had much higher storage requirements than in the United States. Saudi Arabia, for example, mandated at least six months of video retention. Petroleum fields, such as Saudi Aramco, required one-year retention times. Many of the Middle East projects depended on servers connected via the network to external storage units, each holding up to sixty hard drives storing the video surveillance data. These systems were always over a half-million dollars. We found that attractive.

A familiar partner also covered this area. Ingram Micro had a distribution arm in the Middle East, called Network Information Technology (NIT), which was already distributing Axis video cameras, Milestone recording software, and Dell servers. Working through Ingram Micro, with whom we still did a lot of business, we reached a distribution agreement with NIT to resell our recording devices.

Our goal was to have them move away from Dell servers and start pushing BCD's Dell-based purpose-built-for-video appliances. If you were selling Dell, why not sell Dell for Video, especially if your owner, Ingram, was giving a helpful push? Plus, we were still the only video appliance company in the industry guaranteeing the performance of their recording device on a per-project basis. To me, that was the easy button. It seemed like an obvious opportunity.

As it turned out, one party that had a problem with the arrangement was the six-person Dell Middle East salesforce, a smart, energetic group that drove a lot of business. We saw them as occupying a different lane than we did, but we had complementary interests and conflicts.

My son Max, our global sales manager, began meeting with Dell's security team. He discovered that they all shared a passion for football (soccer), and they began regularly communicating via WhatsApp about their favorite teams. As those relationships deepened, Max began to exchange information on our opportunities in their region. He was adept at getting them to present BCD as the best choice for their customer, but only after they were assured they would get the expected order credit on the entire order. Had they lost even one dollar in the deal, they would have just done it directly.

That is where problems began. Although we submitted Dell point-of-sales reports that listed all Dell-based products landing in the META region every month, not all those sales were credited to the local Dell salesforce.

For example, on some projects, we already held the stock in our Illinois facilities. To me, it made sense to build and ship from there. That seemed best for the customer. Unfortunately, what is best for the customer is not necessarily what's best for the Dell sales representative. For reasons we did not then understand, Dell's META sales team got no credit for those sales. Once the salespeople realized that all the trust Max had been building began to evaporate, they stopped driving business through us.

The partner became the competitor.

Through all this, it bothered me that none of these people gave a rat's ass about what was best for the customer. Not once in any of these unfortunate, adversarial conversations did someone on the call even mention that their solution would work for the customer. All that ever mattered was "who was getting the revenue credit?"

It was all about deal credit, and Dell's sales comp plan was negatively affecting our sales. It seemed ridiculous; if we had had that issue going on with HP, we never realized it. Regardless, if the Dell salespeople were not 100% confident that they were to be paid, all our promises in the world certainly were not going to sway them. I realized in short order that I was never going to change them—but I was not sold on changing me, either.

If we were to have any level of success, I concluded, we would need to play the Dell game. I had just the right person to make it work. My son, Alexander, had been managing the supply chain since he joined us back in 2015 as procurement manager, and he had been our main operational contact with Dell.

Alexander's mission was to turn this problem into an opportunity. With the help of Dell's operations team in Round Rock, Alexander learned firsthand about Dell's global flow of goods. He also learned we needed to get BCD's account set up with Dell in multiple regions, with the Middle East heading our list.

Alexander dug deeper and learned that Dell's money trail starts where the goods are built and assembled, a list of sites that included Texas, Poland, Ireland, Malaysia, China, India, Brazil, and Mexico. Alexander made it his mission to set up our BCD accounts so that, whatever Dell product we shipped and wherever we shipped it to, the Dell regional rep named to the end customer account would get full sales credit. In the case of the Middle East, all those goods needed to ship from Dell's European manufacturing facility in Poland, so Alexander set up a new account for BCD in Lodz.

That ended the rivalry. Making this adjustment cost us nothing beyond Alexander's time, and the cooperation of the sales team was worth far more than any commission lost on those sales.

But we still faced cooperation problems, this time from NIT's sales team. Regardless of geographic region, capturing the attention of a distribution partner is a challenge, as we had seen with Anixter and Mayflex. They have so many brands to juggle and so many manufacturers pushing for support. NIT was already selling network cameras, network video recorders (NVRs), video management software, and all the accessories around that, and it was difficult to get to the top of the pile.

It is even more difficult to get another company's sales force to buy into a partnership enough to present the products. They would rather chase a market than make a market; that is, they would rather push whatever was currently hot than try to create heat about something new, even if that new thing is objectively better. After all, sales is "99% confidence and 1% bullshit." Anixter's sales force had never had enough confidence in us to push our line. We would have been lucky had that been at 50% confidence, and 50% bullshit. Regardless, we needed NIT's sales force to have confidence in us.

I had Max lead that charge. Max already had some contacts in the region whom he had met at industry trade shows in the United States. He and I made several trips to Dubai over those first nine months. Regardless of what section you sit in—and trust me, being 6' 5", we flew in business class—thirteen hours there and fourteen hours home are long flights. Plus, something about flying over Iranian airspace makes me a little uneasy as well.

We spent months training the NIT sales reps on our products. We stressed that, by customizing Dell's products for video surveillance, we improved them, yet they still carried the full Dell warranty. We emphasized how easily the products could be adopted by the system administrator at the end user site, at zero risk. To the administrators, it was a Dell. To us, it was Dell for Video. We did not care what they called it, only that they sold it.

To show everybody we were team players, we even drove some of the Dell opportunities we were getting in META through NIT. We worked this out through Jack O'Reilly, Dell's regional sales manager based in Dubai. If the customer's order was processed through NIT and then ordered through Dell's Middle East region, the Dell rep assigned to the deal got full credit. This allowed us to get some "street cred" that we were open to playing with those Dell reps. Forget that it added three to four weeks to the lead time. That was not Dell's concern; only the sales credit mattered.

After a while, this distribution experience seemed to be turning into a rerun of our Anixter experience from a decade before. The salespeople would not push our products; it was easier to sell a Dell. The customer asked fewer questions. Like every other distributor we engaged with, NIT became more valuable to us as a bank that would extend credit to our new customers.

This financial relationship was especially useful in the Middle East, where those higher data retention requirements led to much larger transactions. Rather than trusting a new customer 7,000 miles away to pay an invoice on a $500,000 project, we found it worth the three-to-five points of margin loss to process the deal through NIT.

Ultimately, using distribution partners to promote BCD globally did not deliver the revenue performance we had hoped for, but it did extend our brand awareness on a worldwide basis. The fact we were on their Intranet line card was likely worth something.

With so many paths to the market, we took the initiative to create separate internal divisions. We kept BCDVideo, as the brand was trusted and we had a strong base of customers who helped to evangelize the BCDVideo brand. We also created a unique brand, Video Storage Solutions (VSS), to cover products that were exclusively available through distribution. We even gave the brand its own colors, purple and white, about as far away from BCDVideo's blue and gray as we could get. Creating this separate brand preserved the integrity of the BCDVideo brand. Once we sold our products to a distributor, we no longer had control over pricing; there was nothing to prevent a distributor from dumping our inventory at a low margin, just to move their stock. If the distributor was dumping BCDVideo branded products, our overall pricing plans would suffer. But we did not care if the distributor was dumping VSS products, because it did not affect us.

To separate our North American core business from the global business, we created BCD International, encompassing all customers outside of North America. BCDVideo was still the branded server being sold globally, just under the BCD International umbrella.

Unfortunately, with this move, we inadvertently created confusion about what to buy and how to buy it. That is never a good thing.

Our ability to scramble paid off here. We told all our customers that nothing had really changed and that they all still had access to the BCDVideo brand. The OEM customers liked the fact that these would be BCDVideo systems built to their specifications, marked with their own logos. It just took more explanation than it should have. Poor messaging. And that was on me.

As we ended 2018, we seemed to have withstood the impact of making branding decisions without considering all possible outcomes. We finished at just over $70 million in annual revenue. Once again, we achieved a 20% increase in our annual revenues.

The next year would start to show some cracks in our organization, even as we enjoyed a $94 million year. By this point, it would not be a new year without some new body part replacement. I had a heart valve transplant three years prior, a hip replacement the following year, a year off, and then my knee replacement. People began calling me Steve Austin, the Six Million Dollar Man. "Why would I take a pay cut?" I always replied. Of course, I was only kidding. Well, kinda, anyway.

CHAPTER 49
TWO SHOCKS TO THE SYSTEM

———

January 2019

We had begun the new year riding high. We were working on projects in North America, Europe, and the Middle East. We signed up with new clients. *Inc. Magazine* once again placed us on their list of Fastest-Growing Companies, and *Computer Reseller News* again listed BCD as one of the top solution providers in North America. We ended up with a $12 million January, our largest January ever. The buzz within the company was electric.

But as it turned out, not everyone was happy.

On the last day of January, the Friday before Super Bowl Sunday, the three sales team managers requested an emergency meeting. Right away, I could tell they looked pissy. They were unhappy with the new sales commission plan. They called it unfair. According to them, their team members felt the same way.

That got us off on the wrong foot. They should have come to me with their grievance before rallying the troops against me.

It did not take long for them to get to the real heart of their agenda: they wanted me out of sales. "We'll run sales," they told me. "You focus on the operational side of the company."

I do not know what I expected when we sat down, but a coup was not on the list. Somewhat in shock, I listened to them go on. "You're out of touch," they told me. "Your methods are old and dated, and your sales commission plan is unrealistic."

"It's a plan that would let you double or even triple your base pay!" I countered. "You are coasting along on your $60 thousand salary. That is not all you should be making, but just enough of a taste to drive you to earn more. Your W-2 should be at least twice that!"

"But it takes too much work to get there," they responded. "Sales do not work the same way as they used to."

Wow, thanks for proving my point. You do not even "Know Thy Customer."

This came from rookies who were a few years out of college! I did not want to be that old man who complained about those damn kids making so much racket with their rock 'n' roll, but my irritation was getting hard to repress. "Everyone expects instant gratification," I could hear myself shouting in my head.

Whatever happened to putting in an honest day's work for an honest day's pay? In the 30 years since I first became a sales manager, I never produced a commission plan that did not give everybody on the plan the opportunity to make more money. But you always had to earn it. We were never meant to be a welfare state.

> **Any company needs sales to be profitable. Sales revenue supports the customer service staff that supports your customers. It's the sales revenue that supports the accounting department that manages your customers' invoices and balances. And on and on. I did not create these rules, it is just how business works.**

"We would not be having this conversation if any one of you had maximized his targets last year," I pointed out, earning myself no popularity. "Instead of raising your goals, all I did was modify last year's plan so that you would earn more if you managed to hit the same numbers that you needed to hit last year." Shame on me, I guess.

It was a very heated conversation, and emotional for me. The truth is, I was blindsided. Throughout the company, things were running well. I barely had time to celebrate what was going to be a $12 million month. I had not sensed their dissatisfaction. Even worse, I had not sensed that they had such a very different conception of sales than I did. To me, there was a big difference between getting a sale and earning a sale. I was definitely old school.

I was so incensed that I was close to firing them. Instead, I asked them what compensation plan they were proposing. They did not have one yet. That was enough for me. "Well, go Google one," I said, and brought the three-hour bitchfest to a close.

But the confrontation was not over, at least not for me. On the way home, I replayed the conversation again and again, growing angrier by the moment. Traffic did not help. Every red light infuriated me, and the traffic delays on what should have been the usual 10-minute drive home just gave me more time to play back the tape. I began breathing heavily, and I started sweating so much that I rolled down the window. Yes, in January. It did not help. As I drove down the street towards my driveway, the steering wheel felt heavy, although I was still able to navigate the car onto our long driveway and into the garage.

I pirouetted my legs out of the car, and there was nothing there. It was as if I had no legs. My first impulse was to call 911, but Joanne was out somewhere. The last thing I wanted was for her to come home and see an ambulance. Instead, I decided to suck it up.

I fetal rolled out of the car. Still wearing my heavy winter overcoat, sweating like a marathoner, I shuffled into the house, bracing myself on whatever I could reach—car, door, countertop— to get myself into my chair in the family room. All I needed was to get there, and just suck this thing up, whatever it was.

Once in the living room, I did my best to absorb the blow. I was not sure what the hell was going on. Rallying a bit, I hauled myself over to the bedroom, where we kept a home blood pressure machine. It read 120 over eighty-eight, so nothing out of sorts there. I braced myself back to the chair, trying to absorb whatever was happening to me. I finally texted Joanne to ask when she would be home.

Wives seem to have a hidden instinct for smelling trouble, and Joanne's sonar. *Why, what's wrong?* she texted back.

Nothing, I replied. *Just curious.*

She knew better and got home in less than 10 minutes. Once I told her what happened, she wasted no time in calling 911, all the while scolding me for not calling them earlier. Hoping for mercy, I told her I had not wanted her to see an ambulance here when she got home. She told me I was a "fucking idiot." Once again, she was right.

The paramedics arrived in minutes and took my vitals. "It's nothing," I told them. "I'm fine." The next thing I knew, I was in the ambulance heading to the Highland Park Hospital, with sirens wailing and lights flashing, and Joanne trying to keep up in her car.

That was the last thing I remember until the next morning, when I woke up to find my wife and kids crying in my room. They were full of news. In the middle of the night, the doctors at Highland Park Hospital discovered a blood clot on my brain and decided to transfer me to Evanston Hospital, which has a renowned neurology department. There, I had what was described as a stroke.

Fortunately, it was as clean a stroke as a stroke can be, with no motor, speech, or memory concerns. I did have to do some in-house rehab, primarily walking, sitting down, and getting back up from a chair. Other than being on blood thinners the rest of my life, everything else was as normal as it could be.

My recovery lasted a few weeks, with Joanne closely monitoring my every move. During those weeks, I had a lot of time to think about that contentious meeting with the sales managers. It was obvious that there was a significant culture gap between the sales managers and me. Clearly, I was having trouble getting them to grasp some basics that had always led to success for me. I took that personally.

To me, selling was a process that involved doing your homework first. Go sideways, and first talk to the software and hardware vendor reps. Ask them if they know what hardware a customer currently buys, and from where. Find out what the customer's hot buttons are. Look at their LinkedIn page and see who they follow.

It all falls under the umbrella of "Know Thy Customer" and "Know Thy Competition." By knowing both, you have an edge and can engage in a real conversation on that first customer introduction call. You can come across as a knowledgeable, assured resource on Day One. What could be better than the customer hanging up the phone and thinking, *"This person did their homework!"* That was the expectation I thought I had set with the sales force. I did not invent this process, by any means; I only embraced it and made a small fortune because of it.

These sales managers had a different approach. As soon as they got a call or an email from a customer, they fired back a price quote. Often, they would not even ask for the name of the project, or the video software being used. In my experience, these were huge pieces of intel; once you had this information, you could reach out to the software company, find the right rep for that territory, and ask who else was quoting the project. It is likely most of those software companies would want a BCD server on the project since we had such a low failure rate.

In my mind, pitching quotes is what sales clerks do. I was not paying for these people to be sales clerks; I wanted them to be sales professionals. Whipping out a quote is not how you build relationships. Texting the customer two days later to see if they liked your quote only makes it worse. I never texted customers unless they had become friends, and never about a quote. It makes you look pathetic.

I guess picking up the telephone and calling people has gone the way of the dinosaurs. Maybe that explains why I still like *The Flintstones.* Yabba-Dabba-Doo!

After a few weeks of at-home physical therapy, I returned to the office. I promised Joanne that I would take it easy, and I was sure she had spies within the building checking up on me. I was eager to get back to work. The office was my home away from home, and I was eager to see my team members. It turned out to be, for the most part, mutual.

But there was more to it than that. I took my return as a second chance to reassert myself as the leader of BCD. At the first weekly managers' meeting after my return, I made an announcement. "This company has lost its way," I said, "and that is on me. We need to get back to focusing on the customers."

Going forward, I told them, I would be managing sales. "In my opinion, there is a lack of training going on. This is negatively impacting our numbers and affecting the entire company. We need to teach these kids how to sell. More importantly, we need to teach them how to make themselves indispensable to the customer. I am willing to teach that to anyone willing to put in the effort to learn," I said. Then, matter-of-factly, I added, "For those who aren't, why are you here?"

Change is hard. Some people in the company welcomed it, and others struggled with it. For me, the hardest part of retaking control of my company was coming to grips with the realization that I had been losing control of it in the first place. But taking my eye off the ball was only part of what I was dealing with.

Grappling with the stroke was a huge challenge as well. "At least the stroke is out of the way," Joanne would sometimes say, "so that is a good thing." But the stroke was not out of the way. I could not shake the thought that the stroke could have gone a whole other direction. How fortunate that the blood clot in my brain caused my stroke when I was already in the ICU, in a hospital known for its stroke care. Somebody was sure looking out for me.

Looking out for Joanne, too. How would she have dealt with all the shit around my dying, as well as the family's grief? Would she have been forced to oversee the potential sale of BCD? Or would Alexander have chosen to move from driving BCD's operational engine to running the whole company? These were big questions.

Three days after I had my stroke, BCD threw the company's first-ever President's Club event in Montego Bay, Jamaica. I had done all the planning for this five-day event in the weeks before my stroke. There were going to be dinners and vendor breakfast training sessions. All the external vendors and sponsors, like Intel, Ingram Micro, and Dell, were going to attend. And of course, Joanne and I were going to preside over the whole glorious affair. Instead, she and I spent those days in Evanston Hospital. I was okay with that—more than okay. So was Joanne. Better the hospital than the funeral home.

The show went on. Business was transacted. The Chiefs won the Super Bowl. My colleagues carried on.

They say that life stops when we die, but that is not true. Life goes on. It just goes on without us. For the first time in the two decades since I had founded the company, thoughts of exit strategies began seeping into my consciousness.

CHAPTER 50
WORKING THROUGH A CRISIS

———

March 2020

For several months, I flirted with those exit strategy thoughts. They were never quite silly enough to dismiss entirely, but never serious enough to evolve into a plan. Then a real crisis hit.

In mid-January, just about a year after my stroke, Alexander got wind through his network of international sources that the World Health Organization was sniffing around Wuhan, China to learn about their response to the coronavirus outbreak there two years earlier.

He took note of it, mostly because so much tech is manufactured in China that any sort of disturbance there could lead to a disruption in the supply chain. Still, it seemed like a storm brewing in a faraway place. This was alarming news, but not necessarily something that would impact us.

But this storm kept coming. The infection grew in China, then began ravaging Europe. Our President mocked the virus, calling it the Kung Flu, but it was clear that all the border protection you could dream up would never keep this disease from hitting our shores. All those inbound flights coming from Rome, Paris, London, and Shanghai were ferrying those microbes to New York, Los Angeles, and yep, Chicago. Through January and February, we kept our large-screen security monitors tuned to the various

TV news channels—ABC, CBS, CNN, FNC, and NBC. City by city, we could see cases popping up around the country.

March 11th was the day everything dramatically changed. After more than 118,000 cases in 114 countries and 4,291 deaths, the WHO officially declared COVID-19 a pandemic. The FAA banned international flights from landing in the United States. Tom and Rita Hanks announced that they were infected. The NBA canceled the rest of its season. The Dow dropped by more than 1,200 points. A then-unknown public health official, Dr. Anthony Fauci, told a Congressional committee, "It's going to get worse before it gets better."

The next day, the Illinois public high schools announced they would close. The following week, Governor Pritzker of Illinois ordered employees statewide to stay home. America was shutting down. And like thousands of other companies, BCDVideo had to produce a lot of answers in not much time, and with little information.

Everyone was in full scrambling mode. Our customers wondered what was going to happen with their orders. Integrators wondered what was going to happen with their projects. Everybody was worried about their families and their incomes.

We had no how-to manual to follow. A full century had passed since the last global pandemic. Instead, we had to wing it with what would end up being a mix of common sense and the advice we received from the US Centers for Disease Control and Prevention (CDC) and the Illinois Department of Public Health.

Fortunately, we had a secret weapon—Sue Komarchuk, the rock star who had overseen our human resources since 2018. Sue came from an extensive HR background, and she provided valuable guidance.

First things first: I immediately sent everyone home—everyone except Sue, who agreed to stay. We directed the employees to take with them any personal items, as well as their laptops and anything else they would want or need, since I had no idea when they would return. All we could do was assure them that they would return.

Having sales and support working from home would not be an issue, assuming they did not spend the day watching *Oprah* or whatever they had saved on their DVD players. If they followed my plan, I was confident they would be able to support our customers via their cell phones from home.

The problem would come with the workers who built our servers and shipped them out. They could not work remotely. Our sales team could quote solutions for projects all day long, but our ability to build and ship servers had come to a complete halt, at least for the time being. No server shipments meant no invoicing, which meant no revenue stream. Payroll, on the other hand, never stopped.

This predicament sure was going to make for a long weekend. Sue, however, was calm. Let's start at the beginning, she suggested, and found Governor Pritzker's edict online. Five pages in, we saw our salvation in paragraph nine: *For purposes of this Executive Order, individuals may leave their residence to provide any services or perform any work necessary to offer, provision, operate, maintain and repair Essential Infrastructure.*

We realized that because of our work with the Federal government, the armed forces, and all those Fortune 500 companies supporting the US and foreign governments, BCD qualified to remain open under the Essential Infrastructure and Cybersecurity Operations clause.

It seemed too good to be true, so Sue and I continued to search through the 11-page Stay at Home Order to make sure we were not missing anything, or to see if there was a link provided to apply for that Essential Business exemption. There was none.

I guess you either were an Essential Business or you were not. Perhaps if you were unsure, that meant you were not. As we knew we were, the hell with it; we just went for it. Why call and ask, only to be told no?

Giant exhale. This was great news. However, the responsibility for keeping all our workers safe was on us. And on me.

We decided that first and foremost, if any employee did not

feel safe being in the office, they could work from home. We were rolling the dice a bit here since the workers involved in building and shipping our servers had to be physically present in the building.

In the end, of the forty-two workers employed in Buffalo Grove when COVID-19 struck, sixteen elected to work at home. Of the thirteen workers who built and shipped the servers, no one decided to stay home. Thanks to them, we could continue to fully function.

Of course we made every effort to keep people safe. We took every precaution to keep COVID-19 out of the building: hand sanitizers, air purifiers, and a nurse at the employee entrance to take temperatures. Our cleaning service came twice a week to sanitize all countertops, desks, and tech benches. We went through three canisters of Lysol a day, wiping down anything and everything we touched, from bathroom doors to staplers to the refrigerator door. I wish I had bought stock in Lysol!

Social distancing was more of a challenge. The cubicles in the office were mounted to the floor, so moving the furniture would not be feasible. Instead, we moved people into new spots, each person two or three spots away from the closest team member.

Social distancing was an even bigger adjustment for me. I was used to walking around the facility multiple times a day and saying "hi" to everybody. Now I had to remember to keep my distance. I began to feel somewhat lonely. With almost half of our usual crew absent, the building seemed empty and hollow. We could not even have team lunches anymore.

Wanting our customers to know we were taking this disease most seriously, I ordered a thousand individual wipes with Genetec's Streamvault logo on them to ship inside every Genetec server carton. We added a note: "Please feel free to wipe down the system before deploying."

While all this was going on, Joanne was baking three times a week, so I could bring comfort food to all the team members still working onsite. I was trying to keep her away from the office, which was not easy for the "Company Mom" to hear.

The shutdown was a strange experience, as anyone who lived through it can attest. The quiet streets, the empty stores. It was bizarre to see areas and convention halls where we had installed our systems—Chicago's McCormick Place, New York's Jacob Javits Center, the Superdomes in Atlanta and New Orleans, and Tampa Bay's Raymond James Stadium—being converted from exciting gathering places to emergency health care facilities.

Meanwhile, I made sure all the remote team members realized that although they were out of sight, they were not out of mind. We started having "Let's Stay Connected" Microsoft Teams calls every Monday to ensure everyone was kept informed and felt involved.

A few weeks before Easter, I found a bakery in Florida that made homemade key lime pies ready to ship anywhere in the county. I ordered thirty-three of them, one for each remote US employee, with the note, *Looks like no one will be going to Florida anytime soon, so I thought I could bring Florida to you!*

That went a long way with everyone. I received so many notes of appreciation. Many of the notes indicated that the timing was perfect and that the pies were going to be served at Easter dinner. For a fleeting moment anyway, I felt connected to everyone again.

We also donated a thousand dollars of Girl Scout cookies, through the daughter of one of our team members, to the Greater Chicago Food Depository. When we had sent Girl Scout cookies to local food depositories in the past, one of them referred to them as "happy food," unlike the typical food they receive. That has stuck with me ever since.

As it turned out, one of the most crucial factors that allowed us to stay in business was put in place well before the shutdown crisis hit in March. Back in January, when Alexander got wind of the outbreak two years earlier in Wuhan and things spreading in Europe now, he went into action. Alexander was our supply chain manager, and he knew from his previous experience as a buyer covering China for Grainger International that the Chinese government tended to shut things down quickly whenever a contagious disease broke out.

Relying on his instincts and telling no one—*me included*—Alexander ordered four months' worth of our regular monthly stocking order from Dell. He knew that the bulk of those goods were already located in Dell's Mexico facility, and whatever parts they needed from China were already installed into the finished goods. He got the order in just in time.

Very soon afterward, the pandemic forced Dell to start running its Mexico facility with a skeleton crew. Servers became scarce. But thanks to Alexander, BCDVideo stayed in business. His quick thinking may have made the difference between us muddling through or going under. So, we plowed through.

As happy as Joanne was that the company remained active, she had a different priority. I was not too far removed from my stroke recovery, and she made me promise daily as I was leaving for work that I would stay masked and keep my distance. Our sons were safe as well. Alexander had his own office, and without air travel happening, Max just grabbed a socially distanced sales desk and worked the phones.

Despite the pandemic, the external recognition kept rolling in. BCD was again named one of the Best Places to Work in Illinois (thanks to Sue's diligence) and one of the Best and Brightest in the Nation by the National Association of Business Resources. We made the *Inc.* 5000 list of fastest-growing companies for the second time in three years. We were again named to *Crain's Chicago Business* list of top privately held companies, along with their list of the Chicago area's fifty fastest-growing companies.

We were also named for the first time to *Audio and Security Magazine*'s annual list of the "most influential" companies in the security marketplace. We were number three in North America and number 40 in the world.

Summer brought a temporary respite from the COVID-19 crisis. We could mingle at a distance in the parking lot and bring in food trucks. Unfortunately, the break was short-lived. Come fall, we had to endure another wave of infections. We had to play defense until a vaccine became available the following spring.

Even as we devoted ourselves to maintaining safety, we were able to land some new business. In August, we inked an OEM Agreement with Hanwha Techwin America (formerly Samsung Techwin) to build network video recording (NVR) devices. Within three years, they became one of BCD's largest customers, buying $18 million worth of products annually.

Despite all the turmoil we faced in 2020, we somehow managed 7% year-over-year growth. Granted, we had grown spoiled by our typical 25% annual growth over the past seven previous years, but that 7% was still twice the growth of the average company on the *Crain's Chicago Business* list. This achievement gave me the greatest satisfaction. We really had to earn this one, and we had the scars to prove it. Best of all, we got through the pandemic without a single employee contracting COVID-19 because of a spreading incident within our facility.

We did it! We created a safehouse for our team members who trusted us to do so, and who showed honor by honoring the ever-changing rules. The people in that facility protected each other from this invisible enemy. It truly brought me a sense of parental pride. But the true kudos go to them, not me.

This success would never have happened without Joanne, who served as our off-the-payroll Company Mom throughout the entire ordeal, or without Sue, our Human Resources Director Extraordinaire, who became an expert in all things coronavirus-related. Sue was the main reason the virus never dared to infiltrate our facility for two years, until the COVID-19 emergency came to an official end.

I liked to think this would be my legacy, not the huge deals or the numbers. The greatest win of my career was jointly leading a team effort to keep our people safe.

CHAPTER 51

COVID-19 OPENS THE DOOR

———

May 2020

Each one of us had to adjust during the pandemic. We made sacrifices. We extended ourselves. We adapted to a new normal every other day.

In my business life, the thing I missed most was face-to-face meetings. Thus, I was intrigued when, two months after Governor Pritzker ordered the Illinois shutdown, I received an unsolicited email. It was from Matt Jackson at Morgan Stanley, requesting a meeting. He wanted to talk about my future, what my plans were for the next few years, and whether I had an exit plan. When I looked at my LinkedIn profile, I could see that he had checked me out the day before.

I had been wondering what an exit strategy would look like. I had no clue. My love for my work always seemed to pop that fantasy about the next chapter of my life. But I also knew that I was tired—not tired of BCD, but body-tired. All those past health issues still weighed on me, always taking me to the same painful question: How was Joanne going to deal with selling BCD at some point, should something happen to me? I did have a vague succession plan in place for Alexander to take over someday, but my sudden and untimely death would have created chaos.

I told Matt I would be happy to talk to him, but not on the

phone. As his office in Barrington was a mere two towns west of our office, I was hoping to experience the joy of a face-to-face meeting with a stranger. I was getting desperate for normal human interactions outside my teammates. The fact it was Morgan Stanley was cool, too. We were not talking about Chico's Bail Bonds here!

The next day, Matt came to our offices. Masked and sitting at opposite ends of my 12-foot conference table, we spent three hours together. I started with a 20-minute synopsis of what BCD did for a living, covering our migration from IT to video security and identifying our vendor partners. When I paused to get us both another cup of coffee, I left him with a three-page list of notable sites around the world where BCDVideo was recording surveillance, from Apple to Walmart, from Afghanistan to Zimbabwe. That is my eye candy.

He then walked me through a pre-prepared Morgan Stanley PowerPoint presentation. But Matt was not just reading the verbiage on each slide, he was humanizing it while talking up Morgan Stanley's business model for creating withdrawal plans tailored to businesses like mine.

It was obvious that he was impressed with our geographical reach, as well as the Who's Who list of brand names that relied on our solutions. Then Matt's partner, Ameen Amin, joined us via conference link. Ameen, a native Iraqi, was quite the success story. He spoke multiple languages and lived in six countries before obtaining his master's degree at Columbia University. He was now the Alternative Investments Director and Financial Advisor at Morgan Stanley.

He knew his stuff. Along with Matt, they made a compelling case for taking companies the size of mine out to the market for either a minority or majority sale. Finding out what that would look like would cost me nothing but time—which I had—and would potentially finally answer the question I'd had in my head for years, namely, "What is my company really worth?"

Ameen and Matt told me Morgan Stanley's best customers were businesses just like BCD—family businesses whose patriarch was still at the helm. We discussed how things would flow with either a majority or a minority sale, and what would be needed to make either of those options happen. They warned me that at times, the process would become frustrating. Most importantly, they stressed that they were providing this analysis to me as a free service, without expectations. Matt even confided that should Joanne and I decide to go forward and make a deal with an investor, we were not obligated to house the proceeds at Morgan Stanley.

"Who would do something like that to you, after you did all the work?" I asked. Ameen replied: "You'd be surprised." He was right—I did find that surprising. What is wrong with people?

It did not take long for me to realize that these guys were the answer to my biggest fear. Over the past six years, I had endured a lot of health issues. If I was not long for this world, I did not want to burden Joanne with the job of selling the company. BCD had always been our source of income, and we legally ran our lives through it. I was sure she could capably handle the responsibility, but why should she have to?

I had no idea what a minority sale would look like numbers-wise, but it had to be measured in the millions. Just a month ago, while killing some shutdown-created downtime, I did a seat-of-my-pants estimation of what the company might be worth, based on our revenues, expenses, and liabilities. I came up with $70 million, which our accountant reviewed and said looked about right. Just using basic math, even selling 10% of the company would provide for my family's security well into the future.

Ameen and Matt suggested that, for discussion purposes, we should talk about selling 30% of the company. They stressed, however, that I could sell up to 49.99% of the company and remain the majority owner, which is something I wanted. Based upon that assumed $70 million valuation, 30% would yield more than $20 million. I found that astonishing. I would be able to cash out, provide my family with generational wealth, and remain CEO and majority shareholder of our very successful company. Truly, the best outcome imaginable. Ameen and Matt said the shorthand for someone in my position was UHNW—"Ultra-High Net Worth."

They certainly caught my attention. My thinking about an exit strategy went from "Out there somewhere" to "You've got my interest." This was my chance to make sure Joanne and our family would be set for life should something happen to me. That was all I ever wanted at this point in my life. I truly was doing this for them, and not for me.

That night I shared with Joanne all that I had learned. She asked a lot of good questions: "What about Alexander and Max?" "What about the employees?" Her primary concern was about me. "You have been running BCD for 25 years," she pointed out. "Will you be happy answering to others?" Like I said, good questions.

I reached out to Matt to see if he and Ameen had available time the next day. My plan was to let her hear the answers from the experts. I had done just enough to open the door in her mind.

Over the next few weeks, we talked through scenarios, together and with Matt and Ameen, who made themselves available to us 24/7. As a salesman, I couldn't quite get over that they never tried to sell us anything. Of course, they had nothing to sell. Morgan Stanley would not be getting a cut in the deal; they were only hoping we would bank our anticipated $20 million proceeds with them. Ameen and Matt truly were free advisors guiding us through the process.

Joanne hit it off with both Matt and Ameen, and that was crucial. Had they given her an "icky" feeling, nothing would have moved forward. The truth is, we could not have chosen a better time to explore this decision. While COVID-19 was still ravaging the country, we got to entertain various ways we might become a financially solid couple. Regardless of the choices we would make, it was fun to indulge in a wonderful escape from the reality going on around us.

Eventually, we decided to move forward and Matt and Ameen introduced us to their primary investment banker, Gary Rabishaw of Intrepid in Los Angeles. Gary walked me through the laborious process of creating a pitch book, known as "the Book." This 100-

page document detailed the backgrounds of the officers and key employees of the company, the business plan of the company, including top customers, vendor partners, concentrations, and any relevant deal experience that pertained to the company. The Book was designed to attract venture capital or private equity companies to begin even deeper examinations. Consider it as a giant worm on a fishing hook in an ocean of fish. So many financial and market reports were required. In all, it took close to three months for Intrepid to finalize the Book.

It was now August. The next step was for Intrepid to take us out to the market. There were no guarantees that anyone would even be interested in us, so I set no expectations for myself. At the same time, as we had put so much time and effort into it, I had a good feeling that someone would bite. We only needed one.

CHAPTER 52
CALLING IN THE CAVALRY

———

January 2021

As it turned out, we got twenty serious responses. By the end of 2020, we had whittled the list of potential suitors from twenty down to six. Among them were private equity firms, venture capital groups, and an investment bank. All these firms had experience in funding family businesses.

The team at Intrepid gave me a warning: As attention-consuming as the investment process had been to this point, the next six months would be even more challenging and frustrating. Part of the reason was that the potential investors had an endless appetite for information. This was the full diagnostic. Not only did they investigate every nook and cranny within BCD, but they also scanned the Internet for comments, reviews, and gripes.

Figuring I knew all facets of the company, I appointed myself to handle all data inquiries, either answering the questions myself or passing the requests for data to the right team members. What was I thinking? Every day brought new requests for documents, and more Zoom or Microsoft Teams calls with investors. Half my day was spent on the phone with Gary, Josh, or Eli at Intrepid. Knowing these suitors much better than we did, they prepared us for each call, briefing us on that firm's strengths and weaknesses, revealing their hot buttons, and most importantly, warning us about what would turn them off.

Joining me in representing the company on these Zoom calls were Nick, our CFO, Jason, our VP of sales, and Eugene, our chief technology officer. I would often take the lead in answering questions from the investors, although like an orchestra conductor, I would also defer to the person best equipped to answer. The calls went well, though not perfectly. While Eugene and Jason just went with the flow, Nick seemed a little clumsy at times. I had the impression that Nick felt filtered in my presence. The potential investors likely noticed Nick's guardedness.

Nick had been CFO for about a year. He was one of those people who had said all the right things in the lunch interview, and his references all panned out. After the COVID-19 shutdowns began, he did a good job getting BCD a significant Payback Protection Program (PPP) loan. Lately, however, tensions had arisen. There was friction between him and Sue in Human Resources. Sue was very protective of employee data and strongly objected to using that information as a source for data mining. Nick ignored her, which caused needless acrimony.

All the negativity, on top of the demanding investment process, just added wear and tear on me and I was feeling a little burnt out. Perhaps I was even feeling that I had extended myself too far outside of my comfort zone. First time for everything, I guess. More than ever, I needed the two weeks of the holiday break simply to relax.

As I recharged, I began to reflect on the entirety of my career, from my start in the warehouse in 1979, through founding BCD toward the end of 1999, to now, working with an investment bank on a potential multi-million-dollar sale. Parts of the story made me very proud; other parts seemed surreal.

I returned to the office refreshed, ready to tackle anything. And anything is what I got. On that first business Monday of the new year, Nick walked into my office. He had just come back from a three-week vacation, which had annoyed me. Year-end closings and audits are jobs that fall squarely in the CFO's area of responsibility; while the finished products may be due in January, the process of creating them starts in early December.

We had been telling potential investors that BCD, for the first time in our history, was set to surpass $100 million in revenues. When you are trying to close a deal, however, forecasts are worthless. You need audited numbers. Instead of focusing on the audit, Nick had been getting a suntan. But before I could make Nick aware of my irritation, he shared some news.

"I am leaving the company," he said.

Just as well, I thought. "When is your last day?"

"Today."

No notice? I was shocked by his lack of professionalism. "Why wait?" I said, barely suppressing my anger. "Be off the property in an hour." The words had barely escaped my lips before I texted Eugene, telling him to cut off Nick's company life support—phone and email. He was gone within 45 minutes.

My only regret was not firing him after Thanksgiving. But now we had to complete the audit without a CFO.

The first order of business was to close the books for December. Once we completed that, we could close the fourth quarter and then close the year. Then, and only then, could we prepare for the year-end audit. With the $100 million plus year needing to be certified, I could not close 2020 fast enough!

I met with the three members of our capable, competent accounting team, which, with Nick's departure, had been 25% depleted. We walked through everything together. The good news was that Nick had assigned each of them end-of-year closing responsibilities. The bad news was that he had never bothered to train them to do those jobs. Though surprised, I stayed positive and reassured them that we would get through this together.

An hour later, I got on the phone to begin the search for a new CFO. Given that this was the start of the tax season, I thought this would be a tall order. My first call was to our banker, Amber, at MB Financial, to see if she had any ideas. Better than ideas, the bank had a client, Sutker Moran, which was an outsourcing accounting company—a rent-a-CFO organization. They committed to sending two people to our site. The cavalry would arrive the day after tomorrow. Charge!

With echoes of bugles ringing in my head, I placed a call to Intrepid to fill them in on what had been a very busy and turbulent morning. I did not go into too much detail, and they did not ask for any. They seemed very pleased that we were able to find reinforcements so quickly. We agreed to speak again at the end of the week.

After lunch, the accounting team closed the month of December 2020 without a hitch, leaving us to begin the far more complicated year-end process the following day. A year-end closing has little overlap with a month-end report. The team took it as far as they could. The next day, the duo from Sutker arrived to complete the audit. One of them, Scott Moran, also seamlessly stepped into the due diligence process with the potential investors. On all the team calls, Scott was very matter-of-fact and assured, handling all the questions from the potential investors with ease.

We were lucky to have him on our team, and two years later, remarkably, we still did. Although still outsourced through now-Sutker Moran, Scott Moran acts as our chief financial officer, even though he also works with other accounts. That cavalry bugle charge plays inside my head every time he turns the corner. Likely our greatest "non-hire" ever!

By May, we had narrowed the list of potential suitors from six to two. It was clear that we were closing in on some version of my goal of securing financial security for my family while maintaining control of BCD. Both prospective investors valued the company at $72 million, close to the valuation that I had projected a year earlier; even $2 million higher! The business I had founded 22 years earlier above a Japanese restaurant had reaped a damn good return on investment. All those bumps, bruises, turmoil, and drama had paid off!

Now other issues had to be resolved. What percentage of the company did they want? How much cash were they willing to pay upfront? We also hammered out answers to questions involving equity, board representation, exit strategy, voting rights, and stock percentage.

On June 21, 2021, we finalized a minority transaction by selling a 29.4% share of Burgess Computer Decisions, Inc. to a Chicago-based private equity firm. BCD would continue its journey; the main difference was that we would have to produce a lot more financial reporting. I had achieved my dream of securing security for my wife and family while retaining operational control. The best of both worlds! I was living in the utopia of personal satisfaction.

The days, weeks, and months that followed were unusual times. Everything at BCD was the same, except for all the things that were different. I had to make a lot of adjustments. I was still the master of my domain, except that now I was a master who had to answer questions, explain my reasoning, and accept criticism which I did not always find constructive.

I suppose the biggest adjustment was coming to grips with the realization that my new partners and I did not always share the same values. To our new partners, BCD was a vehicle for making money. Duh! Of course it was. They had paid me a pile of money for a minority share of the company's future profits. I, too, regarded BCD as a vehicle for making money. The difference between them and me is that BCD was also my creation, my baby, my family, and my home.

So yes, I had to make adjustments. Not all of them were easy. But as I had done so often during my life, I thought of my dad. Way back in 1962, Hammermill Paper acquired Burgess Envelope Company. For those next twenty-plus years, as far as I could tell from the outside, it was business as usual. I am sure he had his frustrations; I am sure he got mad. But all I ever saw was my dad multi-tasking behind his desk.

Once again, I felt Dad was showing me the way, and I plowed through. Since the sale, we have had challenges, and we have had victories. Some old and valued customers left us, and a lot of new, forward-looking clients joined. I tried to just keep doing what I had been doing before the deal was struck: I rolled up my sleeves and did my job. I tried to be the same guy after the deal as before. And more than anything, I wanted this to remain business as usual for those loyal BCD team members.

I never was a traditional CEO. Perhaps that was because I did not take a traditional path. I have benefitted from the help and influence of so many people—mentors, friends, colleagues, and, of course, my father, Oscar William Burgess. Sitting in his office for those three hours waiting to go home after he fired me from the summer warehouse job was a turning point in my life, and watching him multi-task and listening to him work was a lifelong gift. (And I have never forgotten the lesson in deflection he gave me a year later in Dean Reiter's office at Niles East High School.)

After those early lessons, I still had much to learn—about business, about people, and about myself. Sometimes I learned quickly, and sometimes only after making a lot of mistakes that hurt myself or others. But through thick and thin, I always knew there was one person who believed in me: Joanne. This did not necessarily mean she always agreed with me, mind you. Her candor has always been part of her love. But I could always count on her, and that has meant everything. Having a wife believing in you makes anything possible.

I was lucky to have another person in my life who believed in me as well: Donna Panfil. She saw something in me, and she was willing to fight for me to be moved from the warehouse into sales. My story happened because of Donna, and I was committed to paying that forward by building a company of opportunity for all. Just like my dad had done all those decades prior.

Along my incredible journey, I was fortunate to work with so many incredible people, and, if you are taking the time to read this, you are likely among them. Thank you all for allowing me that wonderful gift of opportunity. All I ever wanted was a chance to prove myself. Everybody gets an opportunity to do something, perhaps every day. The key is to realize it, then do something about it. I did that tenfold! Much of it with your help.

It was such a privilege having my daughter Lizzie work with us part-time over a number of summers, along with my sons, Alexander and Max, who continue to make a significant difference on a full-time basis.

Now retired, I sit back some forty-five years later remembering my dad calling me on the carpet for being a fuck-up pissing away my life. Two days later, I stumbled into a warehouse job at a computer company. But I had had other warehouse jobs before that one. What was it about Tek-Aids that held my attention for more than two days? Why did I stick with this one for over four months, which was long enough for Donna to notice me?

Because I knew it was my opportunity. Not my opportunity to work in a warehouse, or to break into tech. It was my opportunity to make my dad proud of me. At the time, that was all I wanted. . . and needed. And it worked. For years afterward, even after I opened BCD, he would still refer to me as his "unemployable son." Of course, he laughed when he said it. He was more than just proud. I honored him by building the same kind of company that he did—diverse, with happy team members, all knowing every day that they were key to our success.

BCD was always about seeing, smelling, and then pouncing on opportunity. I was fearless (in some cases, reckless). We won more than we lost, and we made ourselves into a brand name in both the IT and security industries. I believed in people and cherished those who believed in me back, and I tried not to dwell on the handful of haters. And to all those who did believe in me—from the vendor partners to the banks, and most especially to the customers and the great people who worked alongside me—thank you for coming along on this crazy ride with me. Each of you certainly made an impact on me. I hope it was mutual.

However and by whatever means I got here, all I can say is *"It worked for me!"*

POSTSCRIPT

JEFF'S COMMANDMENTS FOR BUSINESS SUCCESS

I built a $100 million company around a simple mantra of OTFD (Out the Fucking Door). We excelled at landing solutions globally in less than 10 days.

But OTFD was never just about delivery speed. It was the DNA of the company. We were a "now" business. We made time commitments and challenged ourselves to beat them, while constantly maintaining our focus on quality. OTFD did not put pressure on us; it made us better. OTFD was our value-add, and our customers fed off the buzz swirling around it.

That said, here are my "Ten Commandments for Business Success," written not on tablets, as Moses did, but on an HP Spectre x360 Laptop. Close enough!

1. KNOW THY CUSTOMER

Do your homework first. This can be as simple as looking at the customer's website—from the brands they sell, to their service offerings, to their mission statement. Nothing lost me more than getting a first-time call and being asked, "What does BCD do?" Do they not have the Internet where you live?

2. KNOW THY COMPETITION

Same as above, but in this case, look for your rivals' weaknesses. Try to identify their Achilles' heels and find a way to make that play into your strengths.

3. SALES IS 99% CONFIDENCE AND 1% BULLSHIT

Speak matter-of-factly and confidently about your company, your products, and what makes you unique. Your confidence is contagious to the person at the other end of the conversation.

4. SHUT UP AND LISTEN

The more the customer shares about their business, the more opportunity you will have to learn their pain points, which you can remedy.

5. THE CUSTOMER'S PERCEPTION IS YOUR REALITY

The customer is always right, even when they are wrong. Just take the hit and find the fix. Share that fix with them and ask their opinion. This inclusion in the remedy forms a bond of trust.

6. TRUST YOUR GUT

Do not overthink things; that will only clutter your brain. Trust your instincts; if you wind up breaking even, that is a win because you are in the game next time. Sure beats the sidelines!

7. FIRST GET THE DEAL, THEN WORRY ABOUT IT

Too much time is wasted on trying to prepare to fulfill a deal that you may never get. Go get the deal, and then everything will fall into place, including profitability. My mentor Jud once won a multimillion-dollar, three-year contract to supply a product from a manufacturer we did not carry. "We will now," he told me. He was right.

8. MAKE YOURSELF INTO THE CUSTOMER'S TRUSTED ADVISOR

Make their business your top priority. Too many salespeople try to sell a product by emphasizing its potential. Better to be the answer to the question the customer is asking, the solution to the problem the customer has. If you cannot supply what they are looking for, point them in the right direction. Trust me, they will be back.

9. LOVE WHAT YOU DO

Have fun earning your living by being yourself. Customers will equate this enthusiasm with the company.

10. HOLD YOURSELF ACCOUNTABLE

Raise the bar on yourself. The people around you will follow, as will the company. The customers will appreciate you more as well.

APPENDIX

Making the move to modifying our high-performing traditional IT computer servers into large-scale, video surveillance recording devices was a game-changer for us.

These systems were never one size fits all; rather each solution was purpose-built for that particular site, based on a variety of parameters—number of cameras, density, retention time, and others.

Over those fifteen years, focusing on the video surveillance market until my retirement in July of 2023, BCD had over a quarter-million devices capturing the surveillance on over four million cameras at the coolest companies and most secure sites in ninety-one countries around the world.

Yet, nothing offered more satisfaction than those installations at our Armed Forces and Government locations—places such as the Pentagon and US Capitol, US Navy, US Air Force and US Marines military bases, Homeland Security, the Federal Reserve, US Border Patrol, US Customs, US Veteran Affairs facilities, the US Treasury, and Arlington National Cemetery.

In addition, my father was a US Air Force pilot flying supply missions over the Himalayas during World War II.

The entire company had a great sense of pride in knowing where our solutions were being installed. For me, it offered the inner peace of "protecting those who are protecting us."

This is why all sales proceeds of IT WORKED FOR ME!! are going to the **Wounded Warrior Project.** Another way to thank them for their service.

ABOUT THE AUTHOR

Born in 1957, Jeff Burgess was blessed with a photographic memory, most likely had Attention Deficit Disorder (ADD), and cursed with a terrible stutter through his sophomore year at Niles East High School in Skokie, Il, where he graduated in 1975.

Jeff attended Illinois State University and spent a little over a year 'playing college'...until the Dean realized no classes were attended, nor books purchased, while he, and his spot as a student was being wasted... Literally.

After making the "Walk of Shame" back into his parents' home, he began a progression of finding jobs, quitting jobs, being let go... being very successful at going nowhere. In 1978, Jeff logged twenty-five federal tax and wage statements (W-2s) at the end of the year. While his father would jokingly refer to Jeff as his "unemployable son", one fateful Sunday afternoon, his father put an end to the jokes, and made Jeff realize that he had all the tools for success--but he needed to get his head on straight and open the toolbox.

The message resonated. Two days later, Jeff found a warehouse job at a local computer peripheral distributor and the rest, as they say, is HISTORIC!

Never satisfied with "selling what everyone else was selling", Jeff began an upward path of bringing in multi-million-dollar opportunities at several computer reselling companies, including his own upon opening Burgess Computer Decisions (BCD) on November 2, 1999.

Fifteen years prior, after getting his life in order, Jeff had met Joanne Aronson on a blind date that neither party wanted to be part of, yet they were engaged and married within six months. Forty years later, they have three married children, Alexander (Joni), Max (Elyssa), and Lizabeth (Michael), one grandson (John Jeffrey), dogs and granddogs.

Jeff has always attributed his success to his work ethic, and his muse – Joanne, who has always been an instrumental voice of reason in Jeff's career growth. Her major concerns always came down to *"will you be happy?"* and *"will they respect you?"*. Joanne excelled far beyond arm-candy at computer trade shows and exhibitions. No one does "Corporate Wife" like Joanne Aronson Burgess! As the unofficial company mom and knowing everyone's name and kids' names, Joanne's personal touches on company holiday parties and other corporate events added incredible warmth, regardless of the coldness of the venue.

In 2009, after selling close to a billion dollars of computer server hardware to several Fortune 500 companies entrenched in the insurance, commercial, and financial industries, Burgess branched out into the video security market, retiring in 2023 with his $100M company's products capturing the video surveillance from over four-million surveillance cameras in ninety-one countries.

Most notably, his company's products continue to protect U.S. Armed Forces Bases around the world, the Pentagon, and, especially, Arlington National Cemetery.

It is Burgess' commitment to honoring our military that led him to the Wounded Warrior Project (WWP). 100% of the sales of this book will be sent to the veterans and active-duty members via the Wounded Warrior Project.

"Years ago, Joanne and Jeff Burgess came to Willow House to collaborate in offering the annual 'Donna Panfil Remembrance Retreat', to honor Jeff's late business mentor. Thanks to their generous support, grieving families have an additional source of sharing and hope to cope with the loss of a special person. Jeff's story explores the importance of hard work, and honoring those individuals that may be gone, but never forgotten."

–David Scheffler, former Willow House Executive Director
and family member

www.ingramcontent.com/pod-product-compliance
Lightning Source LLC
Chambersburg PA
CBHW020433130626
46549CB00001B/121